Published by DC Thomson Media, 2018

A Classic Christmas

Just Like The Ones We Used To Know

Edited By Steve Finan

ISBN: 978-1-84535-727-6

The Sources

THE material in this book has been taken from the vast and rich archive of DC Thomson publications.

These include:

The Sunday Post
The People's Friend
My Weekly
The Weekly News
The Courier
The Evening Telegraph
Weekly Welcome
Weekly Companion
Woman's Way
Lillie London
Annabel

Several of these publications are still printed today — and have gone from strength to strength. Their high quality ensured they remain successful in the modern world.

They have evolved with the times, of course, whereas the 40, 50, or 60-year-old articles lifted from them have not.

Not everything on these pages would work in the modern world. Some of the advice may no longer be good advice — indeed some of the ideas here might be dangerous.

The attitudes and social climate of the past were also very different. The articles are of their time and were intended for an audience of their time.

Please allow them that understanding.

What Was A Classic Christmas?

CHRISTMAS IS the best day of the year. It is a time of wonder, of family, of giving and of togetherness. It is when transgressions are forgiven, good food is eaten and good times are had.

But wonderful though it might be, it isn't the same as it used to be.

Whether it is better or worse is up to the individual to decide, but no-one could deny that the big day of today is quite unlike what the big day of yesterday used to be. A 21st Century Christmas is a far bigger thing than it ever was in the past. It is brighter, louder, a lot more expensive and a lot longer-lasting.

This book intends to take a nostalgic look back at all our Christmases of the past. The things we did, the food we ate, the way we dressed, the presents we gave and received and the way we enjoyed ourselves.

To do this, I have plundered articles, tips, stories, and features from newspapers and magazines of the past. This is how we celebrated and coped with our Christmases, told in the words of the time.

However I would also like to point out what this book is not. It is not intended to be a "how to prepare for Christmas" book. There will be enough articles, TV shows, websites, podcasts and Tweets urging you to do this, buy that, go there, and watch this in your hectic Christmas preparations.

This book, instead, is a comfortable, relaxed look at the way we were. This book wants you to sit back, put your feet up and think of how Christmases used to be. This book doesn't recommend you buy anything, go anywhere, watch anything or feel pressured into making anything.

It is not intended to add to the stress of Christmas. Quite the reverse. It only asks you to remember, enjoy a little nostalgia, and smile.

Steve Finan

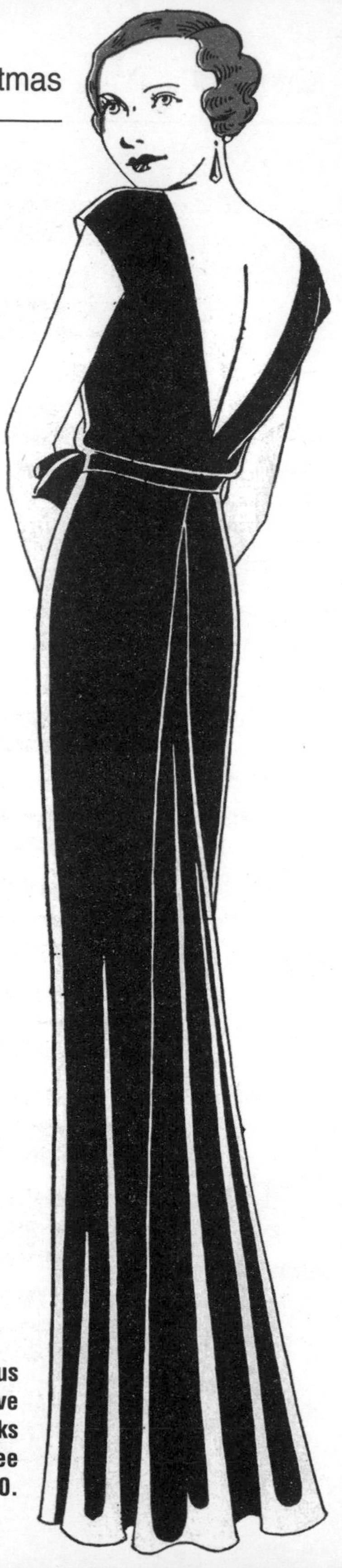

Thanks to:

David Powell, Barry Sullivan, Duncan Laird, Gillian Martin, Sylwia Jackowska, Jacqui Hunter, Deirdre Vincent, Nikki Fleming, Susan Heron, Sara Cunningham, Freya Bigg, Craig Houston, Denise West, James Kirk, Raymond Barr (IT expert), Paul Egan, Fraser T. Ogilvie, and Bill & Chris Nicoll.

Fabulous Festive Frocks **— See Page 170.**

It's Not Like It Used To Be

IT is the one thing that all seasoned, experienced, senior (call us what you will) people agree upon — Christmas isn't what it used to be. And they're right. It isn't.

Whether it is better, worse, more difficult or easier, is up to the individual to say. But, for better or worse, it was different when children got a single present from Santa Claus . Or an apple and an orange in our stockings, with perhaps a florin if we were lucky.

This chapter intends to show articles from the past that illustrate those differences. A Christmas in the time of rationing was a very different thing to what it is today. A Christmas in the very early 20th Century was hugely different to today.

There used to be a bit of mystery and magic around it. It wasn't all about spending ridiculous amounts of money.

We start with a somewhat rambling article from the wonderful, but now gone, Weekly Companion magazine — which has good news for Flappers, but words to be heeded on the subject of women with flat feet.

This chapter also contains stories that have a Christmas slant, or that were published around Christmas, but which show how different the world was just a few decades ago. From children doing alarming things with tomahawks to the tragic story of the woman who declared she'd "spend, spend, spend".

What Weather Shall We Enjoy This Yule?

Weekly Companion — 1926

WHAT weather shall we enjoy — or grumble at — this Christmas?

Judging by forecasts, an open and green Christmas will again be our lot, for the old-fashioned Yule with hard frost and deep snow is now rarely seen except on Christmas cards, and roses in bloom in suburban gardens are much more frequently seen than snow on Christmas Day.

The badly kept roads and the difficulties of locomotion in olden times are largely responsible for the fairly common idea that winters are now less severe than they used to be.

The old chroniclers would make more of slight falls of snow and lighter frosts than we should with all our increased facilities for getting about, to say nothing of the municipal arrangements for the clearance of snow.

Snow has, however, been rare of recent years. During the last 50 years there have been only three really snowy Christmases, and it is only after the "day begins to lengthen" that keen frost and snow set in.

The superstitious may well regard Christmas Day of 1926 with special interest, for it falls on a Saturday.

According to a centuries-old rhyme:—

If Christmas on the Saterday falle,
That wynter is to be dreaden alle,
Hyt shall be so fulle of grete tempeste,
That hyt shall slay bothe man and beaste.

Flappers will be interested to know there is a prospect of plenty of well-berried holly and French mistletoe this Christmas, while Christmas trees are also cheap and plentiful.

This is in contrast with last year, when there were practically no berries and prices ruled high.

Old folks say that, if you would protect your house from fire keep the charred remnant of this year's Yule Log to light its successor next Christmas; and while it is burning see that no person with bare feet or a squint enters — and above all, no flat-footed woman.

Of course, the first thing brought indoors on Christmas Day must be something green; and the first person to enter must be a male — even a tom cat, it is said, can be relied to, bring luck with him.

If a cricket chirrups on your hearth on the fateful day you may look forward to the coming year without a fear; for of all the luck-bringers at Yule-tide, the cricket is king.

Rejoice And Be Glad

Woman's Way — 1919

C — for the Christmas Crib, recreating for us the scene of the first Christmas night. Reminding us of the message of this festival — Peace on earth, goodwill to men.

H — for the Holly with its berries of rich red decorating the house. It has always symbolised joy and merriment.

R — for the Reflections of the Christmas candles left burning overnight in so many windows. In Ireland the old traditional custom of leaving the door on the latch was part of this. It still continues in many areas. The candlelight to guide Mary and Joseph and the unborn Babe to the house — the door unlocked to receive Them with a welcome.

I — for the Ivy which is for ever part of the spirit of Christmas and symbolises happiness. The holly and the ivy, usually joined in a sprig, decorate the Christmas pudding.

S — for the Stocking children all over the world hang up for Santa Claus to fill with fruit and nuts and sweets and little gifts.

T — for the Tree and the Tinsel, all part and parcel of the joy in community spirit and sharing. It was first introduced by a German immigrant to the United States who, in 1847, started the vogue by decorating a tree with home-made paper ornaments.

M — for the Mistletoe, never forgotten by the young. The ancient Druid symbol of goodwill and friendship.

A — for the Alleluia sung by the Angels that first Christmas night, and still be sung by carol singers today. Alleluia — praise ye the Lord.

S — for the Star of Bethlehem which guided the shepherds to where the Holy Infant lay. In some households the custom is for each member of the family to take it in turn to make the star. It is placed over the crib; or on top of the Christmas tree.

CHRISTMAS symbolising love. Not just amongst those near and dear to us, but to all the world. Peace on earth — Goodwill to all men.

Keeping The Peace At Christmas — By An Ex-Police Inspector

The Weekly Companion — 1927

I MAY as well admit that I hated being on duty on Christmas Day, and got out of it if I possibly could.

It used to make me half angry and half sad to see how some people utterly spoilt their own Christmas, and made others suffer as well. It came as a welcome relief to be able to smile now and again at various humorous little interludes.

I'll begin with one of those. At ten o'clock on a Christmas morning a lady, red-faced and boiling with rage, entered the station and dumped the mangled carcass of a turkey on my desk. "Done by Mrs. Brown's brute of a dog," she informed me. " So I want two policemen to come and lock her up. One's no good."

I explained that couldn't be done, and said her remedy was to sue for the value of the turkey.

"But that won't give me a Christmas dinner," she retorted.

Ultimately, much disgusted, she left. About four o'clock another lady, who said she was Mrs. Brown, came and put two shillings on my desk."

"Here's the money to stop the summons," she said, "Although I don't think it's fair after giving her my turkey like you said I was to, and having nothing for our Christmas Dinner but sausages."

I pushed back the money, and said nothing. I was too flabbergasted

Who but a woman would have thought out such a cute plan ?

And the "two shillings to stop the summons" — what an artistic touch!

At about 9 p.m. on Christmas Eve a man was brought to the station, helpless through drink.

Half an hour later his wife, a frail, careworn little woman with two small children hanging on to her skirts — came.

I told her that her husband was in a cell, asleep.

"Could I have some of his wages?" she implored.

"He hasn't been home since he knocked off work, and we've nothing in the house for Christmas."

He had been searched, and all he had was nine-pence. I simply couldn't tell her that, and so the sergeant and I put our heads together and "found" ten shillings for her.

And on Christmas morning I gave the man such a scathing dressing-down that he howled. Whether his contriteness of spirit had any lasting effect, I never heard, the family being strangers in my division.

An hour later a pickpocket was brought in, and although we are not supposed to use opprobrious terms to prisoners I told him he was a skunk.

We can tell from the appearance of purses, and their contents, the circumstances of their owners, and when I looked at those we turned out of his pockets I knew he had been robbing the poor, and so taking the joy out of their Christmas. It made me angry.

The next to enter the station was an old lady, with an orange, a Christmas card, and a mince pie for each of us. "And," she said, "If you have any poor men locked up, do let them go. It's Christmas, you know, and you mustn't be unkind."

After the old lady had gone a young woman was brought in by a constable. She was charged with stealing a fur stole and a bag from a church. A nice Christmas it would be for her!

My next visitor was a woman, with a problem for me to solve — a Christmas dinner problem.

"We've two rooms upstairs and the use of the kitchen where we live," she said. But the landlady has got oven packed-full of things, and there isn't room for another saucepan on the range. And she's done it purposely to annoy me. Can't I make her give me room?"

I sigh, and send a constable along to see if he can make peace. His report tells that the husbands are fighting and the pots and pans are all over the kitchen floor! And Christmas stands for "peace and good will".

And then, to wind up, the leader of a party of "waits" comes and wants me to arrest whoever threw out of the window a number of red-hot coppers. "We've all burnt our fingers," he said, and showed me the blisters on his own hands. I told him he had better apply for a summons.

A horrid trick to play at Christmas.

Do you wonder, after a day like I've described, that if I could escape duty on Christmas Day I did.

Tidying Up For Christmas
Weekly Companion — 1924

JUST about now the housewife decides that a little extra cleaning will be necessary before Christmas, so I hasten to pass on a few hints for lightening the process.

It isn't likely that she will indulge in a wholesale lifting of carpets and orgies of paint-washing, but odd touches with a kinship to spring cleaning will no doubt be required.

Where wallpaper is concerned a greasy mark often mars what is otherwise a perfectly good wall covering. Or some other stain makes its unwelcome presence known, an eyesore to the housewife herself even though visitors may not notice anything amiss.

For Stains

Grease stains vanish if touched very carefully with a piece of sponge dipped in benzene or petrol. I need not add that great care need to be taken that no fire or naked light be anywhere near the spirit.

Another method often employed by professionals is to mix French chalk into a thin paste with cold water and spread it on the stain. Leave overnight, and then brush off.

More ordinary stains, just the kind made round the mantelpiece where a little escaping soot thought nobody would notice it, yield readily to a rub with a bit of stale bread. Rub one way — a downward stroking movement is ideal — and press fairly hard.

Change the bread often, as it rapidly soils. Some painters believe in dipping a bit of bread dough in petrol for very bad stains.

Next — the Furniture

Upholstered furniture has a bad knack of looking grubby just when you want it to look nice. Wholesale cleaning being out of the question, the Continental method of cleaning such furniture might be adopted.

The process requires care, but this is always necessary if cleaning is to be a success. The cleanser is made as follows:—

Dissolve ½ teacup soap flakes in a pint of hot water. As soon as the water is bearable whisk it with the fingers until the suds are stiff as the white of an egg. The mixture must not be so damp as to be sloppy, nor allowed to penetrate to the back of the material.

With a nail-brush, apply these stiff, dry suds to the surface of the upholstery, treating no more than about six inches at a time. Scrub gently and evenly, paying special attention to obstinate stains.

Wring a cloth out of warm water, and while it is still hot wipe over the surface of the cleaned part. A surprising amount of dirt will come away, very dirty parts being done twice if need be.

Velvet can be treated this way, too, a final brush-up with a clean, stiff brush raising the pile again. Where the pile has become very flattened, dampen it and place where the heat of the fire will reach it. The woodwork could be protected with old cushions, dust sheets, &c.

For Paint Work

Any kind of white paint, light-coloured enamel, or unvarnished surfaces can be cleaned easily with a sponge dipped in warm water with some ammonia added. This is followed with a rub up with a dry, soft cloth, using a polishing movement, so that no streaks are left.

Pencil marks on white paint — a not unusual find where children are about — will yield to a rub with a cut lemon or a wipe with fairly strong ammonia and water. Don't rub hard –a soft wipe is quite enough, and does not endanger the surface of the woodwork.

A little whiting sprinkled on a damp flannel will remove marks that refuse to respond to other treatment.

Instead of Polish

To avoid polishing furniture just now, clean it with a flannel cloth dipped in paraffin. This cleanses and shines at the same time, removing an amazing amount of dirt. Rub up with clean soft cloths afterwards.

Even glass can be cleaned this way, and will stay bright in foggy weather.

Linoleum also responds to it. Either add some paraffin to the washing water, or rub the surface with a cloth, well sprinkled with the oil.

A Beloved Light Will Shine Again in John McPherson's Window

The Sunday Post — 1953

IN an empty cottage window, at the head of Loch Nevis, a lamp will burn on Christmas night.

It is the lamp of John McPherson, a shepherd of the hills. For 40 years John lived alone in his little white-washed cottage.

Between him and his neighbours lay 30 miles of desolate country. But John was never lonely, for he loved the wildness of Loch Nevis-side. In winter the sun never struck his cottage. But at night, when wild gales tore shriekingly through the hills, his home was dry and warm.

John never forgot that other shepherds might be out on the hills looking for sheep. Buffeted by rain and wind, they might be lost in the mist and darkness.

So, in his window every winter's night for 40 years, John lit his lamp. Time and time again a weary shepherd saw the light shining through the darkness — and knew that he was safe.

John welcomed them into his home, wrapped them in his plaid, gave them food and shelter, and set them tingling with tunes from his old fiddle.

But one night two years ago the lamp wasn't lit. John, at the age of 82, had died.

Silence came to the little but and ben. The walls lost their whiteness. Seabirds nested in the slated roof.

And the lamp in the window remained unlit.

For two years it has stayed this way — but John himself still lives on in the memory of the men he succoured.

Shepherds — old and young — still speak of him with reverence.

That is why on Christmas night they will light John's lamp again in his little cottage.

It is their simple tribute to the memory of a fine old man.

Good Old Days?

Letter To The Editor — The Sunday Post, 1957

FIFTY years ago, I remember, eggs were two dozen for ls, butter 8d lb., milk 3d a quart.

Women did not powder and paint in public, smoke, play poker or rock ‘n’ roll.

Men wore whiskers and boots and chewed tobacco. Beer was 2d a glass, tobacco 5d per oz.

Labourers worked ten hours a day and never went on strike, folk lived to a good old age and walked miles to wish a friend A Merry Christmas.

Today, everybody rides in motor cars, listens in, looks in, or turns on the gramophone. They go to the pictures, smoke, drink, blame the high cost of living on the Tories, never go to bed the same day as they get up and think they are having a wonderful time.

These are days of high taxes and rocket bases — and if you think life is worth living, I wish you a Happy New Year. — **Mrs E. Tennant, 7 Gairn Circle, Aberdeen.**

Good Old Days?

FIFTY years ago, I remember, eggs were two dozen for 1s, butter 8d lb., milk 3d a quart. Women did not powder and paint in public, smoke, play poker or rock 'n' roll.

Men wore whiskers and boots and chewed tobacco. Beer was 2d a glass, tobacco 5d oz. Labourers worked ten hours a day and never went on strike, folk lived to a good old age and walked miles to wish a friend A Merry Christmas.

Today, everybody rides in motor cars, listens in, looks in, or turns on the gramophone. They go to the pictures, smoke, drink, blame the high cost of living on the Tories, never go to bed the same day as they get up and think they are having a wonderful time.

These are days of high taxes and rocket bases—and if you think life is worth living, I wish you a Happy New Year. — Mrs E. Tennant, 7 Gairn Circle, Aberdeen.

Scalp Um, Paleface

Letter To The Editor — The Sunday Post, 1956

I SAW children of all ages with a great array of toys on Christmas morning, but the one who was enjoying himself most was a boy about five years old in full Redskin outfit.

He had captured a “paleface” — a wee girl’s doll — and was proceeding to scalp it!

I intervened with a few chocolates and the victim was handed back to a wet-eyed owner. — **W. Mitchell, 15 Roxburgh Street, Edinburgh.**

Santa Claus – The Old Man Who Lives For Ever

Red Letter — 1954

THIS is a letter an American editor received from a little girl.

Dear Editor. I am eight years old. Some of my friends say there is no Santa Claus. Please tell me the truth. Is there a Santa Claus?

Virginia O'Hanlow.

And this was the editor's reply:—

Dear Virginia,

Your little friends are wrong; the only things they believe are the things they see. There is a Santa Claus. He exists, as certainly as love and generosity and devotion exist. And you know what a difference they make to your life, how happy they can make you. Just think how dreary the world would be if there were no Santa Claus! It would be as dreary as if there were no Virginias, like yourself. There would be no childlike faith then; we should have no enjoyment, except in sense and sight.

Nobody sees Santa Claus, but that isn't proof there is no Santa Claus. The most real things in the world are those that no one can see — things like love and understanding.

Did you ever see fairies? Of course not, but again, there's no proof that they're not there. Nobody can begin to imagine all the unseen wonders there are in the world. You may tear apart — say, a baby's rattle and see what makes the noise inside. But there is a sort of veil covering the unseen world that not the strongest man, nor even the united strength of all the strongest men that ever lived, can tear apart. Only faith can push aside that veil and let us view the beauty and glory beyond.

And so it is with Santa Claus.

Let us thank God, he lives for ever. A thousand years from now, Virginia, ten times ten thousand years from now, he will still gladden the hearts of all children.

Signed — The Editor.

The Francis Gay Page

The Sunday Post — 1955

THANK God if you have never grown too old for Christmas — even if it can never be quite what it was when you were young.

I suppose (looking back) that, in all, my Christmas gifts were few and rather cheap.

But, I cannot tell you how marvellous the first few minutes of Christmas morning were. Waking suddenly, realising that at last it was indeed Christmas Day...wondering...and then in the dark and cold cautiously feeling for the stocking which had been empty at bedtime.

Oh, the thrill of handling this small parcel or that, and trying by merely feeling to discover whether it was a box of paints or a sugar mouse; guessing if the coin in the toe of the stocking was a penny or a two-shilling piece; opening a tiny cone-shaped paper bag and extracting an unknown sweetie, and lying back under the warm bedclothes and making it last as long as possible.

Most of that has gone, and gone for ever.

But you know, all of us can recapture at least a hint of that old delight if we have planned and conspired in the true Christmas spirit to make some bairn find his or her dreams come true on the morning of the 25th of December.

***There are more tales, memories and thoughts from Francis Gay starting on page 226.**

Can You Remember?
The Sunday Post — 1975

CAN YOU REMEMBER?

WHEN kirks were always full.
When all trains ran on time.
When hard work was rewarded.
When no one worked on Sunday.
When honesty was the best policy.
When criminals actually hated jail.
When prices sometimes came down.
When the £ was a respected currency.
When children listened to their parents.
When your savings grew, not depreciated
When being independent was regarded as a virtue.
When taxes were merely a necessary inconvenience.
When people were proud to buy goods " Made in Britain."
When you weren't afraid to go out alone on a dark night.
When the postie and bobby were friends you knew by name.
When people expected less — but valued what they had more.
When you could go out and safely leave your front door open.
When you could watch any television show without blushing.
When you weren't embarrassed abroad to say you were British.
When you didn't need a fortune to pay a gas or electricity bill.
When a drive in the car was a pleasant trip, and not an ordeal.
When student demonstrations took place only on charities day.
When people stood up while the National Anthem was played.
When you could watch a game of soccer and enjoy it in peace.
When we were individuals and not computer numbers on forms.
When everybody knew the difference between right and wrong.
When men raised their hats, and gave up their seats, to women.
When shop assistants and counter clerks actually tried to be polite.
When you could take the family to any film in town on Saturday night.
When people believed in a fair day's work for a fair day's pay.
When Governments had the interests of all the people at heart.
When Britain was the best country in the world — and everybody knew it.
When people's first thought was what they could do for their country — not what it could for them.
When we looked forward to a New Year with pride, hope and anticipation.

Letters To Santa Claus

The Courier And Advertiser — 1962

TENS of thousands of letters from British children who firmly believe that Santa Claus lives in Denmark's northernmost island, Greenland, will shortly be pouring into the offices of the National Travel Association of Denmark in Copenhagen.

Santa is, however, so busy that he can reply only to letters enclosing a 1s. postal order because he thinks it most appropriate at Christmastime to have thoughts for less fortunate children.

The proceeds are handed to Anglo-Danish Santa Claus Holidays Scheme which works in conjunction with the Children's Country Holidays fund under the patronage of The Queen Mother with Princess Alexandra of Kent as president.

This British fund has for more than 75 years arranged holidays in the country or at the seaside for children who are in need of a holiday but would not otherwise have one. The income from the Santa Claus letters goes towards providing such holidays in Denmark for many of these children.

Last August 120 British children spent a fortnight in Denmark, and in August 1963, 180 children will be able to go. All thanks to Santa Claus's Christmas appeal.

Children who write to Santa Claus and enclose the small donation will receive Santa's acknowledging letter and also a little present of a Hans Christian Andersen's fairy tale.

Address — Santa Claus, Greenland, Denmark. Postage 6d.

The Sunday Post — Christmas 1961

SURPRISING PENALTIES OF A BIG POOLS WIN

THREE months ago Keith Nicholson won £152,319. It was the biggest football pools win of the year.

But has it made life for him or his wife a bed of roses?

Keith was a miner, and lived with his wife Vivian and their three children at Castleford, near Leeds.

When they got the cheque Vivian said frankly, "We're going to spend and spend, and go on spending."

First they invested £100,000 and settled £10.000 on

THREE months ago Keith Nicholson won £152,319. It was the biggest football pools win of the year.

But has it made life for him or his wife a bed of roses?

Keith was a miner, and lived with his wife Vivian and their three children at Castleford, near Leeds.

When they got the cheque Vivian said frankly, "We're going to spend and spend, and go on spending."

First they invested £100,000 and settled £10,000 on each of the children. "That left £22,319 to play with," says Keith with a grin. "We've bought a house and furnished it. We've three cars — a Morris brake, a Zodiac, and Vivian has a Chevrolet.

"A few days ago we were due to sit our driving tests. Vivian failed. I arrived too late for mine.

"We've spent about £700 on clothes. I've bought seven suits and Vivian has a wardrobe full.

"Altogether, we've gone through about £14,000. But after Christmas I think the spending spree will be at an end.

"There's just nothing left to buy."

How has their life changed in three months?

Keith no longer goes down the pit. "Usually he gets up about twelve," says Vivian. Sometimes I get up before that to go and have my hair done.

"In the afternoon there's nearly always something to deal with, either at the bank or the stockbrokers. In the evening we sometimes go down to the local for a drink, or to a dance."

"The main difference," says Keith, "is that if we fancy anything, we don't have to worry about the cost. But we haven't bought silly things."

"I went into a shop where they showed me a mink coat worth £1300," said Vivian. “Eventually I bought an ordinary cloth coat. At £7 7s — I liked it better.”

The Chevrolet was a different matter. Vivian decided she wanted the biggest, showiest car she could find.

“I wanted to give the gossips something to talk about. That has been one of the biggest drawbacks to winning — all the gossip that’s been going on.

“If I go a walk, I’m conscious of people staring, then turning to gossip about me. If I’m out in the garden, in old gardening clothes, I can almost hear passers-by saying — ‘Look at her. All that money and that’s how she dresses!’

“If I go to a dance in an evening frock, they say, ‘Look at her. Even if her husband has won all that money, there’s no need to show off like that.’

“It doesn’t seem to matter what I do, it’s never right for some folk.

“Friends have said — why don’t you go away until it has all blown over? But you can’t go dragging children all round the world just because people are talking.”

And there’s another snag. “Many of the people I’ve known for years no longer speak to us,” said Keith.

“I don’t understand it. I can only assume they’re afraid to be seen talking to us in case others think they’re sponging on us.”

But if it’s tough to live on £152,000 today, the Nicholsons are looking forward to happier times.

“When we get to about forty, then we’ll really live it up,” says Vivian.

“Once the children are grown up and off our hands, we’ll be going to Monte Carlo. We’ll play roulette — the lot. We don’t intend to leave any of the money for the Government.”

Meantime, however, the Nicholsons haven’t been able to spend any of the income the invested £100,000 has brought in.

*The 2018 equivalent of £152,000 in 1961, once inflation is taken into account, is roughly £3,168,000. Keith Nicholson died in a car accident in 1965. Vivian was declared bankrupt shortly afterwards. The couple’s story, and the tale of Vivian’s subsequent chaotic life, was dramatised in a BAFTA-winning BBC Play For Today, which was titled **Spend, Spend, Spend**, and first broadcast in 1977. Vivian died in 2015, aged 79.

Christmas Shopping

IT would appear that shopping at Christmas time has always been rather hectic. Despite all the warnings to shop early, and despite the number of smug people who declare they have finished their Christmas shopping in October (and who therefore shouldn't be clogging up the shops in December) it would seem that panicked last-minute shopping is a habit we have always had.

Yes, Christmas shopping has always been a crowded affair, it's just what was bought — and how much you spend — that has changed.

Ties and gloves seem to have been the favourite gift for men over the decades, while men respond by buying flowers. Or so shopkeepers claim.

And the sales have always sounded enticing...especially if furs are your thing.

If you take a step back from the detail of what is being bought, and just accept that the shops are going to be busy — what stands out is that shopkeepers and managers rarely seem to claim that they are having a good season.

Either people aren't spending enough, or they are spending on the wrong thing, or the shops COULD sell a lot more if they could just get their hands on what it is that everyone wants to buy.

Is there no such thing as a happy shopkeeper at Christmas?

'Twas A No-Austerity Christmas

The Sunday Post — 1948

MONEY may be short — but shopkeepers frankly admit their volume of trade this Christmas exceeds last year, in most cases by over ten per cent. One large store recorded a 33-and-a-third increase in all departments.

There was a drop in the sale of luxury goods. "High-priced luxury goods just won't sell," said one manager. "But women willingly give extra for reasonably-priced clothes, underwear, and blouses rather than buy utility."

Household goods were popular everywhere. Choice ranged from small non-drip teapots at a few shillings to fruit services and water sets at £14 14s.

Does austerity lead to a desire for bright colourings? Shops sold large numbers of small posy bowls, vases, and wall ornaments, all in bright colours.

Most popular gifts for men are ties and gloves. More so this year that they are coupon-free. Shirts, underwear, and kiddies' clothes have all been in big demand. Toy departments all report big business. In one store there was almost nothing left for last-minute shoppers.

At least one man will be a pioneer among model-builders. He bought the first radio control unit on sale in a Glasgow shop. With this radio unit, speed boats and aeroplanes can be controlled like pilotless aircraft.

Sales of books weren't up to last year's record. "More coupon-free goods were available," said one bookseller. Most popular choice was *Came a Cavalier*, by Frances Parkinson Keyes. Close on its heels followed *In Search of South Africa*, by H. V. Morton.

These would have been challenged had more copies been available of Churchill's *Painting as a Hobby* and Henry Cotton's *This Game of Golf* — both best-sellers. Sales of book tokens were also down.

Scottish jewellers report sales of engagement rings were up 50 per cent. on last year. There was no shortage of rings as existed last Christmas.

Type of ring most in demand is the three-stone twist diamond ring. Close runner-up is the three-stone, plain-set diamond. Platinum shanks and solitaires have fallen from grace. To please his sweetheart, the average young man is digging deep into his pocket — to the tune of £25.*

*The 2018 equivalent of £25 in 1948, once inflation is taken into account, is roughly £930.

The Sunday Post — 1949

Happy, Hectic Orgy Of Christmas Spending

FATHER Christmas has chased Dame Austerity right out of house and home. Everywhere the spirit of "To hang with it" has been in evidence.

Quite a spending orgy, in fact, making for the brightest Christmas since pre-war. Salesgirls this morning are resting weary feet after the frenzied rush of thousands of last-minute shoppers.

Buying everywhere was on the happy-go-lucky, lavish scale of old.

City centres were crammed yesterday with arm-laden parents and Christmas Eve theatre-goers. Restaurants everywhere were fully booked, tables jammed tight with excited youngsters having a meal before pantomime time.

Waitresses worked at hectic pace till late at night.

"The people have forgotten austerity," said one chain store manager. "It has been just like pre-war here — except for the prices!"

There was a last-minute panic for Christmas trees. At the market they started off at 1s 3d per foot — then flashed up to 2s. By noon yesterday there was none anywhere.

Fairy lights at £1 vanished from the shops. But there was plenty of holly and mistletoe at 1s 6d per bundle.

And on Christmas tables there'll be thousands of chickens, turkeys, and ducks. Small birds were plentiful at 2s 11d per lb., turkeys more scarce at 3s 11d.

As the zero hour of Chrismas Eve shop-closing drew near it was the male population who made the last all-out effort to get presents in. Busiest shops were florists. "People seem to be making this a floral Christmas," said one.

The folk in hospitals were not forgotten. Every ward was made bright and cheerful. This afternoon toys collected on the trees in cinemas will be distributed to youngsters in hospital.

The Sunday Post — 1950

THE BEST BARGAIN AT THE SALES

THE January sales will be the smallest for several years. But there'll still be a lot of good buys for the sharp shopper.

One of the best will be suits and matching coats will sell at £8. That's normally the price of one garment alone.

About 70 outfits will be offered in one store. The ensemble is in fine tweed, self-coloured or checked. The suit has a straight, wrap-over skirt with a side-slit, and a three-button jacket with patch pockets. The loose coat has a shoulder yoke and inverted pleat.

A range of tweeds and velours will sell at 12s 6d a yard — half-price. They're lengths which were too short for bulk making-up by a manufacturer.

Model gowns, now priced from £12 to £20, will sell at £6.

Another store will have woollen dresses at 15s, 20s, 30s, 40s, 50s, 60s, and 80s.

A draper said he will have a range of wool dresses at £2. Some are worth £8 and £9. He'll sell evening dresses, worth £18, at £5, and others will be reduced to £10 and £12.

There'll be bargains in fur coats — embros lamb coats at £22, short coats at £13. and capes at regular prices are £43, £25 and £12.

Another shop promises to have short beaver lamb coats at 19 guineas. Stock price is £26. The next lot from the makers will cost £30.

Better Than Ever This Year

The Sunday Post — 1952

DID you notice them as you went through the streets last week?

In every street there are one, two, three . . . oh, a dozen uncurtained windows, each with its coloured lights on a Christmas tree.

Never before have there been so many Christmas trees. And not just in the big houses, the villas, the bungalows. Every block of tenements has its half-dozen, telling the message of Christmas.

And have you seen the shops?

Shopkeepers will tell you they've sold more presents this year than any Christmas in the last ten years.

Not expensive presents — but the number of small presents is greater.

Christmas cards are melting away from the counters like snow off a dyke. One woman shopper bought 100!

A customer in another shop bought a Christmas gift for the assistant who served her. What a nice thought!

This tremendous upsurge of the Christmas spirit is greater than ever before. Into our office pours more and more evidence. A phone call from a Government office, for example, said — "Can you dispose of a collection of toys which the staff have gathered?"

A Great Opportunity On January 2

The Sunday Post — 1953

"IF we sold furniture, suites would be going for 4s 11d!"

That's what one shop manager said, and that's to be the trend of the sales that begin on January 2.

Prices will be keenest and bargains the most outstanding for many years.

Biggest reduction will be in winter coats, suits, furs, &co.

Due to the long spell of fine weather, stocks have been piling up in the shops. It is estimated that over 40 per cent. of the womenfolk haven't bought a winter coat or suit yet and over 60 per cent. of the men!

These stocks have to be cleared to make way for the spring collection, no matter what the reduction.

Here are some of the bargains that will be going:— Coat which cost up to £20, going for £6.

Suits, were from £8 to £24, going at £5. Real Harris Tweed suits were 14 guineas, going at seven guineas.

Model hats, were £4 8s, going for £1.

Cheaper hats, reduced to 10s, 7s 6d, and 5s.

Beaver lamb, embros lamb, moleskin, marmot, and pony mink fur coats all at less than half price.

Bed and table linen will also have big reductions. One shop will be selling fine-quality sheets at 35s a pair. Original price, 69s 9d.

Coloured tablecloths were 16s 11d. Sale price, 8s 6d.

Round the store bargains will also be exceptionally good. Yes, it'll certainly be a case of first come, first served this time!

P.S. — When you see a garment or article marked "half price", you can be sure that it is. A new law passed by the Government makes it illegal to describe anything in any way calculated to deceive the customer.

The Sunday Post — 1953

Have You Ever Seen The Like?

YES, anything can happen in the shops at Christmas time!

A woman was wandering round Lauder's, of Kilmarnock, looking for presents for a long list of friends. In the china department she spotted dainty powder bowls, 15s each. The ideal present, she decided — and promptly asked the assistant to wrap up 12 for her!

THAT'S the way to solve your Christmas shopping problem!

A young man went into a florist's shop and ordered 19 red roses for his girlfriend's Christmas — one for each year of her life. Due to the Christmas rush, a mistake was made and the young lady was sent 29 roses!

Her boyfriend had a lot of explaining to do!

Can you imagine a crowd of customers bursting into song in the middle of a crowded store? Well, it happened at J. & R. Allan's, Southbridge, Edinburgh.

Fifty-one children from a nursery school swarmed into the toy bazaar to see Santa Claus. And for his benefit they gathered round him and sang "Away in a Manger."

Customers and staff stopped in their tracks to listen.

And what a cheer the children got when they finished!

Imagine anyone pinching a poker! Yes, it happened in the grate department of a department store. It was not only the most expensive poker in the shop — it was also the heaviest.

A fine Christmas present for the wife — or the old man!

A small boy walked up to the manager of a toy department, "Please, mummy says to ask you if I can change my letter to Santa Claus. I asked him for a cowboy set — but I'd much rather have a covered waggon. Mummy says I can't have both."

"Why, that will be fine," said the manager. "I'll tell Santa Claus right away." A very satisfied small boy marched from the shop, leaving with the grown-ups some of the lost magic of Christmas.

A woman went into a shoe shop to buy a pair of fur-lined boots. She tried a boot on one foot and with difficulty zipped it up.

When she tried to take it off, the zip stuck.

The assistant tried to loosen the zip, then tugged — and ripped her nylons.

The zip was now loose, but entangled with the nylon. The more they tried to free the boot, the worse things became.

Finally, the manager was called in and gave the woman a new pair of nylons. She put them on, and said she would come back and buy the boots some other day.

So far, she hasn't shown up!

In a Littlewood's store, a small boy punched one of the tills and suddenly found himself in possession of the day's takings!

Many children think the tills are little pianos and try tapping the keys!

A little boy walked into a china shop and bought a china sandwich tray for his mother.

He laid on the counter a little heap of shillings, sixpences, threepennies, and pennies to pay the 8s 11d.

"I'm sure Mummy will like that," he said.

He got his parcel and made for the door. But as he fumbled with the door handle, the parcel dropped. Crash!

He stared crestfallen at the wreckage and his eyes filled with tears.

The shopkeeper then called him back and gave him a free choice of another tray at the same price.

The relief in the little boy's face was worth seeing!

A woman visited a cosmetic counter. In less than ten minutes she bought more than £30 worth of cosmetics!

Yes, anything CAN happen in the shops at Christmas time.

Christmas Chaos In The Streets

The Sunday Post — 1958

SHOPPERS yesterday caused the biggest traffic chaos of the year as they flocked in their thousands to towns and cities for the Christmas shopping peak.

It was "parking pandemonium" in many places.

Cars and buses stayed stationary for 20 minutes at a time and bus queues doubled and trebled their normal Saturday length.

Bad weather during the week had kept many shoppers at home and they grasped their last Saturday before Christmas with both hands and open purses.

Stores ended the day well satisfied with their share of the spending spree.

The Automobile Association last night issued a round-up of some of the most seriously congested areas, based on reports from patrols.

Manchester — Extensive traffic jams. Cars were taking 15 minutes to move 100 yards.

Wolverhampton — All car parks full. Traffic three times as heavy as normal. Serious congestion. Up to 20 minutes' delay in clearing traffic lights.

Bristol — Parking spaces non-existent. Cars and buses crawling bumper to bumper. The situation would have been worse but for the heavy rain.

Nottingham — All car parks full. Motorists parking their cars in side streets considerable distances from main shopping areas.

Birmingham — Very heavy traffic, but little congestion.

Traffic was also very heavy in Newcastle-on-Tyne, Gloucester, Bath and Leicester.

In London, A.A. patrols said the central area was reasonably clear, but in the suburbs many more cars than usual were reported.

And what have been the most popular "buys"?

A popular gift for men will be pyjamas. Lots of women will get lingerie and stockings. Other firm favourites are gloves and scarves. Add hand-bags and cosmetics to the list if you're a woman.

2 The Sunday Post, December 21, 1958.

CHRISTMAS CHAOS IN THE STREETS

SHOPPERS yesterday caused the biggest traffic chaos of the year as they flocked in their thousands to towns and cities for the Christmas shopping peak.

It was "parking pandemonium" in many places. Cars and buses stayed stationary for 20 minutes at a time and bus queues doubled and trebled their normal Saturday length.

FIRE—BUT PARTY WENT ON

The Shy Bride Of 16

Minister's 12,000 Miles A Year

ISRAELIS SHOOT DOWN EGYPTIAN PLANE

FOREIGN NEWS

STRIKE HITS SHOPPING

MANDRAKE TAKEN ILL AT THEATRE

IN BRIEF

Christmas Card Delay In Dundee

5 Alpine Avalanches

Mr Rountree Flies

• For Friends Abroad

★ VICTOR SILVESTER

Courier & Advertiser

Manager of a big department store also found that more money was being spent on food this year.

"Busier than last year," said the manager of another store. "They are buying everything, though the average spent on each gift is slightly less than last year."

A member of a large drapery firm said hire purchase was affecting their Christmas trade.

"People are spending less than last year. They aren't buying the big things. But, all the same, business is remarkable," he said.

The main tendency has been towards small gifts.

Toys and games for children were selling well, and many were sold out in certain areas.

The secretary of a large store commented, however, that where people spent 15s last Christmas, they were probably spending 10s this year.

A china shop has a gigantic "piggy" bank in the window labelled "start saving now for NEXT Christmas."

It costs 84s.

IT'S A RECORD CHRISTMAS FOR THE SHOPS

The Sunday Post — 1967

THE main London stores reported Christmas sales records — and the picture was the same in most parts of the country.

Mr Elson Gamble, vice-chairman of the House of Fraser, Glasgow, said, " There is no doubt this is a record Christmas. People seem to be buying more expensive gifts."

Aberdeen shop managers reported the best day's business for the festive season. Some found their stocks inadequate.

Most city centres seethed with last-minute Christmas buyers. Shops and stores were jam-packed and queues were the order of the day. Sales increases of between 10 and 20 per cent. were reported by the larger stores.

A spokesman for one said, " It's been a fabulous Christmas."

A G.P.O. spokesman said last night that with this morning's collection still to come in. the Christmas mail would be near last year's record.

On the railways, all regions reported smooth running.

A Christmas warning came from the Automobile Association, who pointed out that few garages will be open on Christmas Day and reminded motorists to ensure they had enough fuel.

The A.A. in Glasgow said motorists were taking breathalyser tests seriously and this was having an effect on festivities.

Women drivers were much in evidence after closing time.

The Sunday Post — 1974

Stand Yourself A Car For Xmas!

CAR dealers are having a record Christmas for new sales.

It's been the best December ever for the sale of new models in many areas.

Foreign cars in particular are going well. But home-produced vehicles in the lower engine size range are also selling briskly.

The latest increase in petrol prices has brought many motorists with larger cars to the end of their tether.

Also influencing buyers is a recent survey which advised people to buy consumer goods right away rather than later.

With money depreciating in value because of inflation, cash in the bank has almost become a liability.

So cars, like many other luxury items, are enjoying a mini-boom.

British Leyland recently announced their cars will shortly go up in price by 8-and-a-half per cent.

So many garages selling British Leyland vehicles are offering their existing stocks at pre-increase prices.

On a £1500 car, buying now instead of next spring can save the purchaser £127.50 — enough to pay the tax and insurance for the first year.

Ford agents say December sales are up 20 per cent compared to the same period last year.

Another foreign car retailer's sales are up by a third.

Most popular models — small Renaults, Fiats, and Citroens.

One phenomena noticed by the trade is that fewer motorists are offering their cars as trade-ins.

Trade-in prices have never been lower, and many motorists are finding they can get a better price for their old faithful by selling it privately. This allows them to get a better discount on a new car for cash.

The Magic Of Christmas Presents

CHRISTMAS, some might tell you, is all about presents. The giving and receiving, which is really the satisfaction of giving "something just right", and the surprised joy of getting "just what I always wanted".

Asked to think of one definitive image of Christmas, certainly Christmas as a child, many people would choose a picture of giftwrapped parcels around the tree, put there by Santa Claus who also ate his biscuit and milk, and fed the proffered carrot to Rudolph.

We all loved the excitement of presents on Christmas morning, didn't we? Even if the presents might not quite bear favourable comparison with the sort of stuff Santa lugs down chimneys nowadays

Choosing what to buy, however, has never been a simple task, as the new husband who got his wife a steam iron would tell you.

There is a clear message in this chapter, though. The unusual, the remarkable, the amazing . . . these are the stuff of Christmas magic. The woman who was given 50 guinea shoes, in 1959, will never have forgotten that Christmas morning. The child who got the £110 "gleaming red racing car" probably regards 1956 as "the best Christmas ever".

A surprise "just right" present lives in the memory for a lifetime.

Mind you, 50 guineas is a bit steep for a pair of shoes, isn't it?

The Sunday Post — December 25, 1959

ONE young lady in the Borders received the Christmas present of a lifetime this morning — a pair of shoes.

But no ordinary shoes, these. They cost 50 guineas*.

For some time, these shoes have been the centre of a window display in Mr John Rennie's shoe shop at 10 Bourtree Place, Hawick.

They were evening shoes made of cream satin, slip-on courts with a pointed toe and a three-inch heel.

Embedded all over the shoes were £45 worth of semi-precious stones — among them garnets which gave a dazzling orange, green and red effect.

People from all over the Borders travelled to Hawick to see the sumptuous shoes.

Women gazed for minutes at them — and the price.

Then a man came into the shop and bought them.

By now someone has slipped the size three-and-a-half shoes on — and will be feeling like Cinderella!

THE WOMAN WITH THE 50-GUINEA SHOES

ONE young lady in the Borders received the Christmas present of a lifetime—a pair of shoes.

But no ordinary shoes, these.

They cost 50 guineas.

For some time, these shoes have been the centre of a window display in Mr John Rennie's shoe shop at 10 Bourtree Place, Hawick.

They were evening shoes made of cream satin, slip-on courts with a pointed toe and a three-inch heel.

Embedded all over the shoes were £45 worth of semi-precious stones—among them garnets which gave a dazzling orange, green and red effect.

People from all over the Borders travelled to Hawick to see the sumptuous shoes.

Women gazed for minutes at them—and the price.

Then a man came into the shop and bought them.

By now someone has slipped the size three and a half shoes on—and will be feeling like Cinderella!

*The 2018 equivalent of 50 Guineas in 1959, once inflation has been taken into account, is roughly £1,170.

Now I MUST Get Something For The Wife Today

The Sunday Post — 1962

I'M an assistant in a ladies' outfitters. And on Wednesday afternoon I make the acquaintance of well-meaning but lazy husbands.

Husbands who've been meaning to get a Christmas present for their wives ever since October — but never seem to get round to it until the afternoon of December 24.

Christmas has practically arrived — and no present for the wife. Help!

They get away from work early, and pour into the shops wild-eyed and panic-stricken. You never saw such a collection of lost-looking souls in your life.

"I'm looking for a Christmas present for the wife," they tell you.

"Yes, sir," you say brightly. "Was there anything particular you had in mind?"

"No," they reply. "Something round about three quid — no, better make it four quid."

The Yuletide spirit!

These last-gasp Santas all have one thing in common — utter ignorance of their wives' tastes and measurements.

I suggested a pair of gloves to one of them last year. "Fine, fine," he said eagerly.

"Any idea what size the lady takes, sir?" I asked.

He shook his head blankly. Then, suddenly he brightened.

"I know this much — I can't get my hand into her gloves," he said helpfully. His hands were as big as spades. He couldn't have got them into her handbag!

Another man, after racking his brains, said he seemed to remember his wife saying something about needing a new skirt. The poor woman had probably been hinting her head off for weeks.

"We've some lovely skirts," I assured him. "What's your wife's waist measurement?"

"Forty," he stated emphatically.

"Forty!" I said. "Are you sure?"

He nodded. "I remember her telling me just the other night," he asserted. "Waist 40. Hips 27."

I eventually convinced him that he had things the wrong way round. He didn't look the type who worked in a circus side-show.

One gentleman started off with a great show of confidence. "I'd like a woollen cardigan for my wife, please," he said.

"What colour, sir?" I asked. That stopped him for a moment.

"Oh, any colour at all," he said, with obvious satisfaction at having solved this problem so cleverly.

But I had another poser for him. "About what size, sir?"

He was stumped. "Would it be large, medium, or small?" I suggested.

He thought hard. "Well, I wouldn't call her exactly small. But I wouldn't say she was large, either. She must be medium."

That man was about 40. Presumably he'd been married for nearly 20 years. Yet he didn't even know whether the woman he'd married was large, medium, or small.

Oh, yes, 1 have some beauties in the shop, I can tell you. And they'll be back again this week — the same old lost sheep.

Well, boys, before now and Wednesday, find out by devious means —

(1) Your wife's size in gloves.

(2) Her size in shoes.

(3) Her size in hats.

(4) Her favourite colour.

(5) The colours she can't stand.

(6) Her bust, waist, and hip measurements.

Believe me, it'll make my job a lot less complicated! **T. K.**

Now I MUST Get Something For The Wife Today

I'M an assistant in a ladies' outfitters.

And on Wednesday afternoon I make the acquaintance of well-meaning but lazy husbands.

Husbands who've been meaning to get a Christmas present for their wives ever since October—but never seem to get round to it until the afternoon of December 24.

Christmas has practically arrived—and no present for the wife. Help!

They get away from work early, and pour into the shops wild-eyed and panic-stricken.

You never saw such a collection of lost-looking souls in your life.

"I'm looking for a Christmas present for the wife," they tell you.

"We've some lovely skirts," I assured him. "What's your wife's waist measurement?"

"Forty," he stated emphatically.

"Forty!" I said. "Are you sure?"

He nodded. "I remember her telling me just the other night," he asserted. "Waist—40. Hips—27."

I eventually convinced him that he had things the wrong way round. He didn't look the type who worked in a circus side-show.

ONE gentleman started off with a great show of confidence.

"I'd like a woollen cardigan for my wife, please," he said.

"What colour, sir?" I asked.

That stopped him for a moment.

"Oh, any colour at all," he said, with obvious satisfaction at having solved this problem so cleverly.

Not Pleased With Their Presents

The Sunday Post — December 31, 1959

THOUSANDS of women all over Scotland went to the shops last week to change their Christmas present.

On its first day open after the holiday, one store was besieged.

The situation became so difficult that in the middle of the afternoon assistants were told to make no more exchanges except where a wrong size had been given.

One Glasgow woman brought back a diamante dress clip her husband had given her as a present.

"This isn't the kind I wanted," she said. She paid £2 more to get something more to her liking.

Another woman went back with a 7s 6d bottle of hand cream She swapped it for a box of powder.

"Many women are far too fussy about the kind of brooch they'll wear or the kind of perfume they'll use," said a shopkeeper.

"Others want to change the nature of the gift altogether."

For instance, one woman wanted to exchange a bottle of expensive French perfume for something more practical — a handbag, she suggested.

It couldn't be done. In most shops, exchanges can only be made in the department where the gift was bought.

MORE AND MORE PEOPLE AREN'T PLEASED WITH THEIR PRESENTS

THOUSANDS of women all over Scotland went to the shops last week to change their Christmas presents.

On its first day open after the holiday, one store was besieged. The situation became so difficult that in the middle of the afternoon assistants were told to make no more exchanges except where a wrong size had been given.

One Glasgow woman brought back a diamante dress clip her husband had given her as a present.

"This isn't the kind I wanted," she said. She paid £2 more to get something more to her liking.

Another woman went back with a 7s 6d bottle of hand cream. She swopped it for a box of powder.

"Many women are far too fussy about the kind of brooch they'll wear or the kind of perfume they'll use," said a shopkeeper. "Others want to change the nature of the gift altogether."

For instance, one woman wanted to exchange a bottle of expensive French perfume for something more practical—a handbag, she suggested. It couldn't be done. In most shops, exchanges can only be made in the department where the gift was bought.

"Happy Christmas Darling!"

the Revolutionary New HOOVER Steam or Dry IRON

UP-it STEAM IRONS

DOWN-it DRY IRONS

What a very clever way of saying 'Happy Christmas'! It's proof at once you're a really *thoughtful* husband. Because a Hoover Steam-or-Dry Iron is exactly what she wants! It gives the crispest, smoothest results ever — a really professional finish! Saves damping down. Weighs less than normal irons. And marvellous value — two irons in one — £4.19.6.

See your Hoover dealer now!

IMPORTANT!
Only the Hoover has these essential features

1 To change from steam to dry, you just flick control on handle — that's all! (No need to empty iron.)

NO BOILING UP IN THE TANK

2 There is no boiling up inside the tank. The steam is formed by water dropping through from the tank on to the hot interior of the iron one drop at a time.

EVEN DISTRIBUTION OF STEAM

3 Slots in the base distribute steam evenly — not just in patches.

Give Happiness — give HOOVER

Toy Car — £110!

The Sunday Post — 1956

IN the toy shop window at 273 High Street, Kirkcaldy, is the super-toy of the year.

It's a long, gleaming red racing car—price £110.

It's powered by an electric motor housed in the boot, and gives a top speed of 6 miles an hour.

It has an electrically-operated horn (press the button in the middle of the steering-wheel.)

It has an accelerator, and foot and hand brakes. A little lever, operated with a foot switch, gives three gears — two forward and a reverse.

The battery which supplies the motor is under the bonnet. It has to be recharged every 10 miles.

The mammoth price tag hasn't deterred parents. Toy dealer Mr Peter Montgomery has had several inquiries, and one firm offer to buy the toy car.

"That was from the parents of a three-year-old boy just a few days ago.

"I had to explain to them the boy wouldn't really be able to enjoy it. It's really suited for the five to 11 age group."

Toy Car— £110!

IN the toy shop window at 273 High Street, Kirkcaldy, is the super-toy of the year.

It's a long, gleaming red racing car—price £110.

It's powered by an electric motor housed in the boot, and gives a top speed of 6 miles an hour.

It has an electrically-operated horn. (Press the button in the middle of the steering-wheel.)

It has an accelerator, and foot and hand brakes.

A little lever, operated with a foot switch, gives three gears—two forward and a reverse.

The battery which supplies the motor is under the bonnet. It has to be recharged every 10 miles.

The mammoth price tag hasn't deterred parents.

Toy dealer Mr Peter Montgomery has had several inquiries, and one firm offer to buy the toy car.

"That was from the parents of a three-year-old boy just a few days ago. I had to explain to them the boy wouldn't really be able to enjoy it. It's really suited for the 5 to 11 age group."

*The 2018 equivalent of £110 in 1956, once inflation has been taken into account, is roughly £2,750.

The Sunday Post — 1959

HE'S SENDING £10 WORTH OF FLOWERS TO HIS WIFE

IN the last few days some fabulous Christmas gifts have been bought in Scotland.

One Edinburgh man did all his shopping at the perfume counter of a Princes Street store. Included in his gifts was one bottle of French perfume at 19 guineas, and another at almost £12.

Women have clamoured for a new bath oil imported from New York at 65s a bottle.

Even cakes of French toilet soap at 10s each have sold freely.

Last year's average price for perfume was £3. This year it's almost £6.

Elegant long-handled umbrellas at 8 guineas each have been popular gifts in Glasgow. One topped by a chunk of rock crystal sold at £15.

£20 and £30 a time has been paid for handbags. Top price so far is £45. Others may sell before Tuesday at £60 and £70 each.

One Glasgow man has ordered £10 worth of flowers to be delivered to his wife on Christmas morning.

A few Scots boys and girls will get toy baby grand pianos at £15 15s each!

IN the last few days some fabulous Christmas gifts have been bought in Scotland.

One Edinburgh man did all his shopping at the perfume counter of a Princes Street store. Included in his gifts was one bottle of French perfume at 19 guineas, and another at almost £12.

Women have clamoured for a new, bath oil imported from New York at 65s a bottle. Even cakes of French toilet soap at 10s each have sold freely.

Last year's average price for perfume was £3. This year it's almost £6.

Elegant long-handled umbrellas at 8 guineas each have been popular gifts in Glasgow. One topped by a chunk of rock crystal sold at £15.

£20 and £30 a time has been paid for handbags. Top price so far is £45. Others may sell before Tuesday at £60 and £70 each.

One Glasgow man has ordered £10 worth of flowers to be delivered to his wife on Christmas morning.

A few Scots boys and girls will get toy baby grand pianos at £15 15s each!

*The 2018 equivalent of £10 in 1951, once inflation has been taken into account, is roughly £326.

Gifts Go Gay

The People's Friend — 1965

EVERYONE loves to be given intriguing parcels at Christmas. So this year, when you come to wrap your presents, why not try some of these gay ideas?

Christmas Cracker — Are you giving anyone a magazine subscription as a present? Then why not buy one issue of the magazine and roll it into a tube?

You'll find it's easier to manage if you cover it with tissue paper and fix with tape. Wrap with gaily patterned paper, leaving about 3 inches free at each end, fixing the overlap of the paper invisibly with clear sticky tape.

Gather in at each end like a cracker and finish off by tying with narrow ribbon.

Silver Scroll — It's often awkward to wrap a scarf or blouse into a flat parcel, so try making this scroll.

Cut a piece of thin cardboard to the length required, making it about 6 inches wide. Roll scarf inside this and fix into a tube with sticky tape.

Cover with plain paper, then wrap broad satin ribbon round from top to bottom, finishing it off with a matching bow.

Our parcel looked most effective with deep blue paper and silver ribbon.

Charlie The Clown — This makes an ideal way of wrapping a long, narrow gift.

Choose a gaily patterned paper for the clown's shirt — striped, checked or spotted kitchen paper is very effective.

Measure up two-thirds of the way from the foot of the box. Cut enough of the paper to fit this and fix on to the box neatly.

The face is made from pink paper – we used three thicknesses of extra-large paper hankies. Cover the remaining part of the box with this, then draw on eyes, brows, nose and mouth.

Stick the join of the two papers with sticky tape and hide with a broad ribbon, finished with a jaunty bow. For the hat, cut a circle from red wrapping foil, snip into the centre and roll into a cone. If you like, add buttons or pom-poms of cotton wool to the front of the clown's shirt.

Twice The Gift! — To make a double present for any small boy who's a keen stamp collector, wrap the gift in fairly plain paper first.

Cut a circle from stiff white paper and fix on to the front of the parcel. Using stamp hinges, arrange a selection of foreign stamps on the circle.

This idea can be adapted for small girls by using scraps in place of stamps.

Christmas Tree — Wrap gift in self-coloured paper or use several thicknesses of white kitchen paper.

The tree is made from gummed paper shapes that can be bought from any stationery shop. We used coloured circles for the tree itself, but you can vary it by using stars or triangles that look equally effective.

Drummer Boy — Do you always find that wrapping round boxes or tins stumps you?

But the shape's ideal to make a drum that will charm any small child.

First cut a strip of very stiff paper long enough to go round the tin, making it about 2 inches deeper than the actual depth. Fix round the side, making the join as invisible as possible.

Snip the surplus paper at top and foot and fold over firmly. Zig-zag gaily coloured fine cord round the sides, leaving enough free at one end to form a cord to carry the drum.

Cut two circles of coloured foil and paste one at each end of the tin — the folded pieces of white paper make a firm base. Finish by fastening the free end of the cord to the opposite side of the tin — and the drum's complete!

Can You Pack Parcels? Madge Advises You How to Safely Send Christmas Gifts

The Weekly Companion — 1916

I WONDER why it is that so many people exercise great care in choosing Christmas gifts for their friends, yet when it comes to packing them, they are so hopelessly careless.

Last year I was rather unfortunate. Some of my presents reached me in a sad condition, and I find that some of my friends suffered in the same way. And the fault in every case was that of the kind-hearted senders.

I should say that if a gift is worth sending it is worth careful packing. Some presents I have received were packed so carelessly that they really could not be expected to arrive in good order.

The Handiwork of a Belgian — One of my dearest girl friends, who has been Red Crossing in France, sent me last Christmas a perfectly lovely portrait of herself in a very quaint style of frame – the handiwork of a wounded Belgian soldier.

The note which accompanied it told me something of the history of this particular Belgian hero, my friend no doubt thinking that such would cause me to prize the frame all the more.

But, alas! The glass was broken, and the frame quite spoilt.

She had tied up the parcel quite neatly, but not in a manner to withstand rough handling. In posting it, she had stuck the stamps on the fragile box, and in stamping the regulation marks the postal officials had probably broken the glass.

A Fragile Package — From a friend in Cheshire I got such a beautiful sachet. She had designed it herself, and had worked such exquisite embroidery on it.

It was the loveliest thing imaginable in blue satin, the embroidery being carried out in shades of pale pink – an effective contrast.

But I much regret to say that my friend had packed it with just one covering of thin brown paper. Perhaps in taking it to the post office it had been exposed to the rain, thus softening the outside wrapper, and thus got torn in the Christmas crush.

The sachet, I need hardly say, arrived so soiled that I could have cried with vexation over it.

Now, if I'd been sending it, I should have wrapped it up in folds of tissue-paper, and then put it in a box, or between two pieces of cardboard. The final wrapping would have been of strong brown paper.

Photos, Calendars, and Books — Anything in the way of unframed photographs, calendars, or books I pack between two pieces of cardboard.

The cardboards bear the brunt of any knocking about the parcel may get. When buying calendars or any other such thing for my friends, I always ask the shopkeeper to tie it up suitably for postage.

In this way I get the necessary wrapping materials, and I am thus saved any trouble afterwards.

For anything that is at all fragile, I make a point of getting a box, and I stuff round soft paper or shavings, and I never fail to put such packing over any glass with a strong piece of cardboard on top.

Then I never make the mistake of sticking the stamps on the box. I put a tie-on label and use that for the stamps. With this, the stamping at the post office can be done without damaging the package.

Some people may argue that tie-on labels are easily torn away. There is that danger, of course, but I get over it by writing the address twice — once on the box itself, and again on the tie-on label, and to this last I attach the stamps.

The Joy Of The Unexpected

My Weekly — 1957

ONE plan we have found to be splendidly satisfactory is what we call the "direct opposite" gift. Such as giving Granny a bottle of perfume in a deliciously daring "modern" fragrance, or a bit of costume jewellery in contemporary design.

These will shine out like beacons of delight among Granny's collection of hot water bottle covers, bed socks and lavender water — and make her feel deliciously young and frivolous and dashing.

You can depend upon it that great-aunt Emma, who is known to be rather staid and studious, will get her usual quota of book tokens and good, sensible, fleecy-lined gloves and definitely winter-weight stockings.

Go on — give her a bit of nonsense this year! An amusing china animal for her mantelpiece or dressing-table, a gay record (providing she has a gramophone!), a box of "special" chocolates, a jar of preserved ginger — and see your stock go up as a "clever present chooser".

Give the young girl who's sure to get lots of lipsticks and bath salts, a growing plant or a little picture for her room, or a magazine subscription.

All of them with the virtues of being "different" and of long-outlasting something in the cosmetic category.

You see the general idea? Why should housewives — however house-proud – always get "something for the house"; the old, something elderly: the young and carefree, something frivolous?

But whatever you choose, whether for someone in your own age group or out of it, whether with tastes similar to your own or as different as can be, isn't' this the acid test: "Would I like to keep this for myself?"

If as you wrap up our gifts this Christmas you do a little yearn over each of them, feel you really are a noble, unselfish creature to give this and that to your friends, when you'd so much adore to keep them for yourself — then your Christmas shopping this year has been completely successful.

My Dear Readers . . .
Woman's Way — 1928

IT isn't difficult to realise that Christmas isn't far off. Already women are running around jingling bunches of small parcels, and stores are more alive.

The very wise take time and buy their gifts early; but we can't all be wise, so there will be the last-minute scramblers in spite of all the good advice in the world.

Christmas is a birthday. Let us not forget that. We may become so worried and perplexed over the gift problem that we let slip the real reason for giving at all.

A woman who has very little to spend, but gives the little she has to those she really cares for, will have in her heart a quiet happiness — a peace that the woman who gives lavishly and carelessly will never know.

To give to those who have plenty brings less joy. But to remember a friendless, lonely, or unfortunate soul — to plan a little surprise for your true friends, your home folk, sincerely putting your heart into it — is to know the real joy of Christmas.

New Things We'll See In The Shops Next Year

The Sunday Post — 1954

WHAT'S to be new in the shops in 1955? Lots, ladies!

After the glut of girls in shirts and trousers, the female is to become more feminine again.

You'll soon be seeing the shops full of the most luscious bouffant can-can petticoats. They'll be permanently stiffened cotton or paper nylon. They'll have layers of coloured or pleated frills, and trimmings of ribbon, net, or lace.

Some even have tiny silver bells attached to the hemline. These jingle musically as you walk! Prices will vary from about £1 up, according to material.

Leather gloves will come more into the picture again. And the great news about the new leather gloves is:—

(1) They're coming in all the new spring shades like petrol blue, peacock, sage green, and sherry.

(2) Practically every pair of leather gloves will be washable.

Teenagers will like the new pyjamas. One pair has three-quarter length trousers, slit at the hem like jeans.

They're in pastel colours spotted with white. Cost — 19s 11d a pair.

Another pair have a very feminine — hoorah for femininity! — Victorian air! They're made in the same spotted fabric, and have a smocked, lace-trimmed top, and the trousers are gathered in at the ankles with lace-edged frills.

Home dressmakers, especially the more timid ones, will welcome a new type of pattern.

Instead of a blank shape of tissue paper, with one or two odd holes and notches in it, these patterns will have the instructions printed on them. You're told just where to join, alter, tuck, or stitch.

Also of interest to dressmakers is new interlining.

It's warm and fleecy, drapes well, and is extremely light, although made of pure wool.

It looks just like fluffy white cotton wool! Ideal for children's clothes, coats, bedjackets, dressing. gowns, &c., it will cost about 5s 6d a yard.

Another new thing in the glove line will be jewelled woollen gloves. Yes, we'll be able to be glamorous and warm at the same time!

A pair of black angora gloves has backs studded with pearls, and costs 12s 6d.

There will also be a white woollen glove with a dice-check design in tinsel and black. The price will be 10s 11d.

And we'll also see crepe nylon gloves, one size only, which stretch to fit any hand.

Counter Intelligence
Annabel — 1966

FINDING your Christmas shopping a problem this year? Perhaps you'll find something to help here.

First of all, for your husband, father, son, boy friend – if you know that he hankers after a watch that tells the date as well as the time, but simply cannot afford to buy one, why not give him a set of watch-strap calendars?

This is an ingenious notion which can be very useful to the business man. The tiny, metal printed calendar folds on to the strap, showing a month's dates at a time.

Made of smart golden aluminium by Austin Reed, they make an unusual gift, and cost 7s. 6d. for a year's supply of twelve.

I always think food packs are ideal gifts for the elderly, although young wives would like this, too.

Spring and Co. are doing a gift pack of their Traditional Christmas Pudding and mincemeat, both with brandy added.

The attractive scarlet box decorated with Dickensian Christmas scenes contains a 2 lb. pudding in a basin, and a jar of mincemeat. Complete, it costs 15s. 6d.

The postal pack costing 12s. 6d. has the same contents, but without the basin to avoid the risk of breakage.

A gift pack, containing pudding only, costs 11s. for the 2 lb. size, and 6s. 6d. for the 1 lb. size. These also have postal packs at 8s. 9d. and 3s.

There is a strong but lightweight metal rocker which is four feet long and is ideal for children from three years to seven. There are removable canvas seats and it cannot tip over. By James Galt it costs 76s. 6d.

Young sisters and daughters may fancy a mini miner!

Not as expensive as it sounds, it is a gift pack by Miners containing seven mini lipsticks – ideal for experimenting with. A pack costs 4s. 2d. Would make a novel stocking filler.

Any three year-old will love a tractor made by Selcol-Fairchild, Ltd. Complete with trailer it costs 59s. 11d. and will take a child's weight easily.

It can be steered and the trailer is hitched on to a hook at the rear.

If you know anyone who likes the idea of pre-heated rollers, the new concept in hair care, they will be delighted with Dateline.

They heat up in five minutes and come in a sleek box containing sixteen rollers in three sizes and a drawer containing pins. It is neat, portable and costs £9 15s. Guaranteed for one year, too.

More conventional but an equally welcome gift is the portable hairdryer. One by Prestige-Edison has some interesting extras. Inside the lid is a useful-sized mirror, a warm air vent for drying the varnish on your nails while you wait, and the compartment is large enough to hold rollers, pins, etc.

The motor is almost inaudible and fully T.V. suppressed. The hair dryer costs £8 19s. 6d. but if you buy it with a special overnight case to carry it in, the cost is £10 19s 6d.

There has been a revolution in electric shavers – the Sunbeam 777 claims to give the efficiency of a soap and water blade shave with the ease and speed of an electric razor.

This shaver, costing £12 10s., has two heads, each with three blades, thus giving a greater shaving area. Other features — a powerful motor, aero-dynamic styling so that the shaver fits comfortably and securely in the hand, a flip-top opening for easy cleaning, multi-volt operation for the busy traveller and a luxurious case.

Chocolates always go down well with children — in every sense! There are several items in the Cadbury's range, costing from 4d. up. Milk Tray assortments are always popular, too. A new-style box (3 lb.) with a framed picture lid costs 32s. There are kittens (1 lb.) 9s. 6d. and a vintage car box (1 lb.) 7s. 6d.

How about a desk set? Features of a new on the market are a jotting pad, a Parker ball-point pen, a letter opener and, wait for it — a mini transistor radio! It only measures seven inches by five inches and is made in smart black simulated leather trimmed with shiny chrome.

You can, if you wish, have his name engraved on the self-adhesive metal plate which comes with the set.

Cost? Eight and a half guineas.

Festive Health And Beauty

SLIMMING, preparing . . . finding a way to do something about your "dingy neck" — it's all part of the lead up to Christmas. And then there are the parties to prepare for, the problem of getting your hair in peak condition, and of course the best way to apply silver make-up.

You have to look good for Christmas.

And if you go further back in time, a girl to be aware of how she will maintain her looks through long shifts in a munitions factory.

Then there is the worry about what it will do to your general health if you tuck heartily into the turkey, trimmings, and strong stuff on the day itself. Whisky is (it seems) largely OK, but watch out for the Port!

Looking good and being healthy has always been important.

These lycra-clad, fit-as-a-fiddle young things these days didn't invent health and vitality, all they did was invent the habit of wearing gym clothes 24 hours a day.

Fashions change, of course. It is the duty of the young to look at what their parents do and wear and declare it to be "old". They never seem to realise that their parents did exactly the same in their own teenaged time. It is an ever-turning circle.

Being young, healthy and bonny, and made-up and dressed according to the fashions of the time, is as good a way to celebrate Christmas as was ever invented.

Remembering the way it was done in the past is nostalgic as well as amusing — a great way to remember those fun-filled years.

My Weekly — 1978

A THREE-week series to help you become fitter, prettier and completely prepared for Christmas.

Week 1 — Looking Lovely All Over

Bulgy Thighs — Sit in a chair, put a book between your feet, and then stretch your legs out straight in front of you, heels on the ground. Now squeeze your legs in towards the book, using all your muscles from your hips to your toes. Hold for a count of 5 and then relax. Repeat 5 times.

Waist And Hips — Stand about a foot away from a wall, sideways on. Reach your outside hand over your head and push against the wall as though you were trying to knock it over. Hold for a count of 5. Repeat 5 times on each side.

Tired, aching feet — They'll never look good in flimsy party sandals. Try this long-term care over the 3 weeks to Christmas: while you're in your bath, rub heels with a soaped-up pumice stone; treat them to lots of body lotion afterwards. Rub hand cream all over your feet every morning; if they're really rough and dry, rub a thick layer of hand cream over them at bedtime, pop on cotton socks, and leave the cream on all night.

Quick reviver: Splash tired feet with hot and cold water alternately; spray them with Scholl's Foot Refresher Spray (which can, incidentally, be applied through tights, if you want to cheer up your feet during the day).

Dingy neck — Dingy neck from wearing too many cover-up sweaters? A twice-weekly face pack from now to Christmas will help to cheer it up. Always remember, though, to moisturise your neck before and after using the face pack. Or try this: Slice a lemon very thinly and rub the juice over your neck, allowing it to dry on your skin. Leave for about 10 minutes, and then rinse off with cool water.

Goose Pimples On Your Upper Arms — Whip up the circulation of the skin there by scrubbing them briskly with a loofah sprinkled with ordinary household salt. Dry your arms with a fairly rough towel and then smooth in lots of hand cream or body lotion. Rinsing your upper arms in hot and cold water alternately is also good for this kind of condition.

Rough Elbows — Every morning and evening smooth a little of one of the lotions intended primarily for dissolving hard, dead skin away from the feet (e.g., Pretty Feet, Scholls' Rough Skin Remover) into your elbows, and then cream them well with hand cream or skin food. The old trick of "cupping" your elbows in lemon halves for 10 minutes or so, to whiten them, still works, too!

Spotty Back — Scrub it well every day with a soaped-up loofah or backbrush, and then apply some astringent on a pad of clean cotton wool. Check, too, to see whether dandruff is at the root of your problem — if it is, then switch to a good medicated shampoo, and adopt, for the time being, a hairstyle that doesn't fall over your back. Wear cotton next to your skin if you can.

Only 14 More Beauty Days Till Christmas
Week 2 — Hair Care

DON'T let your hair be your downfall. Follow our simple tips and be proud of your crowning glory.

First things first. No hairstyle, however pretty, is going to look any great shakes if your hair is not in good condition, so your first aim must be:

Work to get your hair in peak condition — Take a good look at your hair first, then feel it. What's it like? Strong and supple with a healthy sheen? Or dry and brittle, full of split ends? Or is it, perhaps, fine and flyaway, impossible to manage, or lank and greasy, hanging in clumps? Good haircare should be a long-term policy, but start rescue tactics right now and you should see an improvement by Christmas. Here goes:

1. Your first step, whatever your hair type, should be at a hairdresser (and do remember how busy hairdressers are at this time of the year). A good cut will trim away the worst of any split ends, to help stop them spreading up the hair shaft; give shape and body to fine flyaway hair or lank, greasy hair.

2. Take a long look at your diet. Healthy hair demands a good balanced diet, basically, that's especially rich in proteins, iron and the Vitamin B complexes. Up your intake of fish, meat (especially liver), cheese, eggs, fresh milk, yoghurt, butter or margarine, fresh and dried fruit, salads, cabbage, spinach, watercress, onions, potatoes, cauliflower, wholemeal breads, wheatgerm, Marmite. Eliminate from your diet as far as possible all fried foods that are heavily starchy or sugary. Go on a course of brewer's yeast tablets (following the instructions on the bottle) — excellent for hair health! And take a spoonful of cod liver oil every day.

3. Invest in a really good shampoo — here are our suggestions:

For dry hair — Coromist; Wella Care Almond Shampoo.

For fine, flyaway hair — Linc-o-Lin beer shampoo; Leryss Golden Maidenhair and Safflower Oil shampoo.

For greasy hair — Silvikrin Wheatgerm shampoo; L'Oreal's Elseve Frequence.

Always condition your hair after shampooing to add lustre and bounce to your hair, and to make it more manageable. Again, be careful to use a conditioner for your particular hair type.

Shampoo your hair gently, always, and in tepid to warm water — never use icy cold or very hot water. Don't rub and scrub, and don't wash until it squeaks! Squeaking hair has been overwashed; the squeak is of pathetic protest! Blot hair gently with a warm towel, and then dry it naturally (when you can) or if you haven't time, on the lowest setting of your hairdryer.

4. Massage your scalp lightly every morning to improve circulation, and to loosen up any tension. Use slow circular movements; work from the nape of your neck up and around the head to the hairline. Don't drag at your scalp, just move it slightly.

5. Give your hair a super deep-conditioning treatment for Christmas; here's one that's suitable for all types of hair. Beat together two eggs, a tablespoonful of olive oil, a tablespoonful of glycerine and a tablespoonful of cider vinegar. After you've washed your hair as usual and rinsed out, apply this to your hair. Leave it for 20 minutes, and then rinse hair well.

6. Brush your hair every night (but gently!) between now and Christmas. Don't batter away unthinkingly with the traditional 100 strokes — you might damage your hair. Bend your head and gently brush your hair from the nape of your neck downwards for a full minute, to encourage the natural oils to work their way down the shaft. A natural bristle brush is much the kindest. Do avoid prickly nylon brushes and combs. Anything that feels harsh to the fingers is going to be too harsh for your hair.

7. Polish your hair in the good old-fashioned way — with a silk scarf or handkerchief — to bring out its natural shine.

How To Get By When There's No Time To Shampoo — A dry shampoo (we recommend Batiste) can really revive your hair. Here's how to use it to get the best results:

1. Brush your hair gently but thoroughly to rid it of surface dust and dirt and loose hairs.

2. Dampen a pad of cotton wool in toilet water, make partings all over your head and pat the cotton wool pad over your scalp to freshen it.

3. Spray the dry shampoo (important – don't use too much; this is one case when more is very definitely not better) evenly all over your hair, holding the can a good 10" away from your head.

4. Lightly massage the shampoo in, and leave it on for about 5 minutes.

5. Brush it off thoroughly, using a clean natural bristle hairbrush.

Heated rollers can revive limp locks in a jiffy — but don't rely on them too often, or you may damage your hair.

A steam styling wand can also be a useful tool to restore bounce. If you haven't heated rollers, or a styling wand and are out of dry shampoo, try this: run yourself a bath, or turn on the shower and pop your hair into rollers — the steam will help set your hair. If you have one of the new curly perms, you don't even need the rollers — just relax in the steam!

If you have a fringe, sometimes you can revitalise the look quickly by washing that only – separate your fringe from the rest of your hair with a shower cap, use just a teeny dot of shampoo, and rinse well.

If you're caught on the hop with your hair really in a mess — wrap it up in a super-pretty scarf that matches tones with your dress. Here are three simple ways of tying it:

1. Fold a small square scarf into a triangle. Bring the ends back under your hair and knot the scarf at the nape of your neck.

2. Use a long floaty scarf and encircle your head twice from your hairline to the centre of your head, leaving the long ends to float.

3. Wrap completely, turban-wise, knotting your scarf (you need a 40" rectangular one) at the side, either tuck the ends in, or leave them to float.

How To Blow-Dry Your Hair Successfully:

1. First, do remember that much of the success of blow-drying depends on a basic good cut. Have your hair cut into a simple, easy-to-manage shape that doesn't require complicated manoeuvring.

2. Practise! It's easier to learn if you practise on a friend, blow-drying is quite difficult until you've picked up the knack. It's one of those things that would be so much simpler if only one had three or maybe four hands!

3. If you have the type of hairdryer that has a styling brush and comb fitments, that's fine, but you can manage just as well with an ordinary hairdryer and a small styling brush. Again a natural bristle one is best.

4. It's also worthwhile using a special blow-drying lotion on your hair (there's a good one in the Wella range, for instance).

5. Start by making sure your hair isn't sopping wet — blot it gently with a towel, and then comb through your hair using a good quality wide-toothed comb that won't damage your hair. On the other hand, remember that you won't be able to blow-dry successfully if your hair is practically dry; it should be pretty damp.

6. Hold your hairdryer in your right hand, your styling brush in your left. Now, starting with the underneath hair at the front, each side in turn, brush hair lightly and then guide dryer with fairly rapid up and down movements, not lingering too long at any one spot, and keeping the dryer a good 6" from your hair to avoid damage. Dry roots first, working through small sections at a time. Don't be in a rush, and don't move to a new section until the previous one is thoroughly dry. Keep the dryer moving.

7. When you dry the uppermost layer of your hair, lift small sections of hair gently with the brush, out at an angle — almost as if you were back-brushing — to add bounce and fullness, and then smooth back down into the shape you want it to go. Or, if you have a circular brush, fold a small section of hair round the brush and focus the dryer for a few seconds.

PARTY TRICKS — Try, if you can, to make your hair look a little different, a little special, if you're going to a party.

Here are some suggestions to get you going! Hunt around your local department stores for unusual combs, hair ornaments, artificial flowers to wear in long hair piled high in a French pleat. Spray your hair, just for fun, with Nestlé's Streak 'n' Tips — this is a purely temporary hair colour in a can, in shades gold, silver and blonde, that washes out in the course of normal shampooing.

Have your hair crimped, Renaissance-style, for a special occasion (many hairdressers offer this service).

Section off side hair into two tiny plaits — twist them to the back of your head and secure with a ribbon or comb.

Or braid all of long hair into two plaits, wind them into a bun at nape of neck or twist them on top of your head.

Only 7 More Beauty Days Till Christmas
Week 3 — Party Make-Up

General Hints Before You Begin — Don't simply apply your usual daytime make-up with a heavier hand for an evening occasion — artificial lighting calls for warmer cosmetic colours as well as more definition. A slightly warmer toned foundation, for instance. Subtler shades of eye shadow. A non-blue toned lipstick and blusher.

Never apply a party make-up — any make-up, come to that — without considering what you're going to wear. If your dress is in a neutral colour, like black, or white, or beige, or brown, you can go to town with a glamorous sparkly gold or silver look — there are gold and silver toned foundations, blushers, lipsticks, eye shadows, nail polishes.

If your dress is in a fairly vivid colour, however, you want your make-up to complement the dress, not compete with it, or clash with it — go for a subtler, more subdued effect with muted grey or brown eye shadows, and a lipstick and nail polish to tone with the colour of your dress.

Use lots of mascara — but always allow each coat to dry before proceeding to the next. Use a build-up mascara which has tiny filaments to give a bit of extra oomph!

Special Make-Up: The Silver Look

1. Make-up must be applied to a scrupulously clean face only. Cleanse your face, tone it — and then while it's still slightly damp — moisturise it. Wait a few minutes before applying any make-up; it will give your skin time to "breathe."

2. Use a camouflage stick to cover up any blemishes; you'll get the best results if you first brush on the cover-up from the stick, and then blend it in with your fingertip.

3. Now, foundation. Slightly dampen a cosmetic sponge, if your foundation is a liquid or pancake type; squeeze a blob on to the palm of your hand to warm it and help it spread more evenly, if it's a cream. Pat foundation lightly all over your face, up to hair line and out to ears, under jaw.

4. Brush brows with a dry mascara brush. If they need a little more emphasis, use a soft grey eyebrow pencil. Use very small, feathery strokes so you're actually colouring the hairs and not the skin underneath.

5. Brush a silver base coat all over your upper lids right up from the roots of your lashes to your eyebrows (Boots 17 Pearly Shiner, for example). Blend it in with a cotton bud.

6. Now brush either a strongly silver shadow (examples: Boots No. 7 Mexican Silver Eye Slicker; Charlie Fresh Eye Colour in Silverfrost White) or a silver-frosted colour that goes with your dress (like Rimmel's Frosted Blue or Frosted Green Eye Shadow Stick) over lids from roots of lashes to the crease of the lid, and then under the lower lashes. Blend well.

7. Mascara, next. Grey will look best with a silver shadow. Use three coats, allowing each to dry thoroughly before proceeding to the next.

8. Face shaping next. Suck in your cheeks, and apply a silvery blusher (examples: Charlie Real Live Blush in Silverfrost Plum; Rimmel's Pearly Blush Stick in Pearly Pink) in the hollow below each cheekbone. Blend it out carefully to the sides of your face.

9. Highlighter is important for evening light. You don't have to buy a special product (although Helena Rubinstein's Silver Accent Powder is very soft and shimmery — ideal for dusting over cheekbones, forehead, bridge of nose, chin, to reflect light) — you can, if you like, use a pearly white eye shadow, if you have one — or even, Johnson's Baby Powder!

10. Go very easy on face powder. Use a translucent powder that adds no colour to your face, simply gives a "finished" look. Dust it on with cotton wool and then dust off the excess with more cotton wool.

11. Choose a silvery lipstick to complete your look (e.g. Charlie Silverfrost Pale Pink or Silverfrost Rose). Use a lipbrush for the best results. Blot lips with a tissue and re-apply lipstick. Blot again. If you like a really shiny finish, you could then slick a little transparent lip gloss.

Have Yourself
A Merry Little Christmas
Words and Music by
HUGH MARTIN
and RALPH BLANE
CHORUS Slowly in strict time
Have your-self a mer-ry lit-tle Christ-mas let your heart be light, Next year all our
trou-bles will be out of sight.
Have your-self a mer-ry lit-tle Christ-mas
make the Yule-tide gay,
miles a - way.
Once a-gain as in old-en days
BLACK & WHITE
SPECIAL BLEND OF
BUCHANAN'S
CHOICE OLD SCOTCH WHISKY
DISTILLED, BLENDED AND BOTTLED IN SCOTLAND
DISTILLERS
GLASGOW & LONDON
PRODUCT OF SCOTLAND
70° PROOF CONTENTS 26⅔ FL. OZ
Black & White
The Golden Oldie

Weekly Companion — 1916

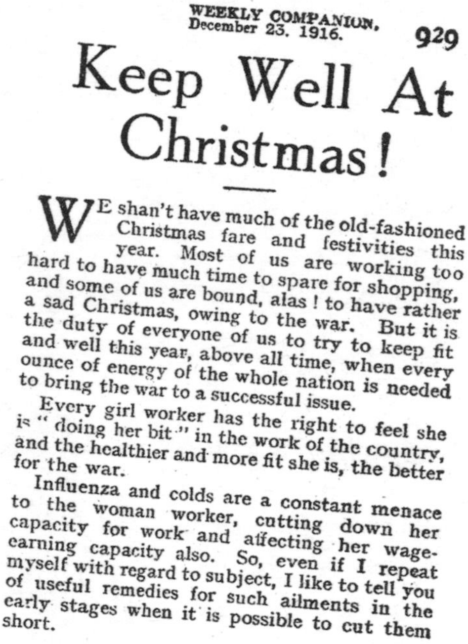

WE shan't have much of the old-fashioned Christmas fare and festivities this year. Most of us are working too hard to have much time to spare for shopping, and some of us are bound, alas! to have rather a sad Christmas, owing to the war.

But it is the duty of every one of us to try to keep fit and well this year, above all time, when every ounce of energy of the whole nation is needed to bring the war to a successful issue.

Every girl worker has the right to feel she is "doing her bit" in the work of the country, and the healthier and more fit she is, the better for the war.

Influenza and colds are a constant menace to the woman worker, cutting down her capacity for work and affecting her wage-earning capacity also. So, I like to tell you of useful remedies for such ailments in the early stages when it is possible to cut them short.

WEEKLY COMPANION,
December 23. 1916. 929

Keep Well At Christmas!

WE shan't have much of the old-fashioned Christmas fare and festivities this year. Most of us are working too hard to have much time to spare for shopping, and some of us are bound, alas ! to have rather a sad Christmas, owing to the war. But it is the duty of everyone of us to try to keep fit and well this year, above all time, when every ounce of energy of the whole nation is needed to bring the war to a successful issue.

Every girl worker has the right to feel she is " doing her bit " in the work of the country, and the healthier and more fit she is, the better for the war.

Influenza and colds are a constant menace to the woman worker, cutting down her capacity for work and affecting her wage-earning capacity also. So, even if I repeat myself with regard to subject, I like to tell you of useful remedies for such ailments in the early stages when it is possible to cut them short.

Don't Neglect that Cold — Commencing "flue" or commencing cold in the head should never be neglected. Guard against such ailments of course by wearing warm woollen underclothing, good knickers, short skirt, and woollen jersey under your coat.

Try this prescription at the beginning, when the stuffy, headachy feeling is so worrying — Sodium salicylate, 10 grains; potassium bicarbonate, 10 grains; infusion of cloves, 2 drachms*; water to half-an-ounce.

Ask the chemist for eight ounces of this mixture, and take half-an-ounce thrice daily after food.

After a day or two, if cough develops, take half-an-ounce of this mixture in water thrice daily: Ipecacuanha wine, 10 minims*;

ammonium carbonate, 5 grains; chloroform emulsion L. T. P., 5 minims; water to half-an-ounce.

Types of Influenza — It is an interesting fact that many cases of the influenza as now going about have symptoms of sickness and diarrhoea, rather than nose, throat, and chest symptoms. If you have sickness and vomiting you should try a little judicious starvation. Don't imagine you have to take milk or beef-tea or gruel every two hours "to keep up your strength." A sick stomach will be grateful for a little rest and quiet, and six hours without food won't hurt anyone. Rather the reverse.

For the diarrhoea, after a dose of castor oil two or three doses of this every hours will be useful: Aromatic powder of chalk, 30 grains; water to half-an-ounce.

Do you rest enough? — The girls who have been working hard these last few months will be all the better of a little rest at Christmas time. Spend one day of your holiday in bed, having a real rest. Try to get extra sleep, and a ten minutes' rest during the day will also help to chase away some of the wrinkles of fatigue.

Try a little beauty treatment — For a rough and tender skin, try this ointment: — Prepared calamine (levigated), 80 grains; water, one drachm; spermaceti ointment, B.P. 98, to one ounce. If the skin is too dry this cream can be applied during the day, and at bedtime as well: Zinc oxide, half-an-ounce; olive oil, half-an-ounce; lanoline one drachm; aqua calcis, 3 drachms.

*A drachm was a unit of weight formerly used by apothecaries, equivalent to 60 grains or one eighth of an ounce.
* A minim was one sixtieth of a fluid drachm, about one drop of liquid.

The Sunday Post — 1955

It's The Mix That Matters — By The Doc

WHEN you sit back today after polishing off your Christmas dinner, you'll probably say to yourself, "Goodness, I'll pay for all this!"

Well, perish the thought. Eat as much as you like!

A real good tuck in of rich food is not bad for you. Indeed, it'll more than likely do you a power of good. You'll feel on top of the world for the next two days. You'd be amazed at how much your tummy can take in at one go.

It can expand from the size of a large orange to bigger than a football — with little or no trouble.

"That's all very well," you may say, "but I've a poor stomach at any time." There's also the folk with an ulcer. What about them?

I've known many a patient with tummy trouble and they eat as well as anybody on Christmas Day. And no bad after-effects either.

The reason is that everybody's digestion is on top form today. When you're happy, the tummy is happy, too — yes, even a poor one.

After two months of winter the system is crying out for proteins — the very thing that rich food has. Foods like steak pie, roast duck, turkey with stuffing, mince pies, black bun, marzipan cake, are all certainly heavy and hard to digest. But they all jolt up the system and, if you finish with fresh fruit, will replace vitamins we've lost.

One important thing to remember is this — make the biggest meal of the year the longest meal of the year. Even an hour and a half isn't too long.

The best time for gorging is really between 6 and 7.30 p.m. But between 1 and 2.30 is a fairly good second.

The stomach is empty then and ready for the job. A light breakfast this morning will not only add to the enjoyment of the main meal, but also to the good you'll get out of it.

What's the best way to tackle a Christmas dinner? Always start with soup or a glass of tomato juice. These are grand for stimulating the digestive juices. The main course dishes you shouldn't take too much of are pork, fatty steak, and duck.

Don't eat too much dumpling after these, either. Go easy, too, with black bun. There's as much goodness in a big slice of black bun as in a whole meat course!

But at the very top of rich foods is double cream. A tablespoonful is enough for anyone.

You can eat as much chicken, lean meat, turkey as you fancy. The advantage of these foods is that you can really delve into the dumpling afterwards!

Just one more word about a big, rich meal be careful with the port — and beer — afterwards. Whisky, gin, sherry, and other wines aren't quite so overloading.

Now, some tips for New Year's Eve. If you're out there's nothing better than a glass of warm milk before you set out. This coats the stomach lining and slows down the effect of alcohol. Keep to shortbread at every house — or sponge cake, chocolate cake, or iced cake.

These all help you to keep your energy, and, again, any drinks you have won't affect you so much. In fact, you'll likely be in bed and asleep before the effects do come. And you've more chance of dodging a hangover!

But here's a warning. Although one big meal today is grand, it isn't wise to repeat the "dose" tomorrow.

Two big dinners on consecutive days can be a strain. As for three days running — that's asking for trouble. You see, on an ordinary day, we take in about 2000 units of energy. On Christmas Day that jumps to as high as 7000 units. It's obvious we can't go on eating rich food without some harm.

And the system, especially the liver and kidneys, is put under strain trying to get rid of the energy. So those who have a craving for rich foods should cut out the habit after New Year.

If you don't, when you catch a cold or flu, you'll be more likely to get a worse than average attack. It's not that you're more prone to infection. You're more likely to lose the battle with it. Years of too rich living can cause thickened arteries, premature old age, even death from flu or colds.

But once in a while there's nothing better than a good tuck in — and now's the time to enjoy it!

Decorations, Trees And Cards

THE Christmas festivities only really began when your family got the paper chains out, and tacked them to the ceiling. There was also that strange paper "thing" that lay flat and hidden away in the loft for 11 months of the year, but opened out to become a 3D circular shape (with the "book ends" Sellotaped together). It was often the form of a pear (which was never quite explained), or had fold-out wings to become an angel.

Then there was the tree, of course, either real or plastic. And the raggedy strings of tinsel and the baubles that seemed to have been owned by your family for a thousand years — but which couldn't be thrown out as they were your "traditional" decorations.

Strangely, however, the hooks (or odd bits of fuse wire) that attached the baubles to the tree always got lost between January and early December.

There was an angel to go on top of the tree, sometimes a star. And who got to put it in place was the cause of many a sibling spat.

It was all part of the magic.

A few of the things reported here merit a mention because they were new ideas, or unusual for their time — though they certainly wouldn't count as remarkable these days.

But Christmas trees appearing in wintry windows are always a sure sign that the wonderful day is drawing near. Fairy lights used to be rare, then everyone had them, then the strings of lights crept out of houses to festoon the windows, eaves, roofs, unsuspecting garden shrubs, various garden elves, gnomes, reindeer, sleighs and (it's a modern world) life-size statues of the members of Little Mix (a popular beat combo of modern times).

Times have, indeed, changed.

It's Good Fun Making Your Own Christmas Decorations

The Sunday Post, 1935 (By Our Woman Correspondent)

HALF the fun of Christmas and New Year festivities lies in the decorations, without which the atmosphere seems all wrong. Why not, this year, try to get away from the usual holly and our old friend the paper chain?

There are some equally gay effects to be achieved with other methods. In a room where there is, perhaps, flowered wallpaper and cretonne furnishing you would be delighted with the effect of plain white and silver decorations.

If brown and red tones predominate, try white and gold.

Take laurel, holly, and any other pretty leaves you can get, and dip them in whitewash thinned down to a creamy thickness. When they are dry give the leaves little splashes of the gold or silver paint, which may be purchased for a few pence a bottle.

If you like a dash of colour, touch up the leaves with scarlet or orange paint, or colour the holly berries, which are now white.

Cellophane may be bought in sheets in all bright colours. Cut out as many small circles — about three inches across — as your patience will allow, and thread them on to tinsel thread, making a knot below each disc of paper about an inch apart. An alternative is to have two contrasting circles at each knot.

Strings of these discs suspended in the corners of a room, or round a lamp bracket, give a lovely Oriental look.

Cellophane may also be cut into petals, three or four being fastened to a wire stem, which can be covered with tinsel or bright green wool. Sew a coloured bead into the centre of each flower, or put a dab of bright paint.

Balloons strung on to silver tinsel — the spiky kind used on Christmas trees — and taken round the picture rail of a room look most festive.

Take care, however, that the balloons are well blown up, and very well fastened, otherwise they will present a wilted appearance before their usefulness is at an end.

If for some reason you cannot obtain a Christmas tree, try placing a large branch — or several large branches — of holly into a pot and decorating it with gaily-coloured glass ornaments just as if it were the orthodox fir. The effect is extraordinarily good.

Wear thick and old gloves when planting the tree, however, for holly is spiteful, and, if you are getting pricked, it is difficult to achieve the right result.

Drifts of cotton wool laid around your Christmas tree and lying on the branches to emulate snow always delight children.

Dip the cotton wool beforehand in a solution of two ounces of alum to a gallon of water, and when dry there is no danger from fire. This solution makes materials non-inflammable.

Glass icicles and those of bright foil are sold these days, and can be hung from lampshades and pictures — in fact, from just anywhere, with great effect.

If you have a garden rich with ferns, the fronds look delightful arranged behind pictures in a fan-shape formation.

Sprigs of artificial holly of gold paper with scarlet berries give a gay effect if scattered over dark-coloured curtains.

Strips of paper with Christmassy scenes in black and white and silver, or in varied vivid colours, are obtainable these days, and transform a room if laid around the walls above a picture rail.

A minute tack in the corners will hold it in place without damaging the wall in any way. Cotton wool pulled into balls and scattered with "frost" can be strung on a silver thread and looped across the ceiling from corner to corner.

These are all fascinating things to do, and can be achieved quite quickly by the nimble-fingered.

But don't forget, however pleased you are with your efforts, that they must be taken down by Twelfth Night if you want to keep luck in your house.

Planning Christmas Decorations
The Courier And Advertiser, 1938

CHRISTMAS is all about dressing up the house and laying plans for making the Christmas dinner table something to remember with a thrill.

Merely to stick a piece of holly over an ancestor or two is to insult the ancestor and the festive season. If your holly falls you put it in a vase and set it where it will glow in all its green and red beauty. You can't "spread out" a spray or two of greenery to look anything at all, and it is best not to attempt it. Plain walls, such as are quite usual to-day, are very difficult to dress, but repay the trouble expended upon them fourfold.

A Lovely Effect

Wooden hoops twined round with coloured paper and a bunch of balloons hung in the centre are easily affixed to plain walls, since the weight is not great. Where pictures are present, garlands of silver tinsel and tree ornaments may be fashioned to hang over pictures and mantelpiece. A hanging light in hall or room is a great assistance in any decorative scheme. It can be used as a sort of mooring mast for strands of decorations with perhaps a big central affair to hang from the lamp itself. If the latter is of clear glass it is an easy matter to line it with red, blue, or green tinsel paper to bring it in line with the rest of the decorations.

A Set Scheme

If you are to entertain a lot, it's a good to decorate one room from a purely grown-up standard. Supposing you have hit on a certain colour and mean to use it wherever possible, jade green, perhaps. Begin by investing in a large quantity of glass balls, jade green in colour. The balls can be got very cheaply at any of the bazaars. Assorted sizes are better than all one size, so you could have several dozen tiny ones, a dozen or so larger, and a few very big ones. In addition, candles the same shade will be needed, along with a few good branches of evergreens.

Tasteful and Bright

The quite small balls are very useful for tying on to the branches to simulate fruit in the growing. Avoid over-regularity. One here, two there and three somewhere else give a richer effect than when a lot of singles only are used. The branches should then be arranged in large vases or jars and set where the effect will be seen at its very best. In front of a mirror or near a good light are ideal places from the decorative point of view. Larger balls placed in glass bowls with a few sprays of evergreen are lovely, or you can pile them up in pyramids, if you like. The balls catch the flickering light of candles and firelight and reflect every stray beam, so that the room glows with colour.

For The Table

Table decorations must, of necessity, be left to the very last minute, though a scheme of some sort may be prepared. For the Christmas table it is just as well to rule real flowers out of the question. They are scarce and dear at this time, and should be reserved for other positions, seeing that it is quite easy to devise table decorations that are more typical of the season. An oblong mirror laid flat on the table and surrounded with plenty cotton wool will suggest a skating pond when small figures are arranged thereon. Sprinkle all with frost, and have tall red or green candles set at intervals round about. Berried holly looks nice, too, clumps of it suggesting bushes keeping watch and ward over the pond. Cake decorations come in handy for such a scheme as this.

Always Effective

Red and green are the traditional Christmas colours, but green and white makes a pleasing change. Place a crystal bowl in the centre of the table and set a green witch ball in it. From the bowl have a green and silver ribbon going to each place, ending in a bunch of small silver bells. Set candles at intervals, crystal containers and green candles being the ideal. A group round the bowl would be lovely, while another idea is to have them in one long line the whole length of the table. Artificial mistletoe can be included in this scheme with the happiest effect. Twist it in everywhere you can and enjoy its green and silvery presence to the full. In place of one large ball, a bowl filled with the cheap, coloured glass balls is a decoration by no means to be scorned.

Mr McIntosh's Xmas Tree Goes Round And Round

The Sunday Post — 1962

PEOPLE going along Great Western Road past Kirklee, Glasgow, see a Christmas tree covered with bright lights whizzing round like a whirligig in the window of a house just off the main road!

It was a few years ago that Mr McIntosh, a surgeon, first hit on the idea. He bought an artificial Christmas tree and a small electric motor.

He fitted the motor to a small turntable, and attached the Christmas tree to the turntable. The next part was the hardest — how to wire the lights of the tree? Obviously, ordinary plug-in lights were out of the question as the tree was to revolve. The wires would get tangled up.

Mr McIntosh had an idea. Why not have two little carbon brushes rubbing against two brass rings on the base of the tree as it went round and round?

The carbon brushes would electrify the brass rings, and he'd fix the lighting wires to the rings.

Then he only needed to wire the carbon brushes to the main supply.

It worked a treat. Since then, Mr McIntosh has been asked many times how it's done.

Have Fun Setting The Christmas Scene My Weekly — 1960

EVERY year, when we suddenly realise we're into December, all of us remind ourselves that this year we'll really start early with our Christmas plans.

We'll buy the Christmas cards while the selection is still wide and we can choose ours at leisure in a quiet shop instead of playing a wild game of snatch-as-snatch-can with a million other last-minute searchers.

By the same token, we'll buy all our Christmas presents 'way ahead. And not only have time to select them with leisurely loving care, but bask in a warm glow of accomplishment and virtue.

We'll plan our parties well ahead. We'll plan our decorations too — for everybody knows a house must be dressed and garnished to do honour to Christmas. Ah, well — that's what we always plan.

Whether we always carry out our plans is another matter! But let's try, this year.

Rope in all the family! — We suggest a good thing to start with is the decorative bits and pieces that do so very much to set the Christmas scene and spark off the Christmas feeling. Because when the last-minute rush does start, these are the things we usually skip. And they are such fun. Especially if there are children in the house, or you are planning a children's party. Cute little decorations will delight the heart of any child. Or any party-going grown-up too, for aren't we all children at heart at Christmas time? So what about gathering the older children about you some evening and all get going?

Presents, Packages and Placers — Home-made snowmen and reindeer can have many uses. To hang on tree; to decorate the party table; to set about the living-room; to tuck into a child's stocking; to give a gay and original touch to your present-wrapping. And they're quick and easy to make, and will cost practically nothing.

Pipe-Cleaner Pete — A reindeer that may not rival Rudolph in having a red nose, but antlers can be made from pipe cleaners. The body is an empty cotton reel. And his head a good-sized bead — or it could be rolled from modelling clay. Paint a bright colour, and sprinkle some sparkly "frost" on the paint while it's still wet. Pass a pipe cleaner through the hollow of the reel and the bead, leaving one end out as a tail and the other to twist round the centre of the antlers. Two more pipe cleaners through the reel are twisted into legs.

Sammy's In Cotton Wool — A snowman can be made of cotton wool. Roll it into a soft, fluffy ball, gently pulling out enough to shape into a head and arms, and stick the base on to a circle of cardboard, felt, or stiff paper. Shape a top hat from stiff coloured paper; give him a walking stick of a bit of pipe cleaner — dipped in red ink, perhaps, for extra gaiety — and glue on tiny beads for eyes, nose and buttons.

Sandy's In Towelling — Another snowman is made from a scrap of white towelling. Cut out four circles, two bigger ones for front and back of body, two smaller ones for front and back of head. Sew them in matching pairs and stuff with cotton wool. Two little oblongs of towelling make the arms. A thimble for a hat, a pipe cleaner muffler, silver paper feet, and again small beads for features and buttons. A good idea for a children's party would be to make a Sandy Snowman for each child and use as place cards for the tea table. A drinking straw can hold the names. The children will adore them — and being allowed to take them home with them!

Xmas Card Played Tune!

Sunday Post — 1951

TWELVE-YEAR-OLD Ethel Scoular took a Christmas card into her class at Hutchesons' Girls' Grammar School, Glasgow, one morning last week.

It had come from America. The card was six inches broad by four inches — and three-quarters of an inch thick. It had a beautifully-painted Nativity scene, with a Christmas greeting.

A handle stuck out of the right-hand side. A classmate turned it — then almost dropped the card on the floor. For it tinkled out the tune Holy Night.

Surely the nattiest Christmas card of the year!

People's Friend — 1962

HOLLY and fir, glitter and tinsel — some quick and easy ways to make your decorations.

Christmas cards, with their rainbow colours, bring their own seasonal brightness to a room. Introduce an original note by the way you display your cards. Try fixing them round the edges of a large mirror using adhesive tape.

Another way is to pin them on brightly coloured ribbon, making a matching bow at the top and tying a coloured glass ball at the foot. Fix these strips to the wall.

A variation is to cut different lengths of tape and attach cards to the sticky side, spacing them out well. Sprinkle the rest of the tape with the glitter used for Christmas trees. Fix a coloured ball at the foot before arranging the strings of cards on the wall.

Why not make a Christmas card tree for your sideboard or a table? It can be made by taking a branch of a bush or tree and painting it white or gold. Set it in a container weighted with earth or pebbles.

Tape your cards to the branches and decorate with glass balls and small Christmas tree ornaments.

WITH HOLLY AND FIR — The holly and fir branches of tradition are invaluable for quick and effective decorations. Fill a basket with them and use it as a table arrangement, placing silver balls here and there among the branches to give a little contrast. A simple wall arrangement can be made by bending a wire coat hanger into a circular shape.

Tape branches of fir and holly alternately to the hanger, hiding the hook with a big red bow. You will find that wire coat hangers can be bent into almost any shape, and you can use them as the basis for all sorts of decorations.

Perhaps you would like to frost the leaves of holly branches to make table decorations.

This can be done very easily. Wash leaves thoroughly and leave them to dry in a warm place. Once they are quite dry dip the leaves in melted margarine of running consistency, then strew thickly with fine castor sugar. Leave undisturbed to dry, and keep in a warm place until required.

You can make interesting hanging decorations with balloons. Buy a packet of the balloons made especially for this. These have small loops on the end, so that various shapes can be made by tying the inflated balloons at the neck, then slipping the neck of one through the loop of another.

In this way you can build up stars, squares, circles and so on. One that would be ideal for a children's party can be made by fixing balloons into two squares, using four balloons for each one.

Using another four balloons, join the corners of the squares so that a box is formed.

Tie two lengths of fine string diagonally across the corners of one end, then fill the box with ordinary balloons of all shapes.

Fix to the ceiling with another piece of string tied across the top. During the party you can shower the children with balloons by simply snipping the string that is across the foot.

The Sunday Post — 1960

A Super Christmas Tweet And Happy Mew Year

IT'S all the rage this Christmas — daft, delirious Christmas cards. For instance, you can help your friends to have their own white Christmas! One Christmas card contains a packet of imitation snow, with the inscription — "Do-it-yourself blizzard!" The recipient opens the packet — and, hey, presto! he's covered with snow.

It's only one of the flood of surprising cards on sale all over the country. There are individual cards to send to sweethearts, wives, hubbies, aunties, uncles, bus drivers, waitresses, employers — even to baby-sitters, cats, dogs, and budgies!

Fork-out from 1s 3d up to about a couple of quid, and you can have a card for everything and everybody.

There's a card covered with flies — dozens of 'em. But before you turn away it's not as bad as it sounds. It's for anglers — and they're fishing flies! For 5s you get this one out of fishing tackle shops.

Sweet young things who work as typists or office girls are rushing to buy a "To my boss" card. Inside there's a four-line jingle that's guaranteed to make the sternest heart soften: —

A very merry Christmas card
That's being sent to show
You're very nice to work for
And extra nice to know.

If you're hardly on those terms with your boss, why not try a more conservative "To my employer" card? The verse inside is as deferential as a butler's cough.

Is the man next door the type who seems to have everything? Send him the "Someone Who Has Everything" Card.

Inside this one is a paper clip — to hold all the bills he'll have to face in January!

Cards for pets are going like hot cakes. One is headed "From My Budgie To Your Budgie" with this verse inside: —

A chirp to wish you all the best
With lots of seed to eat.
I hope that Santa brings to you
A super Christmas tweet!

Another, from cat to cat, is headed — Merry Christmas and Happy Mew Year!

There's a special card for the baby-sitter. It has a big, smiling Santa on front, and inside a verse that humbly acknowledges the important place the baby-sitter occupies in the life of the married couple with a young family.

Only trouble is that, after getting one of these, the sitter is liable to put her rates up!

There's a "to my teacher" card that might make all the difference to junior's report card next term — especially if you add this verse, as one dad has done:

The youngster has told me
So much about you
That I find I'm wanting
To come along, too.

A long-suffering tax payer searched in vain for a card for his income tax man, without success. So he's sending one with this verse (which owes more than a little to the Western ditty *Home On The Range*) inside —

Oh, give me a code that's as big as my load
And free me from P.A.Y.E.;
Leave me something to spend,
Before I go round the bend,
And forget all about Schedule B.

Love, Mistletoe, And Other Superstitions

TIS the season of love and goodwill to all men...and mistletoe kisses that mean something, or might mean something, or might not even be welcome at all.

Christmas is a romantic time of year. It conjures soft-focused images of snow-quietened parks, long talks, long walks and a longing to be with the "right one". It is shy glances at the Christmas Eve dance. It is candle-lit, pine-needle-scented and filled with the "what did it mean?" mystery of a slightly long-lingering Christmas hug.

Perhaps more so than any of the other newspaper and magazine articles in this book, those here are "of their time". The "peel an onion and put it under your pillow" approach to finding a husband might not be often undertaken these days.

But cold reality shouldn't be taken into account when reading about love spells and the pitfalls of buying presents for boyfriends who might, or might not, have bought a present for you.

This is romance.

The Christmas Cupid doesn't care or take notice of what the snow-hearted say. The tinsel-tinged magic of Christmas romance was lit by the glow of fairy lamps and drunk in from cups filled with ambrosia and spiced by the thrill of a new love.

Remember when all your romantic dreams might possibly come true? When everything lay before you, exciting and daunting at the same time? Remember that flutter in your breast, that strange feeling in the pit of your stomach?

That feeling was love, and love at Christmas was even better.

Christmas Love Spells

How maidens fair may peep into the future, at their own risk Woman's Way — 1910

THIS is the season of the year when, according to tradition — good fairies permit maidens to have a privileged peep into the future. There are many ways in which it can be done!

On the Eve of St. Thomas, five days before Christmas Day, let the girl who wishes to see her husband-to-be peel an onion — preferably a large red one — wrap it in a clean handkerchief, and place it under her pillow, saying as she does so:—

Good St. Thomas, do me right,
And let my true love come to-night,
That I may see him in the face
And him in my kind arms embrace.

Another method, said to be equally efficacious, is, after peeling the onion, to stick one pin right in the middle of it, and eight others in a circle round it, while the maiden repeats the following lines :—

Good St. Thomas, do me right,
Show me my true love to-night,
In the clothes and the array
Which he weareth every day.

If a girl is anxious (and what girl is not?) to know how Love will treat her in the years to come, she should — also on the eve of St. Thomas — cut an apple in two and count the pips in each half.

If the numbers are equal it is considered a sure sign that she will soon stand at the altar. If one of the pips is cut in two she may not expect the course of true love to run smoothly; while, if two of them are thus cut, widow's weeds will soon follow her wedding-ring!

Still richer in love omens and spells is Christmas Eve. If a girl takes a seat, on Christmas Eve, between two mirrors, with a candle on either side of her, she should, in time, see twelve candles reflected in the mirror.

The figure of her future husband will also be seen.

If this method should fail, she will still be able to try another. She must take her seat at a supper-table laid for two, when, after a period of hopeful waiting, concentrating her mind on her wish, she will see her true lover take his seat on the vacant seat by her side.

It is important, however, that she should not breathe a word of her experiment to anyone. To do this would be fatal to success.

Should her ambition still be unrealised when Christmas Day dawns, she has, at least, three more opportunities.

Before retiring to bed on Christmas Day she should arrange her shoes in the form of a capital T, repeating as she does so these lines :—

Hoping this night my true love to see,
I place my shoes in the form of a " T."

If the spell works her lover will appear to her in dreams. If not, she can try this :—

With a girl friend, also unmarried, she must keep vigil until the clock strikes one, in a room where they are alone. Each will have already extracted a hair from her head for each year she has lived, and wrapped them in a linen cloth containing some true-love herb.

As the clock strikes, the girls should burn every hair separately, saying:—

I offer this my sacrifice
To him most precious
I charge thee now come in forth to me
That I this minute thee may see.

As she speaks the last word the husband-to-be of each girl should appear, walk round the room and vanish into thin air

How they identify the right one, goodness alone knows.

More romantic is the spell of the withered rose, but as this must be

prepared for six months in advance — the tip given now will have to do for next year.

On Midsummer Eve the maiden should walk backwards into a garden — taking care the police do not see her! She must then gather a rose and send it up in a paper bag which must be placed in a dark drawer.

On the morning of Christmas Day she has to open the bag, and place the rose next her heart. Then when she goes to church the man she is to wed should appear, and either ask her for the rose or take it without the formality of asking for it.

Shall I Give My Boy A Present?
Woman's Way — 1935

YOU'VE got a boy friend, and you want to give him a present.

You're wondering if he'll think it forward of you.

Perhaps you're grateful for being taken out; perhaps you hope it'll make him more interested in you!

Or it may be that he has gone away, and you want to be remembered.

Fortunately, in a good many cases, a girl can give her man friend a present without being forward.

The golden rule about giving a present to a man is this. You must have first of all had something from him.

That something need not have been a recent gift.

It need not even have been a gift at all. He may have been responsible for a good time you had, done a job for you, or been a very good friend.

Then there will be no chance of you seeming forward if you make him a present.

But you must not give a present to a man who has done nothing for you at all. This would be bad taste on your part, and would probably embarrass him a lot.

The only exception to this rule is when your friend is very shy.

Some men can't bring themselves to approach that girl in whom they are interested.

In such a case, you may give a very small present without having had something from him first.

But be sure it is shyness on his part, and not indifference.

Now, about the actual giving.

If you have had a lot from him in presents and outings, you can make him a really nice gift. But otherwise a present — especially a first one — should be quite small. Small gifts can be just as acceptable as expensive ones.

A girl ought to think twice before giving a man a tie or any other

thing which he has to wear — even if she arranges with the shop that he can change it if he likes. He may not care to do so, for fear of hurting her feelings.

Think how troublesome it would be if he gave you a beret you simply hated!

Lastly, send your present by post, and in plenty of time. This will give him a chance to rush out and buy you something — if he hasn't already done so!

Evening Telegraph — 1957

FOR most people Christmas has a religious significance coupled with the feasting, parties and pantomimes.

But in the centuries before the birth of Christmas, December was still a month for celebration.

Men worshipped the sun as the source of light and life.

December, in which the sun reputedly reappeared after the shortest day of the year, was always regarded as a festival month.

It was not until the middle of the fourth century that December 25 was decided upon by the Bishop of Rome as being the date of the Nativity.

MISTLETOE'S MEANING

FOR most people Christmas has a religious significance coupled with the feasting, parties and pantomimes. But in the centuries before the birth of Christ December was still a month for celebration.

Men worshipped the sun as the source of light and life. December, in which the sun reputedly reappeared after the shortest day of the year, was always regarded as a festival month.

It was not until the middle of the fourth century that December 25 was decided upon by the Bishop of Rome as being the date of the Nativity.

There is little doubt the move was made in the hope that by making an essentially Christian day coincide with pagan festivals man's thoughts might be turned to spiritual matters.

But the ancient rites of sun were too well embedded to be rooted out easily.

By the end of the fourth century Church leaders were forced to accept the fact that the heathen customs would have to be assimilated into the Christmas celebrations.

Our traditions have grown from these ancient customs and Christmas rituals.

From the ancient Romans comes the traditional feasting; from the Norsemen of Scandinavia the Yule Log, where in pre-Christian days logs were burnt in honour of the gods Odin and Thor.

But what of the other Christmas customs — the turkey, mistletoe, Christmas trees, house decorations?

James I introduced the turkey as the staple fare; decorations came from the ancient Romans, who always decorated their houses with ever-greens and other baubles on festive occasions; and the Danes gave us the delightful custom of kissing under the mistletoe.

To them, mistletoe was a symbol of peace and love, and those who embraced beneath it would never quarrel.

The first time Britain had a Christmas tree was as late as 1839 when a German princess had one at Panshanger (a stately home in Hertfordshire).

Its rapid rise in popularity dates to 1841, when Prince Albert had one at a Windsor Castle party.

Surely the custom with the most universal appeal is that of children hanging up a stocking on Christmas Eve.

But how many of them know the story of Santa Claus?

The legend originated in the fourth century. Saint Nicholas of the Netherlands, who delighted in helping the poor, dropped his purse down a chimney.

It fell into a stocking which had been hung up to dry.

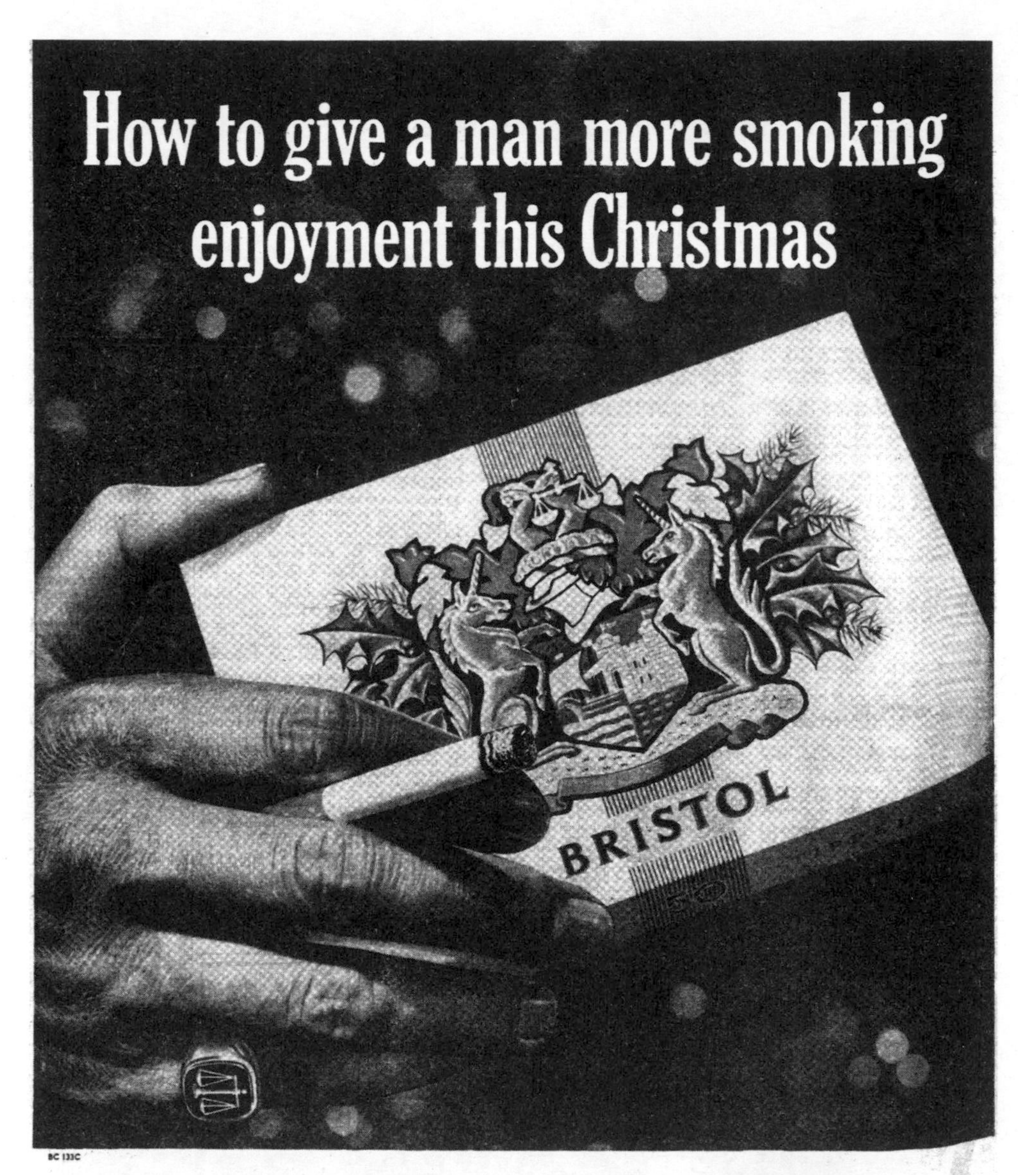

Bristol's unique balance of tip and tobacco actually *increases* smoking enjoyment. The experts call it Tip/Tobacco Balance—and it's something a man appreciates the moment he lights up a Bristol. This Christmas give him more smoking enjoyment. **GIVE HIM**

BRISTOL TIPPED

9/7d FOR FIFTY IN THE CHRISTMAS PACK

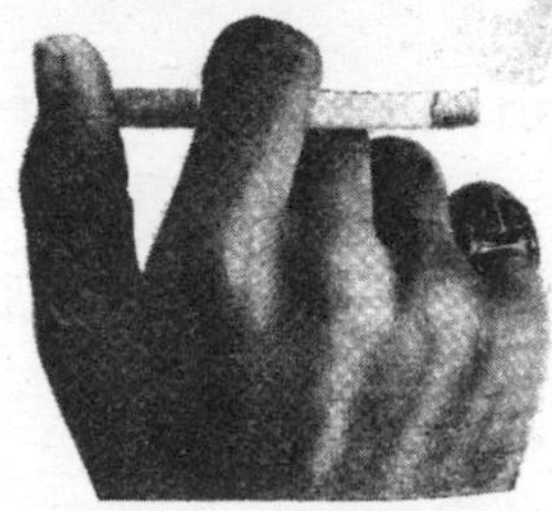

Christmas Superstitions

Weekly Companion — 1924

IT should comfort the superstitious to know that this year Christmas falls on a Thursday.

Any day of the week is better than Wednesday. Christmas omens connected with it are very dark.

According to an old rhyme, a Wednesday Christmas means:—

That yere shall be a hard wynter and strong,
And many hydeous wyndes amonge.

This rhyme goes on to tell of predictions of war, pestilence, earthquakes and "dysasters by lande and sea."

There are many superstitions connected with mistletoe.

You may have as many kisses under it as there are berries on the bunch — but no more.

Any girl who is not kissed under the mistletoe at Christmas will not be married during the next 12 months.

Married people must be as careful about choosing holly as the unmarried must be about mistletoe.

If the house is decorated with prickly holly, the husband will rule throughout the coming year. But if it is smooth, the wife will be in command.

A custom fast dying out is the burning of the Yule Log. It should be brought home by the man of the house on Christmas Eve and kindled by the women with the remains of last year's log.

Girls must wash their hands before setting a fire to the log.

The Devil is powerless to do mischief to households where the Yule Log has been burned properly.

There is no luck in store for the person who does not eat a mince pie at Christmas. To eat one is to be sure of at least one happy month.

But if you want a happy 12 months — you must eat a mince pie on each of the days of Christmas.

The Courier And Advertiser — 1933

"Mistletoe, holly, and ever-green,
After Twelfth Night must never be seen;
Or misery, surely, shall come to ye,
Before the new year out shall be."

CHRISTMAS is now a thing of the past with us, but prior to 1752 the 6th of January was Christmas Day.

Today we now recognise it as Twelfth Day, and if we wish to end up our revels right royally, Twelfth Night allows us a perfectly good excuse.

The occasion itself is shorn of much of its old-time pomp; indeed, only hostesses on the hunt for something novel as an excuse for a party ever give it a thought.

In France before the Republican era, and in Merrie England of the Middle Ages, Twelfth Night revels distinguished by plenty of good cheer were a popular feature, celebrated in commemoration of the three kings who followed a star hundreds of years ago.

SUPPOSED TO BE UNLUCKY

According to superstition, no Christmas decoration should remain in the house after Twelfth Night.

Whether you are superstitious or not, it is as well to take them down then, as they have begun to wilt considerably, and you will have grown rather tired of seeing the same vase of holly for twelve days on end.

In some parts of the country, used holly and other evergreen decorations are never consigned to the flames, while other districts consider that unless they are burned evil will gain a footing.

To find a stray leaf or berry some time afterwards is said to presage an illness for the head of the house.

GAY DOINGS

The baking of a cake with a couple of beans in it is part of the housewife's duties if she wishes to conform to rule on this day of days and night of nights.

Whoever gets the beans rule the revels as King and Queen, not to obey being considered so very unlucky that none dare disregard orders.

The cake is supposed to be cut into slices and handed round, beginning with the master and mistress. In other districts the first slice was kept for or given to a stranger for luck.

No stranger was denied a lodging and food on this night, the door supposed to be kept open for all. This custom died when bands of robbers took advantage of the custom and helped themselves freely to treasured belongings of their hosts.

A QUEEN PAID TRIBUTE

Mary Queen of Scots brought the custom of the bean festival to Scotland, and in the year 1563 made a great party of it.

To beautiful Mary Fleming fell the honour of the bean, and the rightful ruler dropped her sovereignty for the occasion and decked her maid of honour in a wonderful gown of silver cloth and the contents of her jewel caskets.

Holyrood echoed to the tinkle of silvery laughter and the patter of high-heeled shoes, the Queen herself the gayest of the gay.

The revels ended with a dance, "ladies' choice" reigning for the whole evening and causing no end of fun.

Today "Twelfth Night" is but a name, but I am sure it would be revived did it not come so close on Christmas with its plethora of gay doings.

A JOLLY PARTY

If you are having a party tonight songs, dances and games should be indulged in.

The now so popular folk dances, old country dances, and Morris dances are very suitable for such an evening.

In Queen Elizabeth's day, bands of country lads and lasses were called to the houses of the great to help amuse the lords and ladies by their quaint dances, many of them varying greatly with the locality.

In cider counties, Somerset in particular, it is not unusual to "wassail" the fruit trees in hopes that they will bear much fruit next season.

A favourite chant runs as follows:—

"Old apple tree, old apple tree,
We've come to wassail thee,
Hoping thou wilt bear
For us to be merry next year,
So bloom to bear, and merry let us be.
Here's to the old apple tree,
May'st thou grow apples enow,
Hats' full, caps' full,
Three bushel bags' full,
And a little heap under the stairs."

That this is taken as an excellent excuse for a long drink of cider goes without saying, "where the cider apples grow."

To have the best luck it must be taken while the partaker walks round an apple tree.

ARE **YOU** STOCKING-UP FOR XMAS ?
REMEMBER **EVERYBODY** LOVES

Maltesers

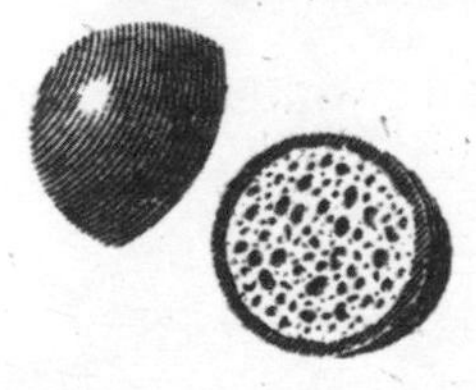

Mm-mm! How their honeycomb crunchiness adds to the fun at Christmas! There's so much *more* to munch in Maltesers! You can hand the big 1/6d box round over and over again — and the more the merrier because they're *so* mouth-watering!

ANOTHER SWEET TREAT BY MARS

The Taste Of Christmas

AH, the food. We all fondly recall the mountainous Christmas dinners. The bird, the joint, the trimmings, the over-indulgence, and the indigestion.

And every family has their favourite Christmas "thing". The dish that Granny/Mum/Auntie made every year. The dish that everyone ate — and had seconds of. The dish that said, "This is Christmas. This is OUR Christmas".

Exactly what the dish is, of course, will be different for every family — the glorious and delicious honey-basted gammon joint with cloves that is the centrepiece of Christmas Dinner table, or the peppermint creams made by the youngest daughter that were handed out when everyone sat down to watch the "big film" on TV.

There are probably several different sweetmeats, savoury delights and showstoppers, eaten over the entire festive period, that qualify as your family's particular taste of Christmas.

Newspaper and magazine editors knew this, of course. And they knew that every tradition starts somewhere. So they provided articles, recipes, and advice on their pages that were the little acorns from which great Christmas food favourites might grow.

And this idea worked. Up and down the nation there are scraps of paper — cuttings from magazines — that only see the light when it is a fairy light. They lie unloved and unlooked-for in drawers or folded into cookbooks for the rest of the year. But at Christmas, they emerge with the tinsel and baubles, and play their priceless part in making the day taste just like it used to, just like it should do.

The following pages are created from those pieces of paper, so if you have never "done" Christmas dinner for the family — this is how to look like a seasoned "pro".

The People's Friend — 1964

Preparing Your CHRISTMAS FARE

THE first thing you should do on Christmas Eve is to take a quick look round and see that you have everything you require to carry you over the holiday. If you haven't, either go out yourself or send someone else to the shops to get what you want, before starting final operations.

—o0o—

Start by preparing and stuffing your bird and placing it in the baking tin ready to slip into the oven. Sieve the crumbs for the bread sauce, and if serving a hard sauce with the plum pudding, make it and place it in a dainty glass dish ready to serve when required.

Collect all the vegetables you need, choosing potatoes of equal size. Trim any damaged leaves off Brussels sprouts. If you haven't any stock to make into soup and enrich your gravy, be sure to have plenty of beef and chicken cubes in your store cupboard.

If you haven't time to make mayonnaise or salad cream to serve with your cold cuts during the holiday, buy a jar of your favourite mayonnaise or salad cream or one or two packets of Danish mayonnaise. Now if you are unable to prepare all this Christmas fare through having to run your home and a job at the same time, let the shops help you.

1. Prepare soup from a packet instead of from stock.
2. Serve cold frozen peas with your bird, and make bread sauce from a packet.
3. Buy the pudding and re-steam and serve on Christmas Day. If you haven't time to make a sauce for the pudding, serve with ice-cream.

I would also buy as many mince pies as you want to serve over the holiday. Just reheat them and dredge them with castor sugar.

—o0o—

To be able to give up all your time to your final preparations for Christmas Day I would have a joint at Wednesday's dinner and serve it cold with jacket potatoes and some pickled beetroot for dinner on

Christmas Eve, followed by hot doughnuts dipped in castor sugar and served with tea or instant coffee. Alternatively, buy one of the complete meals packed in cartons, such as savoury mince beef with mashed potatoes, beef curry with rice, or a spaghetti dinner, which only takes a few minutes to prepare.

For lunch or supper, serve hot, fried fish fingers, heated sausage rolls or sausages and fried bread.

—o0o—

The Christmas Dinner Vegetables

Roast Potatoes — If there is no room to roast the potatoes round the bird, place them in a saucepan of cold salted water to cover. Bring slowly to the boil, cover and simmer gently for 2 to 3 minutes.

Meanwhile, melt enough fat, beef dripping for preference, to cover the base of a shallow baking tin. Heat till as hot as fat round the bird, then drain potatoes thoroughly and place in baking tin. Coat with hot fat.

Place on a rack in the oven below the rack with the bird 1 hour before dishing up bird. Cook for 30 minutes, then turn. If not brown enough when time to dish up, brown on top of the stove, turning frequently. Drain on absorbent paper.

Peas and Carrots — Scrape and slice young carrots. Boil in salted water flavoured with a chicken cube until tender. Drain. Coat with melted butter. Meanwhile, cook quick-frozen peas or canned peas according to directions. Drain thoroughly. Melt enough butter to coat both vegetables in a saucepan. Add carrots and peas. Toss very gently till piping hot.

Dish up. Sprinkle lightly with minced parsley.

Yule Pork Loaf

Ingredients — 1 lb. minced, raw shoulder of pork; ½ lb. minced, raw streaky bacon; ¼ lb. fresh breadcrumbs; 1 minced medium-sized onion; 1 beaten egg; salt and pepper; ½ teaspoonful crushed herbs.

Mix all ingredients together in order given. With lightly-floured hands, shape into a roll. Wrap in buttered aluminium foil.

Steam or bake in a moderate oven (350° F., Regulo 3 to 4) for 1½ hours. Remove from oven. Leave until cold, then spread evenly all over with glaze.

To Make Glaze — Soak ½ oz. powdered gelatine in ¼ pint beef stock till softened. Heat ¼ pint stock. Stir into the soaked gelatine mixture. Add 1 teaspoonful meat extract. Stir till smoothly blended, then apply with a brush. Decorate the top with two sprigs of holly leaves made from bits of cucumber and celery. Garnish with parsley. Serve with shredded cabbage heart, flavoured with minced onion and tossed in dressing to taste.

Stuffings for Turkey

Celery Stuffing — Put 9 large peeled potatoes, 6 celery sticks and 3 peeled, medium-sized onions through a mincer. Melt 3 oz. butter. Add ¾ cupful chopped celery leaves. Fry for 2 minutes, stirring frequently, then add to potato mixture. Season with salt and pepper to taste and add more melted butter as required to thoroughly moisten the mixture. Use for stuffing the carcass.

Chestnut Stuffing — Put 2 cupfuls boiled, shelled chestnuts through a mincer. Stir in 2 oz. melted butter or margarine, ¾ cupful stale breadcrumbs and about 3 tablespoonfuls milk and salt and pepper to taste. Use for stuffing the neck. If liked, add a teaspoonful of onion.

Golden Chicken Shortcakes

A recipe for using left-over cooked chicken for Sunday lunch, high tea or supper.

Ingredients — 8 oz. plain flour; 4 level teaspoonfuls baking powder; ½ level teaspoonful salt; 1 level teaspoonful curry powder; 2 oz. butter; 2 oz. finely grated cheese; about ¼ pint milk.

Chicken filling — Preheat oven to 425° F., Regulo 6 to 7. Sift flour with baking powder, salt and curry powder into a basin. Rub in fat until it resembles fine crumbs. Stir in cheese. Mix to a pliable dough with milk. Roll out on a lightly floured board till ½ inch thick. Cut into rounds with a floured 3-inch cutter. Arrange on a floured baking sheet, keeping them a little apart. Cook near the top of oven for 12 to 15 minutes. When ready, split the hot shortcakes in half and put together with the hot chicken filling.

Serve if liked with baked bacon rolls and with stuffed olives impaled on cocktail sticks. Sometimes a crisp green salad is also served with these shortcakes. Yield: — 5 to 6.

To Make Filling — Turn the chicken soup into a saucepan. Add the chicken. Stir till blended over low heat, then stir in the cream. Use hot.

To Vary — Fill patty cases baked in advance and reheated with the hot chicken filling, mixed with a little minced parsley to taste.

Left-over turkey can be cooked in the same way.

Yule Star Sandwiches

Ingredients — 4 oz. self-raising flour; ½ level teaspoonful salt; 1½ oz. luxury margarine; 4 oz. finely minced lean ham; Pinch of crushed herbs; Milk or water to mix.

Sift flour and salt into a basin. Rub in margarine. Add ham and herbs. Mix to a soft, but not sticky, dough with the liquid, using half water and half milk if preferred. Turn on to a lightly floured board. Knead quickly, then roll out into a large round, just over ½ inch in thickness. Cut into 6 equal-sized large triangles. Place a little apart on a greased baking sheet. Bake in a fairly hot oven (425° F., Regulo 6 to 7) for about 20 minutes.

When cold, split scones in two. Sandwich with a thick layer of cream cheese filling. Decorate tops with more cream cheese, piped through a bag, fitted with a star tube. Garnish with tomato and parsley sprigs.

Transfer to a serving platter, arranging sandwiches so that they resemble a six-pointed star. Place a small dish of olives or olives and sweet pickled gherkins in the centre. Serve with hot coffee.

Cream Cheese Filling — Beat ½ lb. cream cheese till creamy. Season with salt and pepper.

Iced Mince Pies

Ingredients — 8 oz. plain flour; ¼ level teaspoonful salt; 4 oz. vegetable fat; 2 to 3 tablespoonfuls cold water; 8 to 12 oz. mincemeat; 4 oz. sifted icing sugar.

Sift flour and salt into a basin. Rub in the fat until the mixture resembles fine breadcrumbs. Mix to a firm dough with the water.

Roll out thinly on a lightly floured board. Cut out 8 to 12 rounds with a floured fluted cutter, slightly larger than the patty tins and then stamp out 8 to 12 rounds slightly smaller. Line 8 to 12 patty tins smoothly with the larger rounds. Place a heaped teaspoonful of mincemeat in each. Brush undersides of the lids with cold water and lay one over each pie. Press down firmly all the way round to seal edges.

Make a small slit in centre of each. Bake on second shelf of a fairly hot oven (400° F., Regulo 5 to 6) for 20 to 25 minutes. Cool on a wire rack. Sift icing sugar. Mix to a smooth icing with 2 to 3 teaspoonfuls cold water. Place a little on the centre of each pie. Decorate with silver balls.

—o0o—

NOW here are two recipes for drinks that can be served to young and old alike.

Ginger Ale Cup

Ingredients — 8 oz. castor sugar; 1 cupful water; Strained juice of 6 oranges; Strained juice of 6 lemons; 1 quart chilled ginger ale.

Dissolve sugar in water. Bring quickly to boil. Boil for 5 minutes then chill. Add orange and lemon juice. Chill again. Just before serving pour in the ginger ale. Serve in small tumblers. Yield: — About 3 ½ pints.

Pineapple Punch

Ingredients — 1 cupful strong tea; ½ cupful lemon juice; ¾ cupful orange juice. 1 ½ tablespoonfuls lime juice; 2 tablespoonfuls maraschino cherry juice; 3 ½ oz. castor sugar; 6 sprigs of mint; 4 slices pineapple; 2 pint bottles of ginger ale; 2 pint bottles of soda water.

Place tea in a large fancy bowl. Add lemon, orange and lime juice, then sugar. Place 1 or 2 ice blocks in the bowl. As soon as sugar is dissolved add sweetened fruit juice and leaves from the sprigs of mint.

When required, add pineapple divided into small pieces, together with juice from the can, then stir in ginger ale and soda water. Decorate with 1 or 2 thin slices of lemon and orange and arrange round the base of the bowl holly and other evergreens. Serve punch in small tumblers.

Nine servings.

The People's Friend — 1961

A HAPPY Christmas to you all. May your Christmas dinner be the best you have ever cooked, and Christmas Day one of the happiest you have ever spent.

I know that not all housewives like to have Christmas fall on a Monday, because it means that part of Sunday will have to be given up to preparing for Christmas Day. But by Saturday it is possible to get some things ahead and so spread the preparations to relieve Sunday and Christmas Day itself.

So for Saturday I'd allot the following items:—

1. Make your biscuits and cakes and ice your Christmas cake, if you haven't already done so.

2. Complete the decoration of your home in the evening and make some candies and perhaps salt nuts as well.

Then on Sunday continue in the following way: —

1. Crumble bread and sieve for bread sauce.

2. Stuff and truss bird and place on rack. Cover and leave in larder till ready to finish it off for roasting.

3. Prepare butterscotch hard sauce for pudding.

4. Make and bake mince pies only lightly, ready for heating up and browning further.

5. Measure out potatoes to be boiled.

6. Give final polish to table silver.

A CHANGE FOR BREAKFAST — To save time and washing up at this busy season, combine the fruit course with the main course.

Fruit And Bacon Kebabs

Allow 2 kebabs per person. For each, roll half a bacon rasher round a segment of orange. Run on a skewer. Add half a tomato. Repeat.

Finish with a half of tomato. Grill until bacon is crisp, turning as necessary.

Gammon and Grapefruit

Cut gammon into one portion per person. Grill a slice of gammon about ½ inch thick, until golden brown. Turn and grill lightly on other side. Top each with a round slice of grapefruit, ¼ inch thick. Sprinkle with a little brown sugar. Grill till sugar browns and bubbles. Serve at once.

Prepare kebabs, and poise skewers on grill pan, ready for cooking next morning. Remove rind from gammon to save time in the morning.

Soups for lunch or supper

Chicken and Corn — Melt 1 dessertspoonful butter. Add 1 dessertspoonful flour. Stir till frothy, then add 1 cupful hot milk. Cook until thickened, stirring constantly, then stir in 1 can chicken soup and 1 ½ tablespoonfuls drained, canned corn. Stir till piping hot, but do not boil.

Season to taste. Thin to taste with hot milk. Garnish with chopped parsley. For 4 persons.

Pea and Tomato — Pour a can of pea soup into a saucepan. Add a can of tomato soup. Stir till blended. Using one of the cans, measure 2 cans of milk into the soup. Stir frequently till boiling. Stir ¼ cupful cream or top milk into ½ teaspoonful curry powder. Add to soup.

Heat, stirring constantly, but do not allow to boil. Garnish each portion with a heaped teaspoonful of whipped cream.

For 6 or 7 persons.

Christmas Star Pie

Pastry — 2 oz. butter or margarine; 3-4 tablespoonfuls cold water; 8 oz. flour; 2 oz. cooking fat; Pinch of salt.

Filling — 6 rounded tablespoonfuls of mincemeat (about 12 oz.); 8 oz. cooking apples.

Sift flour and salt into a basin. Rub in fats. Mix to a stiff paste with cold water. Turn on to a lightly-floured board. Knead quickly until smooth, then divide in two.

Roll out one half into a round. With it line a well-greased 9-inch round fireproof plate. Prick base with a fork.

Peel and core apples, weigh out 8 oz., then grate. Place a layer in base of pastry case. Spread mincemeat on top. Moisten pastry round the edge with cold water. Roll out most of remaining pastry into a 10-inch round.

Make a ring of 8 stars with a cutter, about 2 inches from outside edge. Place lid carefully over the filling. Press edges firmly together. Arrange star round outer edge after brushing them on underside with cold water.

Bake pie towards the top of a fairly hot oven (425° F., Regulo 7) for 25 minutes, then lower heat to 350° F. (Regulo 4), and bake for 20 minutes. Dust top with icing sugar. When required, re-heat and serve with cream.

Star Shorties

Ingredients — ¼ teaspoonful almond essence, or ½ teaspoonful vanilla essence; 4 oz. flour; 2 oz. fine semolina; 2 oz. castor sugar; 4 oz. butter; Pinch of salt.

Sift flour, semolina, sugar and salt into a basin. Rub in butter, softened with the essence. Add a few drops of water, if necessary, to make a dry dough.

Roll out on a lightly-floured board into a round about 1/3 inch-thick. Cut into stars. Bake, a little apart, on ungreased baking sheets in a moderate oven (350° F., Regulo 4) until crisp and pale gold, for about 20 minutes.

Dredge with castor sugar delicately flavoured with ground cinnamon.

To vary — Brush the shorties with egg white and sprinkle with chopped nuts before baking.

St Nicholas Fruit Plait

Filling — 1 ½ oz. sultanas; 1 ½ oz. chopped nuts; 1 ½ chopped mixed peel; 1 rounded tablespoonful brown sugar; 1 ½ oz. finely chopped blanched almonds; 1 small teaspoonful ground cinnamon; 1 oz. melted butter.

Yeast Dough — 8 oz. flour; ½ teaspoonful salt; ½ teaspoonful dried yeast. ½ teaspoonful sugar; About ¼ pint warm milk; 1 oz. butter or margarine; 1 small beaten egg.

To make filling — Mix all the ingredients together.

To Make a Yeast Dough — Sift flour with salt. Mix yeast with sugar and most of the milk in a jug. Sprinkle 1 tablespoonful of the flour on top. Stand in a warm place for about 10 minutes till a froth forms on top. Rub butter into the flour. Add egg to yeast mixture. Stir liquid into flour. Mix and knead well to a firm dough, adding remainder of milk if necessary.

You need just under ¼ pint and it must be medium hot. Place dough in a greased polythene bag, or in a plastic store jar. Leave in a warm place till it doubles its bulk and springs back when pressed with a floured finger. It takes 50-60 minutes to rise. Turn on to a floured board and knead lightly.

To Make Plait — Divide dough into three equal-sized pieces. Roll each into a strip, approximately 14 inches long and 4 inches wide. Brush tips with water, then spread the filling along the centre. Fold each over to form a thin "tube". Press edges firmly together. Plait the three tubes together, then place on a well-greased baking sheet.

Shape plait into a horseshoe on tin. Cover with greased greaseproof paper. Leave in a warm place to rise for about 10 minutes.

Bake towards top of oven in a moderately hot oven (400° F., Regulo 6), for 15-20 minutes.

When nearly ready, dissolve 1 tablespoonful castor sugar in 1 tablespoonful milk. Bring to boil. Boil for a few minutes. Brush this over plait. Decorate with glace cherries.

Serve with hot coffee.

Meringue Christmas Tree

Ingredients — 6 eggs; 12 oz. butter; 12 oz. castor sugar; 12 oz. self-raising flour; Meringue mixture; Butter cream icing.

Method — Beat eggs lightly. Beat butter till softened. Gradually beat in sugar. Beat till fluffy and white, then beat in eggs, and lightly fold in flour.

Divide mixture between 2 greased sandwich tins, dusted with flour, and an oblong baking tin, 11 by 7, prepared in same way. You need a 7 inch and 6 inch sandwich tin. Bake in a moderately hot oven (375° F., Regulo 5) for 20-25 minutes, then cool.

Meringue — Whisk 3 egg whites till they form peaks. Beat in 3 oz. castor sugar, until mixture is very stiff, then fold in another 3 oz. castor sugar.

Place mixture in a piping bag with a plain vegetable pipe, ¼ inch in diameter. Pipe on to a tin, lined with greased greaseproof paper, in small pointed domes about the size of half a crown. Dry off in a very cool oven (200° F., Regulo 4), with door slightly ajar. They take from 5-6 hours.

Butter Cream Icing — Beat 8 oz. butter till softened, then gradually beat in 1 lb. sifted icing sugar. Beat till stiff, then beat in 2 egg yolks, one at a time, and ½ teaspoonful vanilla essence.

Remove 2 large tablespoonfuls of the icing and colour bright red with carmine colouring. Remove also 1 teaspoonful of the icing and leave uncoloured.

Colour remaining icing in bowl a delicate green.

To Assemble Cake — From the oblong sponge, cut rounds of cake using a 5, 4, 3, 2 and 1 inch cutter. Place the 7 inch sponge layer on a serving plate. Spread with a little green butter icing.

Now, build up a pyramid with the rounds, starting with the 6 inch round and ending with the 1 inch. Sandwich each layer together with green butter icing.

Cover the sides with green butter icing.

Stick meringues in rows round the sides. Pipe green butter icing in the spaces between the meringues, using a small rose pipe.

Use the carmine butter icing to make holly berry clusters on the green butter icing.

Place a small silver ball on the tip of each meringue, making it adhere with the uncoloured icing.

Devilled Almonds — Blanch and peel ½ lb. almonds or chestnuts. Melt 1 tablespoonful butter in a strong frying pan. Toss the nuts over low heat until golden brown, stirring frequently.

Season lightly with salt and paprika, and flavour with a drop or two of Worcestershire sauce if liked. Toss until evenly coated.

To Salt Nuts — Fry blanched nuts in deep hot oil to cover in a small saucepan till golden brown. Or fry in a little melted butter, allowing 1 tablespoonful to 2 cupfuls blanched nuts.

Drain on absorbent paper. Season with salt.

Sugar Coated Almonds — Dissolve 1 lb. castor sugar in ½ cupful water in a saucepan. Bring quickly to boil, then boil until thick and clear. Add 1 lb. unblanched almonds.

Stir with a wooden spoon until the nuts begin to crackle. Lower heat below the pan. Stir nuts until dry.

Remove nuts to a board.

Add just enough water to sugar in pan to moisten it, with ½ teaspoonful ground cinnamon. If liked, add a drop of two of red colouring.

Boil syrup until a few drops, when tossed into the sink, spin a thread. Add sugared nuts. Stir until they separate.

The People's Friend — 1965

A Bird or A Joint?

A BIRD OR A JOINT? Which would you like for Christmas dinner this year? If you are having a large family party, a 10- 12 lb. turkey or a large coronet of lamb or pork will be required. If catering only for two or three, then why not a braised or roast capon which will give you plenty for Christmas and enough cold for Boxing Day, as well as filling for sandwiches later in the week.

Roast Turkey

Ingredients — 1 hen turkey 10-12 lb.; 8-10 cupfuls stuffing; Salt and pepper; butter.

Rinse bird, inside and out. Dry thoroughly. Stuff the breast and carcase with the same stuffing, or use different stuffings for each part. Insert fingers at neck and press the skin from the top of the breast before stuffing. Draw the skin to the back of the bird and fix the back with a small skewer.

After stuffing the body, block the vent with a heel of bread if it is impossible to sew it up, but remove this before carving. Place, breast downwards, on a V-shaped rack or on a flat rack, in tin. Rub all over with unsalted butter. Allowing about 30 minutes per pound, place bird on the middle shelf of a moderate oven (325-350° F., Regulo 3 to 4).

Roast, basting occasionally, until half cooked. Season lightly with salt, turn breast upwards, season again, then dip a square of cheesecloth in melted butter. Baste bird lavishly with butter, then cover with cloth. Bake until the cloth dries out on top, then baste again with drippings from pan.

Remove cloth about 20 minutes before dishing up. Baste again with drippings. Continue to roast until breast is evenly browned, but slit the string between the legs and the body at the same time to ensure the legs are being perfectly cooked.

To Serve Turkey — Untruss. Place on a heated platter. Tuck a cluster of young watercress sprigs into vent. Arrange fried or grilled chipolata sausages around the base. Serve with brown gravy and bread sauce in heated sauceboats, cranberry or redcurrant jelly in a small dish, and roast potatoes and buttered peas in heated vegetable dishes.

Stuffings for Turkey — This year think about a choice of stuffings for the breast. The chestnut stuffing contains no onion, but if you wish you can add a heaped teaspoonful of minced onion to the ingredients.

Chestnut Stuffing — Slit 2 lb. chestnuts. Place in a saucepan with boiling water to cover. Cover and boil for about 20 minutes until the shells and skins can be removed at once. When peeled, put through a mincer into a basin. Stir in one cupful sifted breadcrumbs, about ½ teaspoonful salt, pepper to taste, ¼ cupful melted butter, and ½ cupful thick cream.

Note — If roasting a chicken for two or three persons or a 5 lb. turkey, use above stuffing in quantity given.

Canadian Stuffing — Mix 2 cupfuls sieved breadcrumbs lightly with ¼ cupful melted butter, ½ cupful chopped, stoned raisins, ½ cupful chopped walnuts, ¼ teaspoonful dried sage, and salt and freshly ground black pepper to taste. Use for stuffing breast if chestnut is not wanted.

Liver Stuffing for Body — Mix 6 cupfuls sieved breadcrumbs with salt and freshly ground black pepper to taste, a saltspoonful of crushed mixed herbs, a pinch of ground mace, one teaspoonful minced parsley, one medium-sized onion, peeled and minced, and one cupful shredded celery, fried in ¼ cupful melted butter till soft. Stir in enough top of the milk to make a moist but not wet stuffing. Wash and dry turkey liver. Cut in slices. Fry slowly in enough butter to cover bottom of pan until firm enough to mince. Stir into stuffing. Adjust seasoning if necessary.

Gravy for Birds — Pour off all the fat except 2 tablespoonfuls from the turkey roasting tin. Stir in 1 dessertspoonful of flour into the fat. When frothy stir in ½ cupful turkey giblet stock. Stir till boiling, then add more stock or cream until you have the sauce thinned to taste. Season with salt and pepper. Strain into heated sauceboat. Sometimes sifted boiled chestnuts are used in place of flour.

Saucy Stuffed Chicken

Ingredients — 1 capon 5 lb.;
1 lb. pork sausage meat;
2 oz. butter; Salt and pepper;
2 tablespoonfuls chopped onion;
4 oz. chopped mushroom stalks;
½ pint cider; 2 level tablespoonfuls flour.

Stuff the neck end of bird with the sausage meat. Melt the butter in the frying-pan. Add the capon.

Fry, turning frequently, till evenly browned all over. Remove from pan to a casserole. Add the onion and mushroom stalks to the fat remaining in pan. Fry for 4-5 minutes, stirring occasionally.

Add the cider and salt and pepper. Pour this over the chicken. Cover and bake in a moderately hot oven (400° F., Regulo 5 to 6) for 1 hour.

Remove chicken to a heated serving platter. Pour the liquor from round the chicken into a small saucepan. Blend the flour with cold water to a cream. Stir into the liquor. Bring to boil, stirring constantly, then cover and simmer gently for 5 minutes. Adjust seasoning. Pour into heated sauceboats.

Garnish vent of bird with a bunch of young watercress and arrange round the bird ½ lb. fried mushrooms alternately with ½ lb. boiled button onions, both tossed in seasoned melted butter, or better still, serve them in a heated vegetable dish.

While bird is cooking, fry chips, half the usual width, till golden. Drain on absorbent paper. Serve in a heated vegetable dish, encircled with green peas. Note — If liked, serve also with redcurrant jelly and bread sauce.

Bread Sauce — Peel a small onion. Spear with two whole cloves. Place in a small enamel-lined saucepan. Add ½ pint milk. Season to taste with salt and pepper. Bring almost to boiling point. Cover. Stand in a warm place for 30 minutes, then remove onion.

Add ½ oz. butter and 2 oz. crumbs. Stir till blended. Cook slowly over boiling water for 10 to 15 minutes. Remove from stove. Stir in a pat of unsalted butter and dish up. If a smoother sauce is wanted, blend the pat of butter with a teaspoonful of flour and stir until boiling before serving.

Cranberry Sauce — Buy 1 lb. cranberries and pick them over. Rinse and drain. Place in a saucepan with ¼ pint water. Boil for about 10 minutes until tender. Rub through a sieve into another saucepan.

Add 4 oz. soft brown sugar. Stir until dissolved. Add ½ gill orange juice. Stir till piping hot, but do not reboil. Serve in a heated sauceboat.

Candle of Pork

Ingredients — Loin of pork; Salt and black pepper; 2 or 3 tablespoonfuls orange juice.

Before buying the pork, check how many chops you will wish to serve on Christmas Day, and if you want to serve it again cold on Boxing Day double the quantity.

Ask the butcher to trim the ends of the chops and score the skin vertically. Wrap each chop end in a piece of fat bacon to prevent scorching. Tie on securely. Place joint on a rack in baking tin. Season with salt and pepper.

Roast on the middle shelf of a moderate oven (350° F., Regulo 3 to 4) for 35 minutes.

Baste with the orange juice and finish roasting, allowing 30 minutes per pound. To serve, remove bacon wrappings from chops and substitute paper frills.

Place on a heated platter. Garnish here and there around the base with sprigs of parsley. Serve with apple sauce, roast potatoes and boiled broccoli coated with melted butter.

Apple Sauce — Peel, core and slice three large cooking apples into a small saucepan. Chop a large peeled onion and add to apple, with three lumps of sugar and a squeeze of lemon juice and 2 tablespoonfuls water.

Stir over moderate heat until sugar is dissolved, then add 1 oz. butter.

Cover and cook gently, stirring occasionally, until reduced into a mush. Season with salt and black pepper to taste. Serve in a heated sauceboat.

Roast Potatoes — Allowing two or three potatoes per person, peel and place in a saucepan. Be sure they are of equal shape and size. Cover with boiling salted water. Cover and simmer for about 5 minutes, then drain and place around joint. Baste with hot dripping.

If, when the joint is nearly ready, the potatoes are not browned enough, turn them into a frying-pan containing a little of the hot dripping from joint.

Fry, turning frequently, until evenly browned.

Coronet of Lamb

Ingredients — 12-15 ribs of best end neck; 12-15 small pieces salt pork or fat bacon. Salt and black pepper. Stuffing.

Get the butcher to prepare a joint containing 12 to 15 lamb ribs, or two racks, each containing 6 or 7 ribs, taken from opposite sides of the lamb.

Slice half-way down bones and scrape the rib ends. With your hands bind the two pieces round into the shape of a coronet, joining them together each side with small skewers. Tie string round to keep them in place.

Place on the rack in a roasting tin. Season with salt and freshly-ground black pepper. Pack stuffing evenly into centre. Tie a little piece of salt pork or fat bacon on to the top of each bone to prevent ends charring.

Roast on the middle shelf of a slow oven (300° F., Regulo 1 to 2), allowing 35 minutes per pound.

Be sure to cover the stuffing with greased paper or aluminium foil before starting to roast, and remove it shortly before serving.

To Serve Coronet of Lamb — Dish up on a heated platter. Fix a paper frill on the end of each chop. Garnish round the base with nests of mashed potatoes filled with buttered green peas and with fried mushrooms alternately.

Serve with brown gravy and redcurrant jelly.

Stuffing for Roast Lamb — Dry 3 cupfuls breadcrumbs lightly in the oven. Place in a basin. Stir in ¼ cupful orange juice, ¼ cupful mandarin juice, and 2 teaspoonfuls grated orange rind.

Peel an orange. Separate fingers and peel fingers, removing any pips. Add to crumb mixture. Melt 2 oz. butter. Stir into mixture. Add 2 cupfuls minced celery, 1 beaten egg and salt and pepper to taste.

Gravy for Joints — Pour off all the fat, except 2 tablespoonfuls from the pork or lamb. Add a level tablespoonful flour to the remaining fat. Stir till frothy.

Pour in ½ pint of heated beef stock, using a beef cube dissolved according to directions, if stock is not available.

Stir till smooth and boiling, then add additional stock as required to make a pouring liquid.

Season with salt and freshly ground black pepper. Then add more stock till thinned to taste.

Serve in a heated sauceboat.

My Weekly — 1957

IF husband's an expert carver, then skip this column. This is to help those who have never tackled the job before — or have tackled it with lamentable lack of success and want to do better next time.

We take you step by easy step through the whole procedure, so you can enjoy even this part of the Christmas dinner preparations.

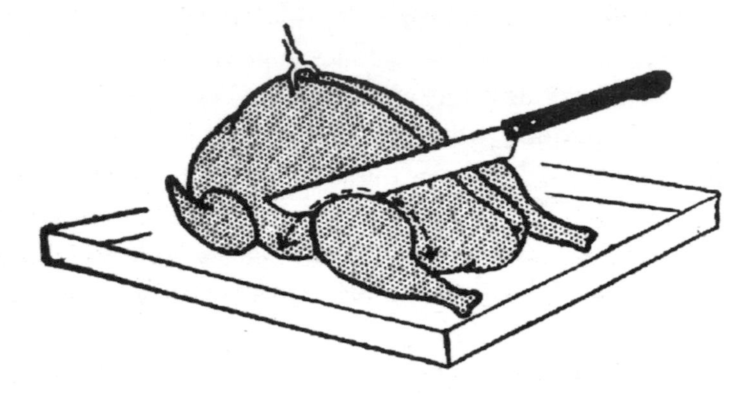

1. Have ready a sharp carving knife, two-prong fork and the cooked bird on a platter. Neck of bird should be to your left. Insert fork so that prongs are at each side of breastbone. Now, starting at nearest side, cut at thigh joint and press leg away from body.

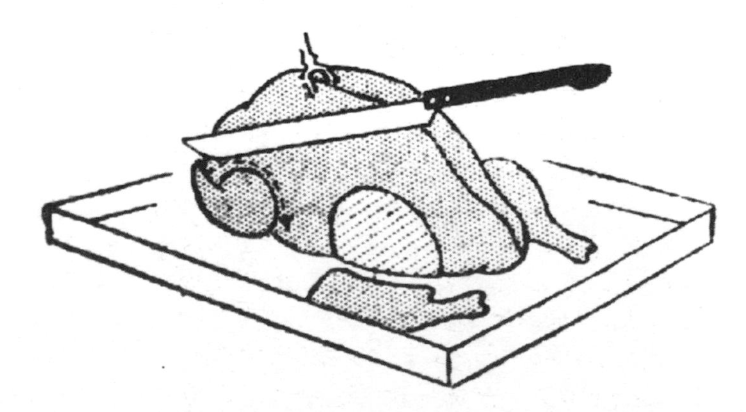

2. Holding fork in same position, separate nearest wing in same way as leg, cutting round wing joint to find dividing point of joint. Sever the wing entirely.

3. Now for breast meat! Commence at an angle near tip of breastbone and carve thin slices of meat, working always towards the joint where wing was removed. Lastly separate thigh from leg at joint and cut off thin slices from these two pieces. Turn platter and repeat process on other side of bird when more servings are required.

The People's Friend — 1964

Igloo Cake

Ingredients — 8 oz. self-raising flour; Pinch of Salt; 8 oz. butter; 8 oz. castor sugar; 1 large lemon; 4 eggs; About 50 white dessert marshmallows; 1 individual swiss roll; Lemon butter cream.

Sift flour with salt. Beat butter till softened. Gradually beat in sugar. Finely grate the rind of the lemon into butter mixture. Beat till light and fluffy, then beat in eggs, one at a time, adding a tablespoonful of flour before beating in each.

With a metal spoon, lightly fold-in remaining flour. Turn mixture into well-greased 2 ½ pint pudding basin that is fireproof.

Bake in centre of a moderate oven (350° F., Regulo 3 to 4) until well-risen and firm, usually in about 1 ½ hours. Remove from oven. Stand for a minute or two, then turn out on to a wire rack. Leave until cold.

Make the butter cream and spread some of it completely over the cake.

Halve the marshmallows and stick them closely together over the cake in rows, like igloo bricks of ice.

Place the swiss roll at the base of the igloo and cover it with butter cream and marshmallows to give the appearance of an entrance tunnel.

To Make Butter Cream — Beat 2 oz. unsalted butter till softened. Gradually beat in 4 oz. sifted icing sugar and a tablespoonful of lemon juice. Beat till fluffy.

Yule Log

Ingredients — 3 eggs. 3 oz. castor sugar: 2 ½ oz. self-raising flour; 1 tablespoonful cocoa; Vanilla butter cream.

Grease and line a swiss roll tin smoothly with greased paper. Place the eggs and sugar in a basin. Whisk until into a thick, light and fluffy consistency.

Sift flour with cocoa. Fold into egg mixture. Pour into prepared tin. Bake in a moderately hot oven (400° F., Regulo 5 to 6) for about 10 minutes.

Turn at once on to a piece of greaseproof paper, dredged with castor sugar. Trim edges quickly with a sharp knife, then roll up carefully so that the greaseproof paper is rolled inside. Cool on a wire rack, and then gently unroll.

Remove paper. Spread cake evenly with half the butter cream, then roll up again. Add sifted cocoa to taste to the remainder of butter cream and spread over outside evenly. Draw a fork carefully from end to end, again and again, over the back to give the impression of a log.

Decorate as illustrated with sprigs of holly or of holly and mistletoe, tied with scarlet ribbon.

Vanilla Butter Cream — Sift 8 oz. icing sugar. Beat 4 oz. unsalted butter until softened, then gradually beat in the icing sugar and vanilla essence to taste.

Yule Pie

Ingredients — 8 oz. plain flour; 2 ½ oz. lard; ¼ pint cold water; Pork filling; 1 teaspoonful salt; ¼ oz. powdered gelatine.

Sift flour into a basin. Place lard and water in a saucepan. Bring to boil. Add salt. Stir into flour.

Knead paste quickly for a moment or two. Cut off a quarter of pastry for lid and keep it warm. Roll out remaining pastry into a round and place in a well-greased 6-inch cake tin, slightly heated.

Carefully mould from the base up the sides till the lining is of even thickness all over. Pack in the filling. Roll pastry lid out to fit the top of pie. Brush edge of pastry lining with cold water. Lay lid in place. Notch edges together.

Decorate centre with pastry leaves made from any trimmings.

Brush leaves and pie over with beaten egg. Make a hole in the centre to allow steam to escape.

Bake in centre of a hot oven (450° F., Regulo 7 to 8) for 30 minutes and then lower temperature to moderately hot (375° F., Regulo 4 to 5) for 1 ½ hours.

When half cooked, cover top of pie with foil or greaseproof paper to prevent scorching.

When cooked, remove pie from tin and return to oven for 5 minutes, for pastry to harden.

Dissolve gelatine in ¼ pint boiling water, or better still, in beef stock.

Leave until almost set then pour into the pie through a funnel inserted in the hole. Serve cold with salad for lunch on Sunday.

Enough for 4 to 6 persons.

Pork Filling — Mix 10 to 12 oz. minced lean pork with ½ teaspoonful crushed mixed herbs and 3 tablespoonfuls stock or water.

My Weekly — 1972

Stollen

Dough

Ingredients — 2 oz. Stork margarine; 1 lb. plain flour, sieved; 1 level teaspoonful sugar; 1 level teaspoonful salt; 1 oz. fresh yeast; Blend together 8 fl. oz. warm milk (78-82 deg. F.) and 25 mg. ascorbic acid tablet, crushed; 1 egg, standard, beaten.

Filling

Ingredients — In 1 tablespoonful of rum marinate together for one hour 2 oz. glace cherries, 2 oz. mixed peel, 6 oz. raisins and grated rind of ½ lemon. 3 oz. castor sugar; 2 oz. chopped almonds; 1 oz. Stork margarine, melted, icing sugar for dredging.

To Make Dough — Rub margarine into dry ingredients. Pour in blended ingredients and egg and work into a dough with a palette knife. Turn out on to a lightly-floured table top or board and knead for 10 minutes. Place in a greased polythene bag and leave to rest for 10 minutes.

Turn the dough on to a floured table top or board and knead in all filling ingredients except melted margarine.

Roll out into an oval about 12 inches by 8 inches, fold in two lengthwise and shape into a crescent. Press folded edges firmly together.

Place Stollen on a greased baking sheet and brush top with melted margarine.

Cover loosely with greased polythene and leave to prove in a warm place for about 30 minutes.

Bake on the middle shelf of a fairly hot oven (400° F., Regulo 6) for 30 to 36 minutes.

Dredge thickly with icing sugar and cool on a wire tray.

Christmas Ring Cake

All-in-One Cake — 5 oz. Stork margarine; 5 oz. soft brown sugar; 3 eggs, standard; 6 oz. plain flour seived with ¾ level teaspoonful mixed spice and ¼ level teaspoonful nutmeg; 1 tablespoonful black treacle; 1 ½ tablespoonfuls brandy; 8 oz. currants; 5 oz. sultanas; 3 oz. raisins; 2 oz. glacé cherries; 2 oz. whole almonds; 2 oz. cut mixed peel; 1 ½ oz. ground almonds; Grated rind of 1 lemon; 1 lb. almond paste; Boiled, sieved apricot jam.

Royal Icing — 2 eggs, standard, separated; 1 lb. icing sugar, sieved; 1 teaspoonful glycerine.

Decoration — Christmas trees and deer.

To make All-in-One Cake — Place all ingredients, except almond paste and apricot jam, in a mixing bowl and beat together with a wooden spoon until well-mixed. Place mixture in a ring tin 8 inches in diameter, bottom-lined with a strip of greaseproof paper and brushed with melted margarine. Smooth top of cake with the back of wet metal spoon. Bake on middle shelf of a pre-heated slow oven (275 deg. F., Regulo 1) for 3-3 ½ hours. Leave in tin for 10-15 minutes, then turn out and cool on a wire tray.

To Marzipan The Cake — Divide almond paste and roll into 2 strips approximately 13 by 6 inches. Brush the cake all over with sieved apricot jam. Cover half the cake at a time, easing the almond paste in the centre of the ring. Cover the other half in the same way. Leave for approximately 24 hours to dry out, before icing.

To Make Royal Icing — Slightly whisk the egg whites together, then gradually beat in the icing sugar and the glycerine. Beat well until icing is smooth and shiny. Keep covered until required.

To Decorate and Finish Cake — Cover cake with a fairly thick coating of icing and using a palette knife, mark in horizontal lines around the surface of the cake. Using a knife or fork, "drag" icing up over the sides of the cake into the middle, giving a "scalloped" effect.

Chocolate Noel Gateau

Ingredients — 6 oz. Stork margarine; 6 oz. castor sugar; 6 oz. golden syrup; 2 eggs, standard; 2 oz. ground almonds; 6 oz. plain flour; 7 level tablespoonfuls cocoa powder and ¼ level teaspoonful bicarbonate of soda sieved together; ¼ pint milk and 2 tablespoonfuls milk.

Icing — 3 oz. Stork margarine; 8 oz. icing sugar, sieved; 2 dessertspoonfuls milk; 2 tablespoonfuls cocoa powder and 2 tablespoonfuls hot water blended together.

To Make All-in-in-One Gateau — Place all ingredients in a mixing bowl and beat with a wooden spoon until smooth (2-3 minutes). Place the mixture in an 8-inch square cake tin, lined with greaseproof paper and greased. Bake in a pre-heated oven (300 deg. F., Regulo 2) on the middle shelf for 1½-2 hours. Carefully turn out of tin. Remove paper and cool on a wire tray.

To Make All-in-One Icing — Place all ingredients except cocoa and hot water in a mixing bowl and beat together with a wooden spoon until well mixed (2-3 minutes).

Reserve a tablespoonful of this icing in a separate bowl and add the blended cocoa and hot water to the remainder. Beat the mixture with a wooden spoon until thoroughly mixed.

To Finish Gateau — Spread the chocolate icing all over the top and sides of the cake. Form peaks round the sides of the cake by gently lifting the icing with the back of a knife. Pipe round the top edges of the cake with a medium star tube.

With a small "writing" or plain tube, pipe the reserved white icing in desired Christmas shapes such as bells, stars or musical notes on to the top of the cake.

IF you feel you want to try something different from the traditional Christmas fare, here are some recipes for appetising alternatives.

Christmas Meat Loaf

Ingredients — 1 lb. minced beef; 1 beaten egg; 2 tablespoonfuls minced parsley; ½ lb. minced bacon; 1 teaspoonful Worcestershire sauce; ¼ oz. bacon fat; 1 tablespoonful minced onion; 2 tablespoonfuls breadcrumbs; ¾ lb. seasoned sausage meat; salt and black pepper.

Method — Mix beef with egg, parsley, bacon, Worcestershire sauce, finely-minced bacon fat or creamed butter, breadcrumbs, onion and salt and pepper to taste. When thoroughly blended, pack half the mixture into a large, greased loaf tin. Cover evenly with sausage meat, then with remainder of beef mixture. Press down lightly. Cover with greased foil. Bake in a moderate oven (350° F., Regulo 3 to 4) for 1 ¼ to 1 ½ hours.

Uncover and baste twice with tomato juice during baking time. When ready, drain off liquid into a small saucepan. Thicken with a teaspoonful of creamed flour.

Unmould loaf on to a heated platter. Spoon tomato gravy over loaf. Place 6 slices of banana, about 1 inch apart, across the loaf. Brush with melted butter. Return to oven and bake for a minute or two until slightly browned. Garnish the base at each corner with a tuft of parsley.

Serve hot with new potatoes and green peas.

If new potatoes are not available, substitute potato croquettes.

Boiled Danish Gammon Hock

Ingredients — 1 gammon hock; 2 oz. demerara sugar; 1 bay leaf; 5 black peppercorns; Whole cloves; 1 ham frill.

Method — Soak gammon in cold water to cover for 4 or 5 hours. Dry thoroughly. Scrape surface with a knife to remove any "bloom." Rub cut end with sugar, pressing it well between the meat and the bone. Leave for about 20 minutes.

Place in a large pan such as a fish kettle or preserving pan. Cover with cold water. Bring slowly to boil, skimming the surface of water when necessary.

When it comes to a full boil, reduce to simmering point and continue cooking for 10 minutes, then add the bay leaf and peppercorns and cover pan. Keep at a slow simmer until tender, allowing 20 minutes to the pound and 20 minutes over.

Remove pan from stove. Stand until cool enough to handle, then carefully draw off rind and trim where necessary. Mark into diamonds with a knife. Insert a clove in centre of each diamond.

Sprinkle fat with a tablespoonful or two of pineapple juice and place on a rack in a baking tin.

Bake in a moderate oven (350° F., Regulo 3 to 4) until glazed and delicately browned. When cold, slip a paper frill over the bone end. Garnish with salad.

Note — When you think the ham is nearly ready, try to slip off the rind, for you must remove it as soon as it can be pulled off. Otherwise, if you intend to glaze it as described, it will be over-cooked.

Annabel — 1966

Cut-the-cost cookery

CHRISTMAS PRESENTS TO MAKE IN YOUR KITCHEN

IF you have any problems with your gift list this Christmas, a little extra time spent in the kitchen could solve all of them. Can you think of anyone — even the lucky person who seems to "have everything" — who wouldn't appreciate a luxury box of handmade sweets or biscuits?

The recipes selected are simple to follow, even if you have never made sweets or biscuits before and one or two do not even involve cooking.

They need no special equipment or hard-to-find ingredients and you will be pleasantly surprised at how inexpensive they are compared to similar delicacies in the shops. And you will certainly want to keep some — or make more — for your own Christmas entertaining.

Attractive packaging adds enormously to the appearance of made-in-the kitchen gifts and will give them a really professional look.

You may have saved some pretty chocolate boxes which can be used again as containers. New boxes, as well as Cellophane wrappers, chocolate coloured and white paper sweet cases, ribbons and paddings, can usually be bought in large stationery departments or in stores.

A shallow box, designed for a single layer of sweets, is the most practical type to use. Sweets should be packed close together and (especially if your gift is to be posted) protected by a sheet of cellophane, securely fastened with Sellotape, plus a layer of padding on top.

Shortbread and biscuits are easier to pack in layers, using greaseproof or waxed paper between each layer and to line and pad the box firmly.

Peppermint Creams

Cost: About 1s.
Quantity: About ¾ lb.
Preparation time: 15 minutes.

Ingredients — 1 egg white; About 8oz. icing sugar; ¼ teaspoonful peppermint essence; Few drops of green colouring.

Method — Beat egg white until frothy but not stiff. Add enough sifted icing sugar to absorb all the egg white and make a very stiff paste. Add peppermint essence and knead it in well. Colour half the mixture pale green with one or two drops of green food colouring.

Turn on to a board which has been liberally sprinkled with icing sugar and shape into a long roll, about ¾-inch diameter. Press lightly with the back of a fork to make a design on top, if you wish.

Cut into rounds ¼-inch thick. Leave to dry overnight, on greaseproof paper. Place in small, green or white paper sweet cases.

Marzipan Dates

Cost: About 5s 5d.
Quantity: 28-30 sweets (roughly 1 lb.)
Preparation time: 20 minutes.

Ingredients — 3oz. ground almonds; 3oz. sifted icing sugar; 1 egg yolk. Few drops almond essence; Few drops green food colouring; 1 box dessert dates.

To decorate — a few shelled walnut halves and blanched almonds (shelled almonds dipped in hot water to remove the skins). A little castor sugar.

Method — Mix the ground almonds and sifted icing sugar together and bind with the beaten egg yolk, plus a little cold water, if necessary. Add a few drops of almond essence, to taste; knead until smooth.

Colour half the almond paste pale green with one or two drops of green colouring. Make a split in the dates down one side and remove the stones.

Fill with a small roll of almond paste. Top the white filled dates with a quarter of a walnut and the green filled dates with a blanched almond. Roll lightly in castor sugar and place in small, chocolate-coloured paper cases.

Marzipan Fruits

Cost: About 2s 6d. per ½ lb.

Ingredients — Almond paste, using the same ingredients, in the same proportions as for the marzipan dates; Yellow, green and red food colouring.

Method — Make up the almond paste as in the Marzipan Dates recipe and model it into small apples, oranges, bananas, pears. Set the paste aside in a cool place overnight, to dry out. Paint the fruit in realistic colours, using a clean, small, soft paint brush and diluting the food colouring with a little cold water, as necessary.

Stick the centres of the oranges with a clove and use the stalks from real apples, cut to appropriate size, for the apples and pears.

Pack in small paper trays or plates and cover with a sheet of Cellophane, secured underneath the tray with Sellotape.

Shortbread

Wooden shortbread moulds are available in attractive patterns but these are fairly expensive. Instead, the shortbread can be cut in rounds, using a teaplate as a guide, or into fingers about 1 inch across and 3 inches long.

Cost: About 1s. 7d.

Quantity: 2 rounds.

Preparation time: 15 minutes. Plus baking time: 30 minutes.

Ingredients — 4 oz. plain flour; 2 oz. rice flour; 2 oz. castor sugar; 4 oz. fresh butter.

Method — Sift flour, rice flour and castor sugar together into a large basin. Add butter and knead ingredients together into a smooth ball.

Roll out on a floured board to a thickness of ¼ inch to ½ inch and shape as desired.

Dredge a buttered baking tin with a little flour, place shaped shortbread on the prepared tin and prick all over with a fork. Bake in a very moderate oven (325° F. — Gas Mark 2) until it turns a pale, straw colour — 25-30 minutes.

Leave to cool on the tins before removing.

Crystallised Pineapple

Cost: About 2s. 4d.
Quantity: 48 sweets (about 14 oz.)
Preparation time: About 3 hours (plus overnight standing).

Ingredients — 16 oz. tin pineapple rings; 8 oz. granulated sugar; 2 oz. castor sugar.

Method — Drain the pineapple rings, reserving the juice, and cut each slice into quarters, then eighths. Dissolve granulated sugar in the juice, make up to ½ pint with water, in a medium-sized, heavy-based saucepan.

Put in the pineapple pieces and cook very gently over a very low heat until the fruit looks clear. (The liquid must not be allowed to boil and this cooking period will take up to 3 hours.) Remove pineapple pieces carefully, using a perforated spoon, and toss gently in the castor sugar.

Place on a rack to dry and leave overnight in a warm atmosphere. Toss again in castor sugar and place in white paper sweet cases.

Coconut Ice

Cost: About 1s 5d.
Quantity: About 1 ¼ lb.
Preparation time: 20 minutes.

Ingredients — 1 lb. granulated sugar; ¼ pint milk; Small pat of butter; 4 oz. desiccated coconut; Few drops cochineal.

Method — Put sugar, milk and butter into a fairly large saucepan. Bring slowly to the boil and simmer over a low heat, stirring continuously, for about 7 minutes or until a little of the mixture forms a soft ball when dropped into cold water.

Remove from heat, add coconut and beat vigorously for a few seconds. It will thicken very quickly so have ready a well buttered square or oblong tin.

Colour half the mixture pale pink with a few drops of cochineal and quickly pour on top of the other half in the tin. Score into squares and cut when cold.

For packing, wrap in small squares of Cellophane.

Turkish Delight

Cost: About 2s. 4d.
Quantity: About 1 ½ lb.
Preparation time: 1 hour (plus overnight standing).

Ingredients — 1 oz. (2 envelopes) powdered gelatine; ½ pint water; 1 lb. granulated sugar; ¼ teaspoonful citric acid; 1 tablespoonful fresh lemon juice, strained; thinly peeled (use a vegetable peeler) rind of 1 orange; ½ teaspoonful rum essence; few drops cochineal; 2 oz. icing sugar; 2 oz. cornflour.

Method — Add the gelatine to ¼ pint of the cold water in a small bowl. Place bowl in a pan of hot water and stir gelatine until it dissolves.

Put remaining ¼ pint of water and the granulated sugar into a saucepan and stir until sugar dissolves. Then bring slowly to the boil and simmer for three minutes. Allow this syrup to cool slightly, add the dissolved gelatine and the citric acid and simmer gently for a further 20 minutes, stirring continuously.

Remove from heat, add strained lemon juice, orange rind and rum essence and leave to cool for about 10 minutes. Add sufficient cochineal to colour the mixture pale pink.

Strain into a square pan (about 7 inches square and at least an inch deep) which has previously been rinsed in cold water. Leave to set in the refrigerator or a cool place overnight.

Cut into small squares or oblongs, using a sharp knife dipped in icing sugar.

Sift icing sugar and cornflour together and toss the squares in this mixture, to coat them thoroughly.

It is just as well to leave the Turkish Delight in this sugar and cornflour mixture for a few hours before packing. If they are being packed in combination with other sweets, place in white paper sweet cases — if packed on their own, line the box with waxed paper and sprinkle liberally with the icing sugar and cornflour.

Christmas Tree Biscuits

These make a popular gift where there are young children in the house. You can save time by using biscuit cutters, available in Christmassy shapes, but "Christmas trees" are quick and easy to cut by hand.

Cost: About 3s.

Quantity: About 4 dozen biscuits.

Preparation time: 55 minutes. Plus baking time: 10-12 minutes.

Ingredients — 4 oz. butter or vegetable shortening; 4 oz. sugar; 1 egg; 8 oz. plain flour; ¼ teaspoonful baking powder; pinch of salt; 1 tablespoonful top-of-the-milk; ½ teaspoonful vanilla essence;

Icing — 4 oz. sifted icing sugar; about 1 tablespoonful water (just enough to make a stiffish paste); one or two drops green colouring; coloured and silver balls and coloured sugar, to decorate.

Method — Lightly grease shallow baking tins. Cream the butter and sugar together, add the unbeaten egg and mix well. Sift flour, baking powder and salt together, and combine with first mixture.

Add just enough milk, along with the vanilla essence, to make a stiff paste. Roll out on a floured surface to one-eighth-inch thick, cut to shape.

Bake in a moderately hot oven (400° F. – Gas Mark 5) for 10-12 minutes, or until golden.

Remove from baking sheet when slightly cool.

When cold, ice the Christmas tree biscuits with white or pale green icing and decorate the "branches" with silver or coloured balls, or sprinkle the icing with coloured sugar before it sets.

TV Becomes An Important Part

ONE of the biggest changes in how we used to celebrate Christmas then, compared to how we celebrate Christmas now, is how television took over the entire day.

TV's invasion started slowly, indeed we hardly noticed it at the start. But then began a relentless march that eventually conquered all before it. We are different types of people to who we were before we all became addicted to the cathode ray tubes.

And we didn't really realise it was happening until it was too late. We should have looked at what Mr George Percy, of Dumfries, was doing and just said "No".

But then we didn't know then what we know now. We didn't know the extent to which we'd become interested in a man called Bruce saying it was nice to see us to see us nice. We had no idea that we'd ever care what happened in a street named after the coronation of King Edward VII. We'd never even heard of gentlemen named Mr Morecambe, or his friend Mr Wise.

This chapter traces the slow, but very tight, grip that television took on Christmas. All the clippings are from The Sunday Post.

1949 **The news of TV signals being picked up in the south of Scotland was greeted with a small, but fairly enthusiastic article. A full TV programme, eh? This possibly amusing, but hardly relevant, piece of information didn't look like it would ever amount to much...fog or no fog.**

GEORGE PERCY, of Dumfries, tipped by The Sunday Post as the first man in Scotland to pick up test signals from the new Midland television transmitter, has become the first man in Scotland to receive a full TV programme.

After disappointing conditions during the opening programme from Sutton Coldfield, Mr Percy tried again last Sunday.

He obtained perfect pictures and sound all evening for two and a half hours, in spite of foggy weather.

MR (TV) PERCY DOES IT AGAIN

George Percy, of Dumfries, tipped by "The Sunday Post" as the first man in Scotland to pick up test signals from the new Midland television transmitter, has become the first man in Scotland to receive a full TV programme.

After disappointing conditions during the opening programme from Sutton Coldfield, Mr Percy tried again last Sunday.

He obtained perfect pictures and sound all evening for two and a half hours, in spite of foggy weather.

1950 **There were no listings for TV programmes in 1950. It was largely pointless because so few people had a TV set and they could barely get a signal even if they did. There was radio, and an article telling which movies readers should watch out for (at the cinema) in 1951.**

There's A Big Treat In Store

1951 is to be a big year for the film fan. Here are a few of the outstanding films you'll see.

King Solomon's Mines — Stewart Granger and Deborah Kerr in the great adventure by H. Rider Haggard. Sun, grandeur and thrills galore.

Captain Horatio Hornblower — Gregory Peck plays C. S. Forester's famous sailor. Action and humour at sea.

Soldiers Three — Walter Pidgeon, Robert Newton, Stewart Granger and David Niven in an adaptation of Rudyard Kipling's yarn.

Quo Vadis — Promises to outdo any previous "spectacle", with Deborah Kerr, Robert Taylor, thousands of extras, and a few lions.

Tales of Hoffmann — Made by the **Red Shoes** team.

An Outcast of the Islands — Carol (**Third Man**) Reed's production of a Joseph Conrad story. New star is Kerima, for whom Reed searched half-way across the world.

Three Little Words — Fred Astaire, Vera-Ellen, colour, music and dancing.

And of special interest to sports fans will be the film version of David Walker's book, **Geordie**.

Looks like a good year.

RADIO

Scottish Home Service

(371 m.)

7.55 a.m. — Weather Forecast. **8.0** — News. **8.20** — Morning Melody. **9.30** — God Speaks. **10.15** — Sunday Morning Prom. **11.15** — Red Letter Day. **11.30**—Music Magazine. **12.10 p.m.**—The Critics.

1.0—News. **1.10**—Country Magazine. **1.40**—Eat, Drink, and Be Merry. **2.5**—Are We Better Gardeners Than Our Fathers? **2.30** — A Christmas Carol. **3.0**—Festival of Nine Lessons and Carols. **4.20** — Stories From the Ballet. **5.0**—Children's Hour.

6.0—News. **6.15** — Makers of Music. **7.0**—Chapbook. **7.45** — A Child This Day Is Born. **8.25**—Week's Good Cause. **8.30**—The Reverend Micah Balwhidder. **9.0**—News. **9.15**—Christmas in Europe. **10.30**—Chamber Music. **10.52**—The Epilogue. **11.0**—News Summary. **11.3 app.**—Close down.

Light Programme

(1500 m.; 247 m.)

8.0 a.m. — Dutch Serenade. **8.20** — Way Out West. **8.40**—Bill M'Guffie at piano. **9.0**—News. **9.10**—Silver Chords. **9.30**—Marching With the Guards. **10.0** — Have a Go! **10.30** — Family Favourites. **11.30**—People's Service. **12.0 noon**—Calling All Forces.

1.0 p.m.—We Beg to Differ. **1.30**—Billy Cotton Band Show. **2.0** — Educating Archie. **2.30**—Lester Ferguson. **3.0** — Life With the Lyons. **3.30**—The Long Shadow. **4.0**—Ray's a Laugh. **4.30**—Down Your Way. **5.30**—Take It From Here.

6.0—Round Britain Quiz. **6.30**—Grand Hotel. **7.0** — Radio Newsreel. **7.25** — Raymond Glendenning on Holiday Sport. **7.30** — Frankie Howerd. **8.0**—Donald Peers. **8.30** — Messiah. **9.0**—Variety Bandbox. **10.0** — News. **10.15**—Ivor Moreton and Dave Kaye at two pianos. **10.30** — Festival of Nine Lessons and Carols. **11.15**—Christmas Moods. **11.50**—News Summary. **11.55** — The First Nowell. **12.0 midnight**—Midnight Mass of the Nativity. **12.50 a.m. app.** Close down.

Third Programme

(464 m.; 194 m.)

6.0 p.m.—Bach and Paganini. **6.30**—Porcelain Sale at Sotheby's. **6.50** — Possession. **7.45**—Chamber Orchestral Concert. **8.45** — Theo Marzials. **9.20**—Mozart and Brahms. **10.40**—Mrs Osborne's Story. **11.0**—Couperin and Bach. **11.35**—I Remember—— **12.0 midnight** — Close down.

1951 **Still no TV listings, which wasn't surprising as there were only two trasmitters in the UK, in London and Birmingham. Radio was still king, and Top Of The Form a jewel in the crown. Success on the show was newsworthy stuff.**

WHAT'S the secret of Morgan Academy's success in **Top Of The Form**?

Last week the Dundee school set up a record score for the series (37 out of a possible 40). And their confidence and speed of answer made it look as though they could repeat the feat any time. Six years ago, Morgan Academy rector, Mr Peter Robertson, appalled at the lack of general knowledge all over the country — made a change to his school's curriculum.

New pupils were told they would be set a general knowledge exam every May — and no special preparation would be done in school for it. A pupil's success would depend entirely on his own reading and observation outside.

All the pupil was given were a few general headings — sport, literature, music, art, &co. The rest was up to him.

Morgan entered the B.B.C. contest and a shortleet of boys was chosen from the results of the general knowledge test. Then Mr Robertson and Mr Collie, the second master, ran a mock Top Of The Form. The boys were questioned exactly as they would be in the broadcast — and they had to answer as if they were on the air.

The team was chosen with two things in mind — first, the accuracy of their answers, and second, their "broadcasting personality" (Freedom from nervousness, quickness of thought, and clarity of speech.)

In the next round — the British semi-final — Morgan meet Llanelly Boys' Grammar. This promises to be the toughest round yet. The lads from Llanelly have a formidable reputation.

1952 **At last, to go with the opening of the first TV transmitter in Scotland, at Kirk O'Shotts, Lanarkshire, we have listings. There is, however, little in the way of true Christmas-themed television, unless Jack And The Beanstalk On Ice counts. Speaking of Jack — the Abbott & Costello movie, in cinemas, was the top Christmas entertainment that year.**

TELEVISION.

5.0-5.5 p.m.—Children's Television. 8.0—What's My Line? 8.40 — Jack and the Beanstalk on Ice. 10.10 — The Epilogue. 10.20 app. — Weather Forecast and News (sound only).

First Win

ABOUT six weeks ago, I bought a raffle ticket. It cost 1s. I put it in a drawer and forgot about it.

Imagine my surprise on Friday, December 12, when I was told I'd won a TV set. Until then, I'd never won anything.—**Mrs P. Stewart, 15 Moredun Park Court, Edinburgh.**

HAVE you booked your seat for the panto yet? If you can't get in, here's Hollywood popping up with one for you!

Granted it's not in true theatre tradition — but who cares provided there's plenty of laughs?

Main mirth-maker is Lou Costello. Lou goes baby-sitting, and starts reading the fairy-tale to the bairn. Then he dozes off...

Before you can say Abracadabra he's planting beans, climbing the stalk, meeting the giant, rescuing the beautiful princess, and being chased for his life. It's still the good old story. But with Hollywood treatment of colour, costumes and settings it takes on a novel and amusing form.

For one thing, Lou's beanstalk makes all the stage beanstalks you've ever seen look like weeds. And exploding eggs and a talking harp will keep the kiddies on the edge of their seats all the time.

And, of course, there are the songs. Completely ridiculous and with rhymes you only find in pantomimes and nightmares!

Partner Bud Abbott has less to do than usual. Buddy Baer gets a change of character from his last role of Ursus. the bodyguard, in Quo Vadis. He makes a magnificent (but not frightening) giant.

Dorothy Ford, his housekeeper, is as glamorous a giantess as I've ever seen — even though she seems about eight feet tall!

Makes a merry Christmas.

1953 **The year it took off, with the help of the Coronation. Except it didn't really. Apart from the Queen being crowned, television was still a peripheral thing. The number of TV licenses rose from 763,000 in 1951, to 3.2 million in 1954, but most of the 51 million population of the UK didn't have a set. But if you did, there was a Hogmanay treat.**

SCOTS TV viewers are in for a treat at Hogmanay.

The highlight will come at 11.10, when the cameras will swing to Govan Town Hall, Glasgow, to follow the revels of a hundred guests at a Hogmanay party and see them bring in the New Year.

There'll be a cabaret, with Jimmy Logan, Jack Anthony, young Scots impressionist Margot Henderson, tenor Kenneth McKellar from the Carl Rosa Opera, and Margaret Miles, who's playing in Puss In Boots at a Glasgow theatre.

Earlier in the evening, viewers can recapture the big moment of Coronation Year in a 60-minute newsreel digest called **Retrospect, 1953**.

This'll be a collection of all the top material from TV newsreels of the year.

And to set the seal on the New Year TV, an edited version of the telerecording of the Coronation Service will be shown on Sunday, January 3.

We Can All Join In The Fun On Hogmanay

SCOTS TV viewers are in for a treat at Hogmanay.

The highlight will come at 11.10, when the cameras will swing to Govan Town Hall, Glasgow, to follow the revels of a hundred guests at a Hogmanay party and see them bring in the New Year.

There'll be a cabaret, with Jimmy Logan, Jack Anthony, young Scots impressionist Margot Henderson, tenor Kenneth McKellar from the Carl Rosa Opera, and Margaret Miles, who's playing in "Puss In Boots" at a Glasgow theatre.

Earlier in the evening, viewers can recapture the big moment of Coronation Year in a 60-minute newsreel digest called "Retrospect, 1953." This'll be a collection of all the top material from TV newsreels of the year.

And to set the seal on the New Year TV, an edited version of the B.B.C. telerecording of the Coronation Service will be shown on Sunday, January 3.

TELEVISION.

5.0-6.0 p.m.—Children's Television. **7.55**—Weather Chart. **8.0** — Harringay Circus. **9.0**—What's My Line? **9.40**—Amahl and the Night Visitors (Christmas story with music. **10.30 app.**—News (sound only).

1954 **If TV was ever to become relevant, it had to be challenging. And the adaptation of George Orwell's 1984, starring a young Peter Cushing, certainly challenged. It was accused of being frightening, subversive and even horrific. Most complaints were about the harrowing Room 101 scenes. Such controversy did it cause that questions were asked in Parliament. Hardly festive fare, but it was shown twice, on December 12th and 16th, 1954. Everything was live in those days, so these were seperate performances. The second was recorded for posterity and is, to this day, regarded as a landmark in the development of TV drama. It was widely discussed on newspaper pages of the time.**

WHETHER you saw **1984** on TV or not, you've certainly heard of it. And that is one good reason why all the shuddering and howling and wringing of hands about the play is utter nonsense.

You HAVE heard of 1984. Thousands of TV owners have been moaning about TV that bores them, TV that doesn't get under the skin of a subject, TV that's trivial. Okay. Now 1984 gives us something with punch, something that makes the rusty brains turn over.

And what happens? Shoals of protests.

What exactly is 1984? It's a look — a sane and acutely intelligent look — into the future. It could be the NEAR future. But it's based, every word of it, on what is happening in the world today. Winston Smith, a minor member of the ruling party of Oceania, is the hero. In Oceania the rule of the party is absolute. Obedience to the will of Big Brother, the Hitler of Oceania, is the only way to stay alive. If he says two times two equals five, then two and two do make five.

But Winston has his doubts. Instead of loving Big Brother, as a good party member should, he hates him like poison.

From then on Winston is doomed. He falls in love with Julia, another party member. This, too, is asking for it, for love between party members is forbidden. However, they have a few brief weeks of happiness in a secret hiding-place.

They even join what they think is a Brotherhood to fight Big Brother. But the hiding-place is a trap. The Brotherhood is a trap. The two people they trust are party spies. They are captured. They are mentally tortured — Winston with rats and a mask for his face, because he hates rats.

Finally they succumb to the will of the party. They even betray each other. Then, with their brains washed clean of all such ridiculous thoughts as love, freedom, unselfishness, and self-respect, they are released.

They no longer love each other. They no longer have any identity. They have become what Big Brother wants them to be — cogs in his machine.

That's the story. It isn't pleasant. But it is not because the story's unpleasant that all the peely-wallies have shuddered and switched it off.

It is because it is too like the truth! Remember the Nazis? Remember Belsen, Dachau, Buchenwald? Remember Hitler Youth children betraying their parents because their thinking had been controlled? Remember the show trials in the Iron Curtain countries? Remember men like Cardinal Mindszenty, who fought heroically before their arrest — and then, after interrogation (you can call it brain washing), sobbed that they were traitors and spies and deserved all they got?

That's the story that 1984 tells. The truth today is terrifying. But the only way to make it less terrifying is to face it, not run away from it.

That's what the B.B.C. is doing in presenting 1984. They're doing the thing they've always been accused of running away from — telling the harsh, unvarnished, unpalatable truth.

Let's hope they go on doing it. And if, as is possible, they show a film of the first atom bomb explosion on Christmas Day, here's one bloke who'll be rooting for them!—**T. J.**

The Play All The Fuss Is About

WHETHER you saw " 1984 " on TV or not, you've certainly heard of it.

And that is one good reason why all the shuddering and howling and wringing of hands about the play is utter nonsense. You **HAVE** heard of " 1984."

Thousands of TV owners have been moaning about TV that bores them, TV that doesn't get under the skin of a subject, TV that's trivial.

Okay. Now " 1984 " gives us something with punch, something that makes the rusty brains turn over. And what happens? Shoals of protests.

WHAT exactly is " 1984 "?

It's a look—a sane and acutely intelligent look—into the future. It could be the NEAR future. But it's based, every word of it, on what is happening in the world today.

Winston Smith, a minor member of

That's the story that " 1984 " tells. The truth today is terrifying. But the only way to make it less terrifying is to face it, not run away from it.

That's what the B.B.C. is doing in presenting " 1984." They're doing the thing they've always been accused of running away from—telling the harsh, unvarnished, unpalatable truth.

Let's hope they go on doing it. And if, as is possible, they show a film of the first atom bomb explosion on Christmas Day, here's one bloke who'll be rooting for them!—T. J.

1955 **By the mid-point of the 1950s, the revolution was well under way and television was at last popular enough to have been promoted above the radio listings in newspapers. Football (although only the second half) was live from Rome on December 18th. The Royal Christmas Message (referred to in the listings as simply "The Queen") was brought to us live from Sandringham at 3pm on Christmas Day — but was a sound-only broadcast. Television, even on Christmas Day, had a Children's slot at 5pm, followed by an hour-long break in transmissions to allow the kids to calm down and be put to bed. And the public was given warnings on the dire consequences of letting their hair dryers or lathes interfere with the TV signal.**

RADIO and TV

TELEVISION.

2 p.m.—Italy v. Germany, 2nd Half (Rome Eurovision). **3.15**—Concert Hour. **4.0**—I Married Joan. **4.30**—The Brains Trust. **5.0-6.10** – Children's Television. **7.30**—News, The Weather. **7.45**—God Rest You Merry (carols). **8.15** – This Is Your Life. **8.45**—The Devil's General (play). **10.15**—Christians Be Joyful. **10.55**—News Summary. The Weather.

RADIO and TV

TELEVISION.

11.0—Welcome to the New Born King **3.0 — Her Majesty The Queen.** **3.15**—A Christmas Visit to Disneyland. **4.45**—Watch With Mother. **5.0** — Children's Television. **7.30**—News. **7.45**—Music For You. **9.0**—Christmas Box. **9.45**—Bird in Hand. **11.15**—Today in Bethlehem. **11.25**—News Summary.

HOME (371 m.)

7.55—Weather Forecast. **8.0**—News. **8.15**—Born This Joyful Morning. **9.0**—Postman's Knock. **9.20** — Christmas Bells. **9.30**—Family Service. **10.15** — From Our Own Correspondent. **10.45** — Music For Noel. **11.30**—Scottish Garden. **12.0**—God Rest Ye Merry. **1.0** — News. **1.10** — Tom Jenkins Orchestra. **1.40**—Josh White. **2.0**—The Star

1955 is to bring a hefty new crop of regulations. They'll affect drivers, pedal cyclists, pedestrians. They'll also affect the housewife.

To prevent TV interference she'll have to see that suppressors are on the vac., washing and sewing machines, hair-driers, &c. Hubbies who have electrically-driven lathes, lawn-mowers, &c., will also have to toe the line.

Don't boggle at the new regulations, folk. They're intended to add to the comfort and happiness of most of us.

1955 IS to bring a hefty new crop of regulations.

They'll affect drivers, pedal cyclists, pedestrians.

They'll also affect the housewife. To prevent TV interference she'll have to see that suppressors are on the vac., washing and sewing machines, hair-driers, &c. Hubbies who have electrically-driven lathes, lawn-mowers, &c., will also have to toe the line.

Don't boggle at the new regulations, folk. They're intended to add to the comfort and happiness of most of us.

1956 **In what was to become, and still is, a major point of contention, the public soon began to believe that they owned TV, and that they should be able to watch what they wanted to watch, not what the programme schedulers thought they should watch. And we told them, in no uncertain terms, what was what!**

So Disappointing On Wednesday evening thousands watched enthralled as two boxers fought on TV.

Two minutes to go. The bout still hung in the balance. The atmosphere was tense.

Then phut! The B.B.C. switched over to a programme about the countryside. It fell as flat as a pancake.

Why? We asked the B.B.C. They said in the case of a BIG event they run the programme on.

Someone should tell them that top amateur boxers in an exciting fight IS a big event.

1957 **By 1957, more than 95% of the UK could receive a TV signal (though there was still a bit of work to do to reach some of the more rural corners). ITV had begun, in the London area, in 1955 but was now available across the country. The concept of renting a TV set, instead of going to the huge expense of buying one outright, was spreading rapidly. Television was at last a mass medium. Daily life for ordinary people in the UK hasn't been the same since. However, small details like Christmas didn't make much of a dent on the late-December TV listings.**

B.B.C TELEVISION.

1.25 – World Cup Football – Italy v. Portugal **3.15**—News Review. **3.45**—Melody Hour. **4.15** - The Brains Trust. **5.0**—Children's Television. **6.5**—Sunday Special. **7.0**—Meeting Point. **7.25** – News Summary. **7.35**—The Thin Man. **8.0** – Thark. **9.30**—Tufty. **10.0**—Handel's Messiah. **10.45**—News. **10.55**—The Epilogue.

SCOTTISH TELEVISION.

2.15—Armand and Michaela Denis. **2.30**—Free Speech. **3.0**—Rosemary Clooney Show. **3.30** - Call of the Blood (film). **4.50**—Hawkeye and the Last of the Mohicans. **5.20**—Robin Hood. **5.50** – Rockets Galore. **6.5**—News. **6.15** – Sign Off. **7.0**—About Religion. **7.25**—News. **7.30** – I Love Lucy. **8.0**—Sunday Night at the Prince of Wales. **9.0**—Highway Patrol. **9.30** – News. **9.35**—Armchair Theatre. **10.35** – Jack Jackson Show. **11.5** - The Colonel (play). **11.30**—Close down.

1958 The explosion. TV is suddenly big business, with entire newspaper pages dedicated to commenting on the shows. Christmas was changed for ever, it was now not only an event we celebrated at home, it was an event we watched on a little screen in the corner of the room.

The **Queen's Christmas Day Broadcast** is traditional. But last Thursday T.V. introduced a new element — cosiness. It was just like a fireside chat — and the Queen's shy smile at the end delighted everyone.

Best actress of the week — a wee Scots girl called Janet Munro. She stole the show in I.T.V.'s Sunday evening play **The Silent Heart**.

Quatermass is back. The pace flagged a bit after a good start, but finished on the usual note of suspense. It looks promising and I'll certainly watch next week.

I've always admired **Sooty**, Harry Corbett's puppet teddy-bear. But why did they spoil their appearance on Children's T.V. last week by forcing a pathetic little puppy and a frightened kitten into a budgie cage and trying to get them to perform? For many it left a bad taste in the mouth.

Shows may come and series may go. But **Sergeant Bilko** is still the daddy of them all for the laughs. Last week he signed up for another three years. Here's hoping we're signed up to stay with him.

What is it about the panel of **What's My Line** that gives them a wrong sense of their own importance? When they are stumped by a contestant they think it clever to say such things as "Are you a bill-poster?" Harding has been doing it so long we've become accustomed. But when guest panellist, Cyril Fletcher, asked a teacher of the Royal Ballet: "Are you a bill-poster?" it certainly wasn't funny.

The Sky At Night is worth watching. Don't think it's too advanced. Last week's was very do very down-to-earth

Poor I.T.V.'s **Stars In Your Eyes**. They're still hunting for amateur talent. And it's proving a most difficult job. But thanks for trying.

> The Queen's Christmas Day broadcast is traditional. But last Thursday T.V. introduced a new element into it —cosiness. It was just like a fireside chat—and the Queen's shy smile at the end delighted everyone.
>
> Quatermass is back. The pace flagged a bit after a good start, but finished on the usual note of suspense. It looks promising and I'll certainly watch next week's episode.
>
> Frankie Howerd, you surprise me. After a mediocre performance mid-week you came on the 6.5 Special and didn't even bring a smile to my face. Yours is one hat-trick I DON'T want to see completed.
>
> I've always admired Sooty, Harry Corbett's puppet teddy-bear. But why did they spoil their appearance on Children's T.V. last week by forcing a pathetic little puppy and a frightened kitten into a budgie cage and trying to get them to perform? For many it left a bad taste in the mouth.
>
> Shows may come and series may go. But Sergeant Bilko is still the daddy of them all for bringing out the laughs. Last week he signed up for another three years. Here's hoping we're signed up to stay with him.

1959 **Previews of shows, hearty recommendations, and strong opinions show just to what a degree the British public had taken ownership of what was on their TV screens. Several of the comments show that the viewers feel they have every right to criticise and make demands of what is being shown — it is their TV, in their house, in front of their family. Christmas and Hogmanay are becoming events owned by TV, with lots of specialised shows.**

IT'LL be the party of the year—and you can be there! The time? New Year's Eve, at 11.35. The place? **White Heather Club**.

Look at some of the guests who have promised to come along — Jimmy Logan. Duncan Macrae, Robert Wilson, Joe Gordon, Jimmy Shand, Anne and Laura Brand and the City of Glasgow Police Choir.

Andy Stewart will play host. And Bobby Watson has been carefully rehearsing his party piece. Don't miss it!

Fancy seeing a bird that flies backwards! In Argentina, **David Attenborough** waited five hours to get good pictures. It was well worth it.

Which Christmas show did you prefer? **Circus**? **Harry Belafonte**? **Hughie Green**'s show? **High Noon** maybe? I liked 'em all. My compliments to both channels for their festive fayre.

I just had to sit through all of James Stewart's camp-fire cowboy version of **Scrooge**. I reckon if all Dickens' stories were told on similar lines there would be quite a few higher marks in the English exam.

Don Juan may have been a good film in its day, but for modern entertainment it didn't click. Even the name Douglas Fairbanks didn't make it any more interesting.

Mr Producer, please do some-thing to safeguard against the same tunes being selected for **Dial For Music**. Denis Lotis has sung Mack the Knife twice already — and there have only been two shows!

Was it the Yuletide spirit or natural good taste that made the first winning contestant in Tuesday's **Concentration** decide to stand down and let someone else have a go? Whatever his reason, I take off my hat to him!

Norman Wisdom's dressing-room capers on **Picture Parade** didn't amuse me, but the excerpt from his latest film did. It's sheer torture to show an extract like that and whip it off as it reaches the climax.

1960 **Perhaps it says something about the TV shows of the time — perhaps it says something about us. But the festive TV comments of 1960 lack the Christmas spirit, somewhat. We didn't like anything, and found fault with everyone. Watching TV had become, like the weather, a subject we all could find common ground to complain about.**

DEAR EAMONN ANDREWS...

YOU know what I'm getting fed up with? The celebrity spot in "What's My Line?"
Somebody comes along, signs in to hysterical applause, and proceeds to answer the panel in a disguised voice.

TV Comment

Glynn did the right thing in taking the £500 on "**Double** Your Money." You **can bet** your life his Stonehouse **Gang**

YOU know what I'm getting fed up with? The celebrity spot in **What's My Line?** Somebody comes along, signs in to hysterical applause, and proceeds to answer the panel in a disguised voice.

This might have been funny originally, but now it seems strangely embarrassing.

So many excerpts from **The Prisoner of Zenda** have been plugged this past week that there can't be very much left to see tonight!

Tamest Western of them all — **The Lone Ranger**. When the youngsters are laughing, it's time for action!

Another good show against the **Ask Me Another** experts. But, in all honesty, I thought many of the questions — to both sides — were, a lot easier than last week.

B.B.C.'s Sunday-nighter **A Time To Fight** wasn't outstanding as plays go. But it was good entertainment and, interesting psychology.

B.B.C. might have picked something a little better than **The Eye Of Allah** for the first televising of a Rudyard Kipling story.

Didn't think **Sid James** was as funny as usual last Thursday. Maybe Sid & Co. are saving their best for tonight? Hope so.

A wee word to S.T.V. sports man **Arthur Montford**. You're getting into a bad habit of mumbling, Arthur.

1961 **Soap Operas would become a staple part of Christmas TV. There are three things you can rely upon a soap opera for: 1. No secret is ever kept. 2. No wedding goes smoothly. 3. Christmas is chaotic. Coronation Street actually debuted in December 1960, but just a year later had grown to become the first show mentioned.**

What About It, Coronation Street?

LET'S hope Coronation Street becomes a little more cheerful over the festive season.

Len Fairclough is niggling at Ken Barlow. Harry Hewitt is wrangling with his wife. Elsie Tanner and Dennis always seem to be feuding. And, of course, there's Ena . . .

Peace on earth, goodwill to men—except in Coronation Street!

○ A moving and telling moment in "This Is Your Life." The mother of a sea-captain who lost his life during the war paid tribute to Lieut.-Commander Kane. Although she couldn't be present and had to appear on the screen, he stood up and snapped to attention.

○ Disappointed with "Scotsport's" offering from the League Cup final. No second half film, no sound to accompany the presentation. Much better on B.B.C.

○ So Maigret can fight! The Patron did rather well in a tough tussle with a village blacksmith who wielded sledge-hammers and chains. Then a chase over half-a-mile of sand-dunes—and you can't do that sort of thing unless you're 100 per cent. fit!

○ Scotland's formation dancers are certainly hitting the high spots! From a seemingly hopeless position, the East team finished sensationally only one point behind their North - West opponents. A great effort.

○ How about a pat on the back for Derek Guyler, one of the regular supporting elements in the "Harry Worth" series?

○ The noisiest two minutes of the week—the music at the end of "International Detective."

○ What on earth would "Mess Mates" do without Croaker?

○ Wish the "Hippodrome" had left off the circus acts. It was too soon after the Glasgow circus. And there are more to come, Billy Smart's tomorrow on B.B.C. and Chipperfield's on A.T.V. We can have too much of a good thing.

○ Sunday's Nativity play, "Man In Time" made clear what it considered the ills in our modern society. But I wish we'd been given a stronger clue as to the cures.

Alan Stewart's TV COMMENT

○ A classic "Candid Camera" where people tried to put up the deck-chair which had the notches on the wrong side.

TRY IT!

○ Looks as if "Tonight" started a popular craze for the party season when they showed a Glasgow man taking his waist-coat off without removing his jacket. I've almost tied myself up like a Christmas parcel trying it!

○ Is it necessary to import

LET'S hope **Coronation Street** becomes a little more cheerful over the festive season.

Len Fairclough is niggling at Ken Barlow. Harry Hewitt is wrangling with his wife. Elsie Tanner and Dennis always seem to be feuding. And, of course, there's Ena...

Peace on earth, goodwill to men — except in Coronation Street!

A classic **Candid Camera** where people tried to put up the deck-chair which had the notches on the wrong side.

First off the mark with a Christmas special — **A.T.V.** Fine festive fare in their circus. The camera made best use of Bartschelly's spinning plates — just the man you can leave with confidence to wash up after Christmas dinner!

Looks as if **Tonight** started a popular craze for the party season when they showed a man taking his waist-coat off without removing his jacket. I've almost tied myself up like a Christmas parcel trying it

Better report on **Harry Worth** this week. He became enmeshed in the web of the Min. of Pen. and Nat. Ins. and turned it inside out!

I enjoyed the singing in **Songs Of Praise**. But why didn't they use the organ instead of the piano?

1962 **The line between a TV show and real life begins to blur. Admiration for policemen is healthy, admiration for the fictional policemen of Z-Cars is...odd. It is another sign of the grip being exerted over the public's imagination. It is also a sign of how well done and realistic the shows were becoming. There is also the first indication of Christmas fatigue, with complaints about too many Santa appearances. How quickly has the new way of celebrating Christmas become jaded.**

Surely there's no shortage of young ladies around BBC who could provide fashion notes on **Come Dancing**. You won't convince me Geoffrey Wheeler enjoys having to describe layered underskirts and elaborate dresses of "frothy turquoise net". You have my sympathy, Geoff.

Mounted Police, river police, police in vans, cars and motorcycles, police on foot, police dogs and police frogmen — as **Z-Cars** searched for a missing kiddie, my admiration for the boys in blue grew greater than ever.

Is it necessary to give a Christmas touch to EVERY programme? There seemed no point in having Santa as a contestant on **Take A Letter**. It's like a football team having a game at Christmas and playing Santa at centre.

I raise my paper hat to **Steptoe And Son** — tops in an unspectacular **Christmas Night With The Stars**. Old Steptoe's story of the Christmas he spent in the trenches was the funniest thing I've heard on TV this year.

For a Christmas edition of **This Is Your Life**, I compliment BBC on their choice of Dickie Attenborough. His genuine surprise at seeing and hearing from so many of his friends was well worth seeing.

A new description of fog by **Bob Hope** — "I saw a light in the distance. It came nearer and nearer. Then I realised what it was — the tip of my cigarette."

Let's hope the news that came over the radio on the **Benny Hill Show** never comes true — a traffic jam stretching from Hyde Park Corner to Edinburgh.

Four thugs and a girl invade an elderly Glasgow woman's home to break through to a bank. That's the set-up for STV's **Thirty-Minute Theatre** tomorrow — **The First Foot**.

The news I've waited to hear — **Tony Hancock**'s ITV debut is a week on Thursday.

1963 **IN 1963, The Sunday Post invented Facebook. It wasn't called "Facebook" of course, but the concept was the same — a look at the opinions of ordinary people. The TV comments of readers were invited to be used alongside those of critics. This idea proved to be a winner. People liked to read about what other people thought....exactly as, almost six decades later but now "online", people still like to read about what others think.**

KIDNAPPED — Keep your Liverpool music. Give me this theme tune any day. Can you tell me what it's called? — **C. Coxon, 63 Greenhow Tce., Newcastle-upon-Tyne.** *(BBC have had many inquiries, Mr C. It's a traditional Highland muster roll (for mustering the clans). It hasn't been published or recorded commercially).*

KIDNAPPED — Badly needs swashbuckling Alan Breck to swash a few buckles at this stage.

CORONATION STREET — You always seem to be knocking it. But I'd like to wish them a right merry Christmas — and that comes from all of us down here. — **R. Edwards, 40 Clarendon Road, Morecambe.**

OLD MAN OF THE MOUNTAINS — The philosophy of hermit Bill Collins made mighty good listening. I raise my paper hat to Fyfe Robertson for tracking him down, although I was tempted at times to ask which was Fyfe Robertson!

UNIVERSITY CHALLENGE — Students and lecturers of Leicester rattle off answers to questions on every subject under the sun. Then comes one that stumps them all: "What was the last team Leicester City played at home? " It's not fair, ref!

LESLIE CROWTHER — Was his first-ever party piece with the Minstrels too good? He hasn't done anything half as good since his debut.

WHITE HEATHER CLUB — A reader wrote last week suggesting it would be better to end it at midnight. But what about the folk who have no first-foot and will be only too glad to welcome Andy and his friends? I know I will. — **Mrs E. Beetham, 1 Mansion House Road, Paisley.**

TOP OF THE FORM — Is it possible? A youngster who didn't know Ringo Starr is the Beatles' drummer. What's education coming to?

Z CARS — Was that Barlow's Christmas spirit? I've had a cheerier time at the dentist.

NEWS — With a newscaster called Peter Snow reading an item about a snowmaker in Scotland, it's hardly surprising the flakes started to fall outside just minutes later!

GERRY AND THE PACEMAKERS — Did you see the sweat dripping from his brow as he sang? Who said this was money for jam?

CHRISTMAS DAY — It just wasn't the same without Max Bygraves.

NO ROAD BACK — Brrr! Judging by what we saw of conditions on the Greenland ice cap, I wouldn't even consider starting out!

CHARLIE CHAPLIN — Don't spread this around, but I much preferred Charlie in the old, silent days.

ELIZABETH TAYLOR — There was a "For Export Only" tag about her London travelogue. Her very presence made it interesting, but black mark, Liz, for talking about the Changing of the Guard and showing film of the Trooping of the Colour.

SPORTS REVIEW — Congrats to Dorothy Hyman, but the film of those wild and wonderful Test matches was the highlight of the night.

JACK HEDLEY — His role in the **First Night** play put me right in the mood for another cracking Tim Fraser serial. How about it, BBC?

JUNIOR POINTS OF VIEW — Surely there's a Scots youngster somewhere in London who could read letters from north of the Border and pronounce "loch " correctly.

THE DEFENDERS — Spoilt by an indecisive ending. The producer has no qualms about the Prestons losing a case. He should have no qualms about them winning one — even if it means a rogue cop being dismissed from the force.

PANORAMA — Not a pleasant prospect — that of Jet airliner accidents in 20 years becoming almost as common as road accidents are today in your own town. About time those safety precautions we heard about were universally approved.

1964 BY 1964, the "Facebook" approach was even stronger. Viewers were asked to name their show, or series, of the year. Again, this proved to be hugely successful. People loved having their letters published and postbags bulged at the seams. Never, throughout entertainment history, had actors, presenters and producers been judged in this way. It is one thing for an actor to suffer the scorn of a reviewer — and dismiss their so-called "professional" opinions as biased bitterness. Quite another to be subject to the praise, and scathing displeasure, of an audience millions strong. If TV changed the profession of acting, then mass-published opinion was the tool used to beat it into a new shape.

LAST week we asked readers what they considered the best single show or series on TV during the year. **Coronation Street**? **Z-Cars**? **Compact**? No! The voting has proved a real turn-up. All the top-rated shows have been pushed down the poll by — **The Count of Monte Cristo** series.

Mrs J. R. Dunn, 4 Middleton Rd., Woodland, Bishop Auckland, says, "It was gripping from first to last. Alan Badel played the part of Edmund Dantes to perfection."

C. S. Morton, 28 Willoughby Drive, Anniesland, asks a good question — "Where has Alan Badel been all this time?" Well, at least we're sure of seeing a lot more of him now, Mr M.

Runner-up couldn't have been more appropriate. It's the man who's been running longer than the Olympic marathon champion — **The Fugitive**, with David Jenssen starring as Dr Richard Kimble. "He enthralled me every Sunday," said **Mrs Mary Manson, 98 Kingseat Avenue, Grangemouth.**

In third place is the couthy crew of Tannochbrae in **Dr Finlay's Casebook**. There was bags of support for Miss Ellen Scollay, 38 Airlie Street, Hyndland, who reckons, "There's just nothing to beat it."

HERE'S a selection from other letters—

GENERAL ELECTION — The best programme of the year was the coverage of the election, and the most disappointing thing was its result. —Mrs Alice Reid, 110 Duff Street, Macduff.

CULLODEN — It made my blood freeze, but it was an epic. — Henry Cowan, 14 Fairbairn Street, Dundee.

DICK VAN DYKE — Definitely the year's top comedy show, with grand support from Rose Marie and Morey Amsterdam. — Caroline Hughes, 84 Wellmeadow Road, Glasgow.

DIXON OF DOCK GREEN — Always a good clear cut story with a sound, solid moral for good measure.— G. Fraser, 56 Hillside Avenue, Alexandria.

HOGMANAY — To find the best of the year you've got to go right back to when the year was only a few minutes old. It was Duncan Macrae's version of how the Highland Fling originated.— Mrs T. Young, 9 Barr Ave., Neilston.

THIS IS YOUR LIFE — Best single show was the one devoted to Barbara Mullen. I think you called it The Magnificent Mullens — and how right you were? — Mrs F. Reid, 41 Lothian Cres., Paisley.

Now to the biggest disappointment of the year. Votes covered a much wider field here, but **Not So Much A Programme . . .** came in for a real pasting. "They could take a tip on satire without venom from Mike Bentine," wrote Mrs J. B. Phillips, 1 Broompark Ave., Prestwick.

Burke's Law was outlawed by many viewers, too. Mrs S. Murray, 26 McAllister Avenue, Airdrie, said, "It was grand entertainment to start with, but now it's just stupid."

ROYAL COMMAND PERFORMANCE — Too many of them were playing to the Royal Box instead of to the audience. — J. Lawson, c/o 3 Lawson's Lane, Buckhaven.

FORTH ROAD BRIDGE — Fog to blame mostly. But I thought Richard Dimbleby was below par. — Mrs Helen Loudon, 14 Glengavel Gdns., Wishaw.

THE AVENGERS — Phony fisticuffs left much to be desired. — J. W. Keith, 191 Lyoncross Rd., Glasgow.

PALLADIUM — I looked forward so much to seeing Tony Hancock, but I had to vote it a miss.— Jas. Robertson, 21 Harlington Rd., Aberdeen.

BOXING — There I was at three in the morning with two flasks of coffee and enough sandwiches for a Sunday School picnic, and the Clay-Liston fight turned out to be the flop of the year. — D. Campbell. 1 Granton Avenue, Edinburgh.

1965 **TELEVISION discovers another thing that will turn out to be a long-standing "truth" — viewers like reality. Two of the top shows in Christmas week (the week all the best shows are kept for) were reality-based.**

A REVELATION to every driver — that was **So You Think You Can Drive**. This knocks parlour games for six. For every point dropped, drivers now know they must react more efficiently in situations they might find themselves in tomorrow. Then, of course, there's the prestige angle. You've simply got to score more than a wife who's never been behind the wheel of a car in her life! It's a tip-top idea, BBC, that should be a regular series.

TOMORROW'S WORLD — The programme on the advances in science enabling newly-born babies to breathe without brain damage when they can't do it naturally was superb. Not even Hitchcock can compete with the suspense of waiting to see if a handful of human life is going to make it. — Mrs J. Nicol, 43 Fernhill Rd., Rutherglen.

DR FINLAY — Always right on the ball when they mix social and medical problems. The story of out-of-work Angus Hendry was a topper.

VAL DOONICAN — Must rank as one of TV's top performers. Good, clean family entertainment, all the time. Let's say a diamond amongst the dross. — Allan Drennan, 89 Bathgo Avenue, Ralston, Paisley.

ALEXANDER BROTHERS — Don't they make a grand job of *Nobody's Child*?

DAVE ALLEN — I liked his Christmas crack, "With so many womenfolk determined to be first with their present to hubby, it's strange that it so often ends in a tie!"

EAMONN ANDREWS SHOW — You either like Spike Milligan or you don't — and I don't. — Mary Twivey, 125 Rosehill Drive, Aberdeen.

PEYTON PLACE — Glad to see Mia Farrow doing something with her hair to get rid of that "little girl lost" look. Let's hope it puts a spark of life into dreamy Alison McKenzie. — Mrs S. Spence, 12 Malcolm St., Glasgow.

THE LITTLEST HOBO — I'm only 12, but I don't think they could have phoned the Sheriff when the telephone wires had been cut only seconds before. — Charles Adams, 175 Holm Street, Glasgow.

1966 **TV companies start giving preview screenings to newspapers, so their shows can get good reviews in advance — in this case STV's Hogmanay offering.**

BETTER than ever — that's how I think the Hogmanay shows will turn out this year. STV have theirs "in the can". Rikki Fulton's the link man, but Roy Castle is the one to watch. He sang, danced, clowned and put so much into this show he had to be carried to a taxi afterwards with a strained back! But my favourite item is a stirring torchlit version of *Men of Harlech* by Ivor Emmanuel. BBC will have Andy Stewart, Jimmy Shand and Moira Anderson "live". They're not giving anything away meantime, but I know there are loads of surprises. Lonnie Donegan will be there as well.

COME DANCING — Just witnessed another defeat of Scottish dancers, and I think they got a rough deal. I reckon the Scots judges on the panel were afraid to give their team too high marks lest they were accused of bias. Isn't it possible to have neutral judges as in international matches? And in case you're wondering, I happen to be a qualified teacher of dancing — and I'm ENGLISH! — Frances E. Hunter, 18 Cherrybank, Dunfermline.

DAKTARI — Come on, that's the second time a half-hearted hunter has been too soft to shoot an animal. And for a man with 65 stitches in his leg, that was quite a sprint from Sean Murphy!

TOP OF THE FORM — Can't recall the questions ever being easier. And in a semi-final, too!

SONGS OF PRAISE — Grand service to celebrate 50 years of the Cub Scout movement. Having been an assistant cub-mistress 34 years ago, it was great to hear them singing again in perfect unison, as always. — Mrs M. Anderson, 16 Newhailes Cres., Musselburgh.

VAL DOONICAN SHOW — The Doonican-McKellar-Castle triple act must run pretty close to being one of the most entertaining items of the year.

WHITE HEATHER CLUB — As an Aberdonian, I had great difficulty understanding the words that Andy Stewart sang on Friday, so how can he expect non-natives to understand them? — Mrs Catherine Cain, 43 Winton Avenue, New Southgate, London.

1967 **The concept of a Christmas blockbuster TV special began. Revered now, and the legends would have you believe that everyone loved the Fab Four in the 60s, but at the time the Beatles didn't get away with what the viewers reckoned was sub-standard fare. The Magical Mystery Tour album came out on December 8th, priced 19s 6d (About £16 today). And the BBC screened the film, amid a media frenzy of anticipation, on Boxing Day. A huge television audience (for the time) of 15 million watched.**

WELL, after all the ballyhoo, what's the viewers' verdict on The Beatles fantasy ***Magical Mystery Tour***? Sorry, lads, but it gets the thumbs-down!

I've always been a Beatles fan, but I'm disillusioned after this. — Patricia Quinn (15), 24 Leith Street, Riddrie.

I waited anxiously to see this, but oh, what a disappointment. — D. Macleod, 217 Moraine Ave., Blairardie.

How dare the BBC show such an insult to our intelligence? — Mrs G. McMurrough, 89 Fellsview Ave., Kirkintilloch.

In countless homes at sometime or other during a week's viewing, someone must say, "That was a lot of tripe". I said it after watching this. — Mrs Helen Wright, 81 Cardenden Rd., Cardenden.

Give me Cliff Richard and The Shadows any time. — E. Keith, 54 Modley Pl., Ellon. Better luck next time, boys.

QUEEN'S SPEECH — It was absolutely splendid, and a striking reply to the critics who said the whole ritual was becoming a bore. — A. Buist, 56 Bruce St., Dunfermline.

STANLEY BAXTER — I hope Santa Claus was kind and gave Stanley an extended run in 1968. That would be a smashing gift for all of us. — Mrs M. Allan, 35 Stratford Street, Glasgow.

COUNT FIVE AND DIE — It dealt with wartime intelligence, and those concerned did not wish their presence to be known to the German spies. Yet, unless I'm mistaken, the British major was wearing the Intelligence Corps tie! — Major W. Poulson, 6 Balmoral Terrace, South Gosforth.

VAL DOONICAN SHOW — His sweaters are smashing! Wonder who knits them? — Miss Rodger, 185 Garrioch Rd., Glasgow. *(Val has most of his sweaters sent over from France and Italy, Miss R).*

1968 **TV is terrible...or, at least, that seemed to be the opinion of Mary Whitehouse who was at the height of her campaign to clean up what was on the box. One of her bugbears was Alf Garnet in 'TIll Death Do UsPart, which had just started a new series. Specifically, it was Alf's use of "bloody" that upset Mary. It may have been Christmas, but all anyone was talking about was bloody Alf and his bloody anti-social views. It is a good example of a TV show reaching a level of popularity, or notoriety, where it transcended its original purpose. It was a sitcom.**

ALF GARNET, hero or villain? That's the question we put last week. And what a tremendous reaction. These are just some of the letters that have poured in —

I loathe Alf. He makes me boil at his stupidity and crudeness. But I just can't stop laughing! — J. A. Williamson, 26 Latimer Road, Darlington.

Someone should tell Alf it's better to remain silent and have people think you a fool, than to open your mouth and prove it! — W. Duncan Weatherstone, 18 Almond Bank Tce., Edinburgh.

Admittedly Alf's use of that six-letter word is a bit overdone, but the only thing wrong with the present showing is lack of fresh material. — M. Scott, 96 Northinch Street, Glasgow.

I'm all for Alf. He must be a real tonic to thousands of lonely people. — L. Calder, 30 Magdalene Drive, Berwick-on-Tweed.

All reference to the Royal Family and religious matters are unpalatable to the majority of viewers. — Miss E. Stevenson, 21 Edward Street, Dunfermline.

If you're honest, you'll admit there's a little bit of Alf in most of us. — F. Spence, 72 Hall Rd., Birmingham.

He goes too far. — Mrs Margaret Meekison, 27 Tormusk Rd., Glasgow.

He says things that most of us want to say about Parliament. But we don't have the guts to say it. — J. Dailey, 59 Kinnaird Dr., Stenhousemuir.

I think Alf is a boorish caricature of the British working man. We may swear like troopers, but not at home. — A. W. Fleming, 1 Smith Avenue, Inverness.

I'd rather hear Alf do a bit of plain swearing than sit and watch some of these sex plays. — Mrs E. Jackson, 32 Cockermouth Rd., Sunderland.

1969 **On the brink of a new decade, TV is firmly, belovedly a part of everyday life. Most people, by this point, couldn't remember what life was like before its rhythms became dictated by the little box in the living room. Declarations of the year's best shows were serious stuff. However, the casual sexism of a "Personality of the year" and a "Female personality of the year" would persist quite a while longer before being addressed.**

TAKE A BOW, LIBERACE

WELL, that's it all for another year. And I'd like to hand out some TV Oscars—

PERSONALITY OF THE YEAR—Maybe I'm putting my neck on the chopping block. But I'm going for Liberace. You either love him or hate him. But his long-running I.T.V. Sunday series went like a bomb.

FEMALE PERSONALITY OF THE YEAR—Moira Anderson has made almost as many appearances as yon revolving globe before the B.B.C. news! Fact that I haven't had a

WELL, that's it for another year. And I'd like to hand out some TV Oscars.

PERSONALITY OF THE YEAR — Maybe I'm putting my neck on the chopping block. But I'm going for **Liberace**. You either love him or hate him. But his long-running ITV Sunday series went like a bomb.

FEMALE PERSONALITY OF THE YEAR — **Moira Anderson** has made almost as many appearances as the revolving globe before the BBC news! Fact that I haven't had a word of complaint speaks for itself.

BEST SUPPORTING ACTRESS — **Effie Morrison**, consistently good as Mistress Niven in **Dr Finlay**.

COMEDY FIND OF THE YEAR — **John Alderton**, long-suffering tutor of class 5C in **Please Sir**. My bet is he'll be bigger and better in 1970.

TOP SPORTS COMMENTATOR — My vote goes to the rugby maestro, **Bill McLaren**. The man talks with an authority few can match.

AWARD FOR BRAVERY — To the news cameramen who've brought the highlights of this troubled year to our screens. The battles in Derry and Belfast. The near-riots at the Springboks games. Camera crews have been kicked, punched and abused. But they never fail to keep the cameras turning.

HAPPIEST RETURN — That of **Morecambe and Wise** after Eric Morecambe's near-fatal heart attack. Their Christmas show was terrific.

1970 **With a new decade, attitudes changed. Scathing opinions on the fare on offer and the highlights of the year have a touch of sarcasm.**

WHAT'S the dullest night of the week for TV? Sunday gets my vote.

Worst Night Of The Week!

Busy For Bill

SINGER Bill McCue says life has never been so hectic.
He has his own series

TV WEDDING of the year on December 27. And John Alderton and Jill Kerman of "Please Sir" have the notorious 5c pupils among their

Take last week. BBC gave us **Dr Finlay**, now on its deathbed, a 1948 **Garbo** film and **Omnibus**, which is strictly for the connoisseur.

ITV's main offering was a two-hour yawn of a film **The Third Day** and the elderly **National Velvet**.

Then came a second-rate play, complete with the apparently inevitable bedroom scene, and **Tom Jones** — not everyone's cup of tea.

On the No. 1 home viewing night, surely TV can cook up better fare. Care to join me in a Bring Back **Sunday Night at the Palladium** campaign? At least there was always something to talk about on Monday mornings.

TV highlights and the not-so-highlights for 1970 —

MOST UNFORGETTABLE MOMENT — When that Aussie athlete doffed his cap as he pedalled a child's tricycle past the Royal Box at the end of the **Commonwealth Games**.

DISCOVERY OF THE YEAR — No, not **Freddie Starr**. **Helen McArthur**. As good as **Moira Anderson** — and that's saying something.

FLOP OF THE YEAR — Marty Feldman in the **Royal Variety Show**.

SERIES OF THE YEAR — For sheer up-to-the-minute topicality, **Doomwatch**.

DELUSION OF THE YEAR — The BBC's apparent belief we're all daft about **show jumping**.

WONDER OF THE YEAR — How **Coronation Street** writers keep coming up with a fresh angle just when you think the show must be on its last legs.

BEST ENTERTAINMENT OF THE YEAR — **The Young Generation**, Full of vim. Worth a series of their own.

1971 A NEW way of approaching Christmas TV, a quiz for the "average TV addict". How many points would you get?

WELL, that's another year's viewing almost over. If you're an average TV addict, it means you watch 17 hours of programmes every week. How much of it do you take in? Here's a quiz to test your knowledge.

1. Which English football club is Eric Morecambe always plugging?

2. Who drinks in The Skinners' Arms?

3. One for TV cookery fans. What are the Christian names of a) Graham Kerr's wife and b) Fanny Craddock's husband?

4. How many husbands has Elsie Tanner had?

5. Watt, Hawkins, Evans, Barlow, Snow. Put these "Softly, Softly" characters in order of seniority.

6. You hear their names night after night. But can you name the BBC's a) political b) diplomatic correspondents?

7. Name three Australians who are regulars on our screen.

8. Which member of BBC Scotland's "Sportsreel" team once played for Hibs and Hearts?

9. Who is "the one with the short, fat, hairy legs"?

10. Name any four members of the original class that Bernard Hedges taught in "Please Sir". For a bonus point, what class was it?

11. Bert Lynch is the only one of the original four Z-Cars cops still in the programme. Can you name the other three?

12. What was the name of the Steptoes' original horse, and what's its successor called?

13. Name three actors who've played Dr Who.

14. What have they in common — Eric Morecambe, Harold Wilson, Andrew Cruickshank?

15. Who's tallest — Hughie Green, Ian Carmichael, Michael Aspel, Tommy Cooper?

16. Name three comedians who wear spectacles before the camera.

17. Have a guess. How many people have been featured in This Is Your Life since Eamonn Andrews had his first confrontation (on both Channels) — 10, 150, 200, 250 or over 300?

18. Who were a) the first b) the last comperes of the Palladium?

19. Name the Scots actor whose TV roles included a) a monk b) a ship's engineer c) farmer d) detective

20. Who's older — a) Cliff Richard or Tom Jones; b) Lulu or Cilla Black; c) Kenneth Kendall or Andrew Gardner; d) David Coleman or Jimmy Hill?

THE ANSWERS

1. Luton Town F.C. He's a director. 1 point.
2. The Steptoes.
3. a) Treena b) Johnny. 1 point each.
4. Three. Arnold Tanner, Steve Tanner, Alan Howard. 3 points.
5. Barlow (Det. Chief Supt.); Watt (Det. Supt.); Hawkins (Det. Insp.); Evans (Det. Sgt); Snow (P.C.) 1 point for each.
6. a) Hardiman Scott b) Christopher Serpell. 1 point each.
7. 3 points if you named three from Rolf Harris, Alan Freeman, Ray Barrett, Frank Ifield, Trisha Noble.
8. Brian Marjoribanks.
9. Ernie Wise
10. Eric Duffy, Peter Craven, Sharon Eversleigh, Maureen Bullock, Frankie Abbott, Dennis Dunstable were the main characters of class 5C. 4 points if you got four names (even Christian names) plus a point for the class.
11. Fancy Smith, Jock Weir, Bob Steel. 3 points.
12. First one was Hercules. Its successor is Dolly. 2 points.
13. William Hartnell, Patrick Troughton, Jon Pertwee. 1 point for each.
14. They all smoke pipes.
15. Tommy Cooper (6 ft. 3 ½ in.). Hughie Green is 6 ft. 1 in., Ian Carmichael is 6 ft., Michael Aspel is 5 ft. 9 ½ in.
16. Ronnie Corbett, Eric Morecambe, Arthur Askey, Ronnie Barker. 3 points.
17. 310. (255 editions on BBC; 55 on ITV).
18. A) Tommy Trinder b) Jimmy Tarbuck. 2 points.
19. John Grieve
20. a) Tom Jones, by 4 months. They're both 31. B) Cilla by 5 years. C) Kenneth Kendall by 8 years. D) David Coleman by 2 years. 4 points.

1972 **The stuff of which memories are made. This was the year when Dad's Army was at its height of popularity, regularly drawing audiences of 18 million or more. John Le Mesurier is the "man of the year". Jon Pertwee's Dr Who reign is also at its zenith, sending children (and adults) scurrying behind the sofa. Great days, great TV.**

THE TV Man of the Year made his bow back in 1938, when there were about 20,000 sets in existence.

With the exception of the war years, he's seldom been off the screen since.

John Le Mesurier has really come into his own this year as the harassed sergeant whose mere facial expressions contribute so much to **Dad's Army**.

When John was first offered the Dad's Army part five years ago, he thought the show would be a flop, and wasn't sure he wanted to be in it!

Why John Is TV's Man Of The Year

MY TV Man of the Year made his TV bow back in 1938, when there were about
20,000 sets in existence.
With the exception of the war years, he's seldom been off the screen since.
Name—John Le Mesurier, who has really come into his own this year.
As the harassed sergeant whose mere facial expressions contribute so much to Dad's Army. With a
spell-binding performance as a foreign office man
who defected to Russia in "The Traitor." As a
Lord in "A Class By Himself," not ITV's greatest-
ever comedy show by any means, but one that
demonstrated yet again the versatility of this
man.
le's one of a handful of gifted British actors who gives 100
per cent. every time.
How marvellous! That's very kind. I'm deeply touched," was
John's reaction when I spoke to him last week.
What pleased me most about the year was being asked to
do 'The Traitor' by BBC. They tend to put people in
compartments. Their choosing me showed I hadn't been
pigeon-holed."
trange thing about Dad's Army. When John was first offered
the part five years ago, he thought the show would be
a flop, and wasn't sure he wanted to be in it!
ohn's had a hard slog to stardom. Behind him are more than
forty years on the variety stage, pantomime, cabaret

NEW MENACE ON SATURDAY NIGHT

JON PERTWEE returns as Dr Who in the first of a new series (BBC, Saturday, 5.50pm). He's joined by the two previous doctors, Patrick Troughton and William Hartnell. The three combine forces to deal with a new menace — the Gell, an all-devouring blob.

FILMS — I'm very fond of the **Lassie** films, and I am rather disappointed they are being shown early in the afternoon when I'm at school. I think it would be a good idea if they were shown in place of the Saturday films at 3 p.m. on BBC 2. — Hazel Macintosh, (age 12), 24 Portal Road, Northside, RAF Kinloss, Moray.

THE SKY'S THE LIMIT — Surely among the Christmas presents there will be new dresses for the girls. Hope Monica will get a bit more material. — Mrs J. Scoble, 201 Admiralty Road, Rosyth.

FAMILY AT WAR — Still smashing second time round. I can now watch it in peace without remarks from the family. They didn't like it. **— Mrs G. Moss, 81a Round Hey, Cantril Farm, Liverpool.**

INTERNATIONAL SHOWJUMPING — Oh no, not again!

1973 **There would be several candidates for the title of "best British Christmas TV show of all time". But Morecambe and Wise must be considered in any era. The British public adored them. In every workplace and playground you'd hear — "What do you think of it so far?" To get the answer — "Rubbish". The early and mid-70s saw them at their formidable and hilarious best. When people talk of great TV of that era, it is Eric and . . . the short, fat one with the hairy legs . . . they talk of.**

MY verdict on Christmas TV? Simply that there's still no one to compete with **Morecambe and Wise**!

They're becoming as much a part of Christmas turkey and plum pud. They did it again this year with a Christmas night show that left almost every other one at the post, in inventiveness, inspired comedy and preparation.

Their Spanish dance sequence with Vanessa Redgrave I rate as just about the funniest three minutes of 1973.

Other Christmas highlights? A delightful 50 minutes with **Perry Como**, which B.B.C. contrived to "bury" at the odd hour of 12.30 p.m. on Christmas Eve.

A gallant try by **Tommy Cooper** — though he was cruelly handicapped by having to compete with M. and W. for part of the time.

By the way, I gather these informal glimpses of Princess Anne's wedding, which were slipped into the **Queen's Speech**, went down well at the Palace. So much so, I'm told we can expect more Royal surprises in the New Year.

SOME MOTHERS DO 'AVE 'EM — Gets funnier every week. I hope Frank won't do himself an injury with his hair-raising stunts. — Mrs I. McGregor, 211 North Anderson Drive, Aberdeen.

STEPTOE AND SON — Aren't they relying too much on the vulgar comments getting a laugh?

THE GENERATION GAME — For good clean wholesome fun, it takes some beating. — J. Hotchkiss, 5 Cloan Ave., Glasgow.

CHRISTMAS EVE — Quite the most unadulterated rubbish imaginable for adult viewing on both channels! — Mrs M. McAllister, 1951 Dumbarton Rd., Glasgow.

1974 **The oil crisis, three-day week, power cuts, inflation at 20%, strikes, two elections in a few months...tough times in recession-hit Britain. The nation needed something to look forward to, something to lift the gloom, and one of the places they looked was in the corner of the living room. Colour TVs, usually rented, were becoming commonplace. There were some good shows to look forward to, though.**

WHAT lies ahead of us in 1975? That's the question I put to TV bosses. Despite gloomy talk of programme cuts, there's plenty to look forward to.

Troubleshooter Geoffrey Keen comes into the hard-headed business world in **The Venturers**. Gerry (**Colditz**) Glaister should be on a winner with **Oil Strike North** set against the exciting battle for North Sea oil.

Terry Nation, Dalek creator, weighs in with **The Survivors**, about a folk rebuilding civilisation after most of the world is wiped out by plague.

Returning are **Sutherland's Law**, **Dock Green**, **The Onedin Line**, **Barlow**, and **Spy Trap**.

A new thriller series **The Hanged Man** is by the same chap who wrote **The Power Game**. I hear it will be peak Saturday night ITV viewing.

Frankie Howerd and **Bruce Forsyth** team up for the first time for a Thames special. There'll be three more **Benny Hill** specials. One more **Tommy Cooper**.

Old favourites coming back on BBC include, **The Likely Lads**, **Two Ronnies**, **Are You Being Served**, **It Ain't Half Hot Mum** and **Second Time Around**.

The Garnetts are back in **'Till Death** on Hogmanay — with a shock. Out goes Else as she decides to visit her sick sister in Australia. Has Dandy Nichols really gone for good? Stories have been rife that she's had too many tiffs with Warren Mitchell.

Sunday serials for the family include a sequel to **Anne of Green Gables**, called **Anne of Avonlea**. Kim Braden stars again.

BBC will use the **Lulu** show to present The Shadows singing this year's **Eurovision** songs. **Cilla Black** comes out with something new — six situation comedy shows for ATV. They begin in mid-January.

From ATV comes the first TV series from the **Carry On** crowd.

BBC are doing some excellent " **In Concerts** " for the youngsters, featuring **David Essex**, **Labi Siffre**, etc.

Biggest new success could be **The Rockford Files**, starring **James Garner** and **Noah Beery**. It's a drama series about a private eye who specialises in unsolved cases marked "inactive" by the police departments. A sort of successor to **Ironside** which is finally ending this winter.

TV's New Cop Is A Tough One

John Thaw still gets the odd rude remark from viewers with long memories — despite the fact it's about eight years since he last played Sergeant Mann in the Military Police series **Redcap**.

Now he comes up as a tough, unorthodox cop, Detective-Inspector Jack Regan, in **The Sweeney** (ITV, Thursday). Thames TV is so confident of success with this series about the Flying squad — alias the Sweeney Todd — they've begun making a second lot before screening the first. "I don't think I'd like Regan", John told me. "He's tough and aggressive".

John's been married to Sheila Hancock since last year. Baby Joanna, five months, is doing well. John's the son of a Manchester lorry driver. At a youth club he was encouraged as a stand-up comic. Then the club leader gave him elocution lessons and John got into R.A.D.A.

In Your View – and mine

MORECAMBE AND WISE — Thanks, Michael Parkinson, for including their musical item with Andre Previn. I still think it's the funniest thing I've ever seen on TV.

GOLDEN SHOT — Ann Aston should be given a note book and pen to save herself the embarrassment of mental arithmetic. — P. Giffen, 64 Haugh Street, Falkirk.

PETERS AND LEE — First show of their own was a big success.

KOJAK — Let's hope BBC never axe this one. It's the best police programme on TV. — Mrs F. Ravensley, 94 Haycliffe Rd., Bradford.

DAY WITH DANA — What a relaxed, professional artiste Dana has become. — Mrs J. Fairclough, 21 Somerville Rd., Waterloo, Liverpool.

SOME MOTHERS DO 'AVE 'EM — Christmas edition suffered from being spun out to 50 minutes.

MAX BYGRAVES — His carol singing on **The Golden Shot** was delightful, — Mrs Gouldsbrough, Darlington.

1975 **IT was the golden age of television... "Don't panic" in Dad's Army, Pan's People on Top of the Pops, "For mash get Smash" ads on ITV, and a lot of sexist jokes. Christmas was the best TV week of the year. Indeed, almost every programme mentioned here might be regarded as a classic. There were only three channels, and no VCRs yet, so everyone — millions upon millions — watched the same thing at the same time and talked about it the next day. Some of the jokes might not be attempted on TV nowadays, but then it was a different era.**

HIGHLIGHTS of **Les Dawson**'s Boxing Day show? "It must be the first show I've done without mentioning the wife. "I had to leave her alone. Why? She's older than me — and German. We met when she crashed in a field in Essex. She'd been shot down by a Spitfire!"

In fact, Les's wife is a lovely, even-tempered lass called Margaret. This'll be the first Christmas in their new house at Lytham St Annes. "It's so big compared to our old place, even the mice need St Christopher medals for safe travelling! "When someone asks where the loo is, I say 'First left, first right, up the stairs, down the passage then phone the A.A'."

ERIC AND ERNIE ARE BACK

"MY wife was sent to me from heaven...as a punishment!" **Eric Morecambe** and **Ernie Wise** still use that gag for sentimental reasons. They used it on the first night they did a double act at Liverpool Empire nearly 35 years ago! Time passes, but Eric and Ern don't seem to age.

Their Christmas Day show (BBC) is the first new TV they've done in a year. "We needed the break," Ern told me, "but it's good to be back."

UPSTAIRS, DOWNSTAIRS — Excellent acting by Lord Bellamy and his son James. They left me in tears. I am 83, so perhaps I appreciated the dignity and good behaviour of earlier years! — Mrs M. Cameron, 15 Main Rd., Low Fenwick.

Strange that Mrs Bridges — so perfect a cook and house-keeper — tolerates Ruby's untidy hair. — Mrs E. Walker, 19 Leebank Drive, Netherlee, Glasgow.

NEW FACES — So it's back with the panel passing snide remarks at each other, and Arthur Askey hogging the show. Nothing new in that. — Mary Sanderson, 61 Rossfield Drive, Bramley, Leeds.

FACE THE MUSIC — Highlight of the week. Joseph Cooper is the perfect chairman — Mrs Hutchison, 124 Queen Street, Castle Douglas.

CELEBRITY SQUARES — Magnus Pike slipped up with his pronunciation of Lochnagar. — Mrs N. Ell, 8 Priory Court, Forfar.

RONNIE CORBETT SHOW — Ronnie and Jimmy Tarbuck made a grand twosome. — Mrs A. Robertson, 13 East Dr., Larbert.

HOUSECALL — Please don't axe Dorothy Paul. I think she's the tops. — Mrs E. Brown, 239 Dickson Dr., Irvine.

POLDARK — I've watched every episode and have been very impressed. — E. Bayne, 24 Edgefield Rd., Loanhead.

ARE YOU BEING SERVED? — Hilarious. I can't remember so many laughs packed into half an hour.

KEN DODD'S WORLD OF LAUGHTER — Today's world is full of gloom and depression. Doddy's was full of happiness and sunshine. Hope it comes back soon! — Mrs E. Brooks, 3 Clovelly Ave., Leigh.

EVEREST — Some of the best photography I've ever seen in a TV documentary. A memorable programme.

THE VIRGIN SOLDIERS — How some of the old sweats must have enjoyed this.

STATE OF EMERGENCY — Gripping stuff. But maybe a bit too near reality for comfort?

MUSICAL TIME MACHINE — For colour and special effects, it gets my vote as the most spectacular series in a long time.

KOJAK — I hope somebody gave him a dummy for Christmas. It would be a change from his lollipop. — Mrs W. Gilmour, 7 Mentone Avenue, Edinburgh.

AND MOTHER MAKES FIVE — I was laughing my head off watching Wendy Craig with her arm-sling. Next morning, I tripped, put my shoulder out, and chipped a bone. I've a sling on and I'm not laughing now, believe me! — Mrs M. Drain, 21 Rutherford Drive, Edinburgh.

1976 **Each year throughout the 1970s, it was another show's turn to be the most-popular, most-talked-about, must-see programme of the year. And 1976 belonged to Bruce Forsyth and The Generation Game...or it might have been Noel Edmonds' Swap Shop — depending on how old you were at the time! There were a lot of good shows on the box, though.**

A Royal Request For Bruce

BRUCE FORSYTH and Anthea are just ending the most successful Generation Game series ever.

Think of all the catchphroses being repeated up and down the country— "Nice to see you," . . . "Didn't he do well?" . . . "Good game, good game," . . . Give us a twirl," ... " Shame, shame."

Bruce will be back with The Generation Game in the autumn.

And he has an unusual job lined up. "Prince Charles was in touch the other day!" Bruce said. "He asked me to do a one-man show at the Theatre Royal. Windsor, in January. "It's for charity — helping young people to help themselves."

Scottish Flavour On Ne'erday Swap Shop

BIGGEST success story of '76 must be Noel Edmonds' Multi-Coloured Swap Shop. I hear it will have a Scottish flavour on Ne'erday — with a film sequence featuring pipe-major Jimmy Pride, sons James and Conn and their new single, "The Funky Beggarman."

Jimmy, you'll remember, was pipe-major of the Royal Scots Dragoon Guards (not to mention senior pipe-major in the British Army) when they made Amazing Grace.

He retired from the army around the time the record was released, moved to a converted mill in the Borders with his wife and three sons and started making bagpipe reeds for export all over the world.

He also teaches piping at schools and now has several hundred pupils working towards their O levels in the ancient art.

THE SWEENEY — Unlike the mounties they don't always get their man! But full marks to the best detective team on TV. — F. Allison, 61 Milnbank St., Glasgow.

COME SUNDAY — No one who watched and listened to the programme from Sherborne Abbey could fail to be moved by the way Michele Dotrice read the beautiful story of Christmas, written by David Kossoff. It brought the whole meaning of Christmas very close. — Susan Farnell, Harrison Road, Halifax.

NATIONWIDE — Normally noted for its original ideas. The stagecoach episode hasn't been one of them.

DES O'CONNOR — Best of the shows he's offered so far. Hope he keeps it up. — Mrs H. McElhinny, 17 Troon Street, Dalmarnock.

RUSSELL HARTY — Warren Mitchell was disgusting. There's a limit to what we should have to watch. — Elizabeth Blair, 62 Grierson Street, Glasgow.

SOFTLY, SOFTLY — It's had a few downs, but a lot more ups in its long career. Sorry to see it go.

THE QUEST — Now the fuss has died down on Starsky and Hutch, how about some publicity for the Baudine brothers? — Georgina Bates, 16 Ashmore St., Manchester.

SONGS OF SCOTLAND — Please pay tribute to all involved in this delightful, joyous programme. It stands unique in these grim days. Tonight's episode should be used again and again by the Scottish Tourist Board. — A. Williamson, 21 Kirkview Cres., Glasgow.

THE DUCHESS OF DUKE STREET — Time to switch off. Last week's episode hit rock bottom. — G. Paton, 1 Victoria Rd., Gourock.

PEBBLE MILL — Fiddler Ally Bain's playing of that slow air against Shetland landscapes was unforgettable. — Ian Drummond, 8 Viewforth Gdns., Edinburgh.

SOME MOTHERS DO 'AVE 'EM — A case of too many repeats spoil the broth of a boy.

1977 **Christmas Dinners were planned around what was on telly. The task was made yet more difficult by the decisions that had to be made on whether you watched BBC or ITV. Christmas Day 1977's listings were:**

B.B.C. 1 TV

11.15 CARTOON.
11.40 FILM. "National Velvet" ★★★ **(1944).** Elizabeth Taylor is the 12-year-old training her horse to win the Grand National. Mickey Rooney's great.
1.40 ARE YOU BEING SERVED? Robot Santa Claus goes berserk in the store, so a replacement must be found. No shortage of volunteers when the staff learn there's to be a £50 fee.
2.10 TOP OF THE POPS '77. Noel Edmonds and Kid Jensen.
3.00 THE QUEEN.
3.10 BILLY SMART'S CHRISTMAS CIRCUS. Jasmine Smart introduces acts from America, Italy, Mexico and Britain.
4.10 FILM. "The Wizard of Oz" ★★★★ **(1939).** It WAS a great film, but I must be honest and say I think it's had its day. Youngsters weaned on colour TV will ask what all the fuss was about.
5.50 BASIL THROUGH THE LOOKING GLASS. Basil Brush meets the Queen of Hearts and comes up trumps in Alice's wonderland.
8.20 NEWS and weather.
8.20 MIKE YARWOOD presents variety from two palaces — Westminster and Buckingham. He'll do Denis Healey as a punk rocker. Guests are Paul McCartney and Wings, courtesy of the Kintyre Tourist Association!
8.55 MORECAMBE AND WISE. Get the kids quiet! In a Cyrano de Bergerac sketch, Penelope Keith is the romantic lead and Francis Matthews plays the Count de Basie! Then there's an extra episode of "Poldark," with Eric as Judd and Ernie as George Warleggan. Angharad Rees — "Hang-glider," as Eric calls her—takes her own role as Demelza. All that plus Elton John—and I've heard rumours of a dancing team with a difference.
10.00 NEWS.
10.05 FILM. "Funny Girl" ★★★★ **(1968).** Based on the life story of Follies star Fanny Brice. It had been a smash-hit on Broadway and in the West End before Barbra Streisand made this.
12.30 NEWS.

STV

11.45 GLEN MICHAEL'S CAVALCADE.
12.30 JUST WILLIAM. William takes the vicar's sermon to heart—and everybody suffers.

1.30 HAPPY DAYS. "Guess Who's Coming To Christmas."
1.55 SCOTSPORT REVIEW OF THE YEAR.
3.00 THE QUEEN.
3.10 TO SEE SUCH FUN. Frank Muir introduces clips from comedy films going back over 40 years.
4.40 EMU'S CHRISTMAS ADVENTURE. Emu's in Toyland with Arthur Lowe, Jack Douglas and George A. Cooper all joining in the fun.
5.40 NEWS.
5.45 THE MUPPET SHOW. Julie Andrews gets the treatment from Fozzie and his friends.
6.15 SALE OF THE (
6.40 STARS ON CHRISTMAS DAY. Moira Anderson introduces Harry Secombe, John Mills, Gracie Fields and the late Bing Crosby.
then the Boer War. That's where it really hots up. Simon Ward made a great job of the role. Robert Shaw and Anne Bancroft are his parents.
10.05 NEWS.
10.15 STANLEY BAXTER'S GREATEST HITS. These include his version of "Towering 'Quake '75" and an underwater sequence based on Cousteau.
11.30 CELEBRATION. Sir Geraint Evans, Isla Blair and the Treorchy Male Choir.
12.30 LATE CALL. Very Rev. Leonard Small, Edinburgh.

1978 The Golden Age is over. How TV jaded were we by 1978 that we started pointing out what was bad rather than good?

THIS is the time annual awards are the order of the day. This year I thought I'd get away from all the mutual backslapping. I herewith offer my opinion of the ten worst programmes of 1978.

1. **It's A Knockout** — Never, surely, did so much misplaced ingenuity and money go into the making of any programme. And what of Mr S. Hall, he of the hysterical laughter, and Mr E. Waring, sadly in need of elocution lessons for the benefit of anyone not born in Batley or Wakefield?

2. **Star Maidens** — This poor man's **Star Trek** is described as a Scottish Television co-production — so they can't blame anyone else for the diabolical scripts and excruciating acting.

3. **Most Wanted** — Roughly on a par with most transatlantic crime offerings. What makes it stand out is the presence of Mr Robert Stack, whose expression hasn't changed one iota since he played federal agent Elliot Ness in a previous existence.

4. **Bruce Forsyth's Big Night** — As far as I'm concerned, a strong candidate for the disaster of the year. Proving yet again that, no matter how many stars they sign up, ITV's comedy touch is less sure than that of the Beeb.

5. **Dallas** — If you think **Crossroads** is bad, try this prime slice of American ham.

6. Pennies From Heaven —Was praised to the skies by the highbrow critics. To the average viewer, it was incomprehensible garbage. And pretty grotty at that.

7. The Incredible Hulk — Makes the **Six Million Dollar Man** and **Wonder Woman** look like Oscar winners.

8. Bernie — Mr Winters just got by when partnered by brother Mike. His own programme is a disaster.

9. Battle Of The Sexes — STV, 21 this year, have come of age with some good programmes like **Hess**. But this nonsense is straight out of the bad old days.

10. Wednesday At Eight — Second rate variety bore with Tom O'Connor suffering from the handicap of not being all that funny.

1979 Morecambe and Wise, the Gods of 1970s Christmas Specials, were with ITV by this time, but it was a by-product of Ernie's home life that was the top festive show.

ONE of the most surprising TV successes of the year — that's **Give Us A Clue**. It pulls in 14 million viewers a week for the oldest of parlour games — charades. The Christmas Eve special has Beryl Reid and Dickie Davies as guests.

Credit must go to the way Mike Aspel chairs the teams. And the versatile Una Stubbs and Lionel Blair, chosen because they're quick-witted and dancers who don't mind leaping around.

We'd never have seen the show if it wasn't for Ernie Wise and his wife, Doreen. They always hold a Boxing Day party and insist everyone joins in charades. Philip Jones, head of Thames TV light entertainment, is a regular guest at these parties.

He confessed, "I'm not that keen on miming, but, the Wise version with teams, points and a time limit really makes people let their hair down. They suggested I try it on TV. I was far from convinced, but eventually gave it a try".

BLANKETY BLANK — Gets my vote as show of the year. The Christmas edition was magic, and I'm not just meaning the switch to the recent panel. — Mrs D. Hamilton, Colinton, Edinburgh.

LARRY GRAYSON — I'd hoped he'd get a handkerchief for Christmas so he'd be able to wipe that ever-perspiring face. — Mrs Jessie Coyle, 33 Ladeside Rd., Blackburn, West Lothian.

BENNY HILL SHOW — Too suggestive for family fare at Christmas. — M. Maley, 3 Greendyke Street, Glasgow.

SONGS OF SCOTLAND —Beautiful scenery, delightful singing. A great advert for Scotland. — Mrs Jenny Robertson, 41 Stirling Drive, Bearsden.

THIS IS YOUR LIFE — The Muhammad Ali show was definitely "The Greatest"— Mrs G. Hickman, 27 Croft Close, Bishops Tachbrook.

1980 A new decade, but a look back. Unusually, a news event was lauded as the top TV show of the year.

WHAT a year it's been on the box! Pleas of poverty by the BBC. Pleas of another kind by ITV companies who find out today if they're to carry on with new franchises — or get the elbow. A moment of truth all round.

And an apt moment to put 1980 into frame with my pat-on-the-back awards of the year.

No doubt about THE TV presentation of the year – it was coverage of the **S.A.S. rescue of hostages from the Iranian Embassy**. And for my money, ITV were points winners over BBC with pictures of the storming of the building which turned into the longest, live newsflash in TV history.

MOST UNDER-RATED SERIES — Mock me not, I've no hesitation in nominating Des O'Connor. And it was highlighted by Ken Dodd being funnier than I've ever heard him before.

SURPRISE PACKET OF THE YEAR — Val Doonican, previously regarded as just a pleasant warbler, turned out to be a brilliant story teller. His memories of his father on Parkinson made a memorable half-hour.

DISCOVERIES OF THE YEAR — I like the look of new singing group Wall Street Crash, virtually unknown till the Royal Variety Show.

DOCUMENTARY OF THE YEAR — Strangeways, by a mile. The team responsible have really earned a New Year cell-ebration!

BUTTERFLIES — For cunningly posing the question of the year — did Ria go off with the other feller?

NOT THE NINE O'CLOCK NEWS — Out on their own with creative mischief. Even if they did go over the top at times, they cut some of the pompous down to size.

MOST HONEST REMARK OF THE YEAR — Magnus Magnusson told me after last week's Mastermind final that he's yet to forecast the winner! And he dismisses critics of the question assembly and delivery with "Who wants another **Sale of The Century**?"

CORONATION STREET — Still streets ahead for crises and cliff-hangers, what with the death of Rene and Emily's bigamy.

It is a little cruel to look back at predictions of the future made in the past. No one can see their future, no one could know how TV would change, and how much it would cost. No one reading this in 1980 would have predicted the average family would one day find it acceptable to pay hundreds of pounds every month for the privilege of having films and sports channels. But this set of predictions isn't too bad. A lot of it came true — although much also didn't come true. The rise of satellite channels, the new-tech breakthroughs of digital television, the innovations in flat-screen, high-definition, giant-sized TV sets took us all by surprise. Who knows what will happen in the next 10 years...but let's hope that they find a way to bring back Morecambe and Wise.

What will TV be like ten years from now? That was what we asked one of Britain's leading experts — Pat Hawker of the Independent Broadcasting Authority.

He's an expert on the latest radio and TV developments.

First of all, he reckons we'll have a screen three feet high and four feet across by 1990. A mini-projector will throw a picture on to a reflective screen. Cost will be over £2000.

There will be two or more stereo speakers placed around the room for sound.

There'll be at least one extra channel — and many homes will have access to news services like Ceefax.

In America, work has started on producing the ultimate "home entertainment centre" — a kind of super deluxe music centre and colour TV with video unit all built into one.

You'll be able to buy any programme from films to fitba' the way you now buy L.P.s.

The most exciting new development could be satellite TV.

Very soon now the French and the Germans will put an orbiting satellite into space. The advantage of satellite TV is it would provide a perfectly uniform TV picture from Lands End to John O'Groats — a tremendous advantage to the more remote areas.

Local TV would still be dependent on ground stations.

One snag is that, twice a year, the satellite would be eclipsed by the moon. Since it will be solar powered, it would stop working for an hour.

What Will TV Be Like In 10 Years' Time?

By positioning the satellite over Brazil, the blank screen period would be 2 am. — when most folk are sleeping.

Satellite TV would mean everyone needing a new aerial. Saucer shaped, three-feet across, made of plastic and aluminium. Cost? About £250 including labour — at today's prices!

There still won't be any chance of picking up American TV. U.S. satellites are almost all on the west coast — out of sight round the earth's curve.

But American TV companies may do a deal with a private satellite — Luxemburg has plans for one — to relay American pictures to a European satellite for beaming down to Britain.

One country ready for satellite TV is Japan. The American and Japanese colour TV system used 525 lines. Britain and most of Europe use 625 lines. It's a handicap if you want to sell TV sets worldwide as the Japanese do. So they're now building sets with a circuit to take both signals just by flipping a switch.

Lillie London's
Frocks
In All Sizes
JOHN LENG & Co LTD.
DUNDEE.
6D.
Free Patterns
of both these Dresses
INSIDE

Fabulous Festive Frocks

YOUR dress for "that" Christmas party is a hugely important part of the festivities.

What is in fashion this year? — And, equally as important, is it a fashion that suits YOUR particular size, height and colouring? Will you look just "OK" in it? Or will you look stunning in it? Will you knock Santa's socks off!

Advice, opinion, news of alternatives and new ideas might be sought on the subject. In the 1930s, the best place to look for inspired inspiration was a magazine called **Lillie London**. It specialised in showcasing, commenting upon, and recommending the latest fashions from the capital of the Empire.

But these were hungry years — there were very few boutique-style dress shops outside the capital, even in major cities — so Lillie London sold patterns to allow readers to make these dresses themselves. It was, of course, just assumed that they had the seamstress skills to run up a small thing like a Grecian-inspired ballgown in Georgette.

Each dress in the magazine was lovingly hand-drawn, with fulsome recommendations on when and how it should be worn. The high quality and truly fascinating insights provided by the brilliant, but now long-forgotten, Lillie London speak for themselves.

If you were going to a Christmas party, then you'd have loved to look like this.

An Entirely New Line

Lillie London — 1930s

THE dresses and coatees on these pages have caught the very essence of the new line, and express it in a form which is simple enough for the home dressmaker to copy triumphantly.

The "cut", the important factor in a stylish garment, is all in the paper patterns; the actual making up you will find surprisingly simple.

The choice of material for evening clothes is always important. I suggest white taffeta for Dress No. 1467 (next page).

Dress No. 1469 would be nicest in lace, although chiffon or satin could be used.

I like the idea of it in dusky brown lace worn with coatee No. 1468 in butter-coloured taffeta.

Stiffened chiffon would be my choice for No. 1471 and its coatee, or this ensemble, too, would be splendid in lace.

Navy taffeta would be my

Dress No. 1471

Dress No. 1470

suggestion for the belt — "navy for evening" is another bit of advance news worth noting!

No. 1471 gains its backward sweep by means of a flared godet low on the back skirt. Flared frills cover the shoulders to the waist at the back.

Just for a change comes coatee No.1470, with the wind behind it, so to speak. Its alluring hem stands out perkily in front. It could be worn with its matching frock for a dinner outfit.

Dress No. 1468

Dress No. 1469

Evening Fashions

Lillie London — 1930s

THE new evening silhouette is quite the most exciting thing that has happened in the dress world for a long time. It is what one might call a "wind-swept" effect. Not a blown-about, untidy effect, needless to say, but everything has "movement".

Almost Grecian in its simplicity and its perfection of line is the lovely satin evening gown on this page.

Bodice and skirt are cut in an unbroken line, with seams at the centre front and centre back as well as each side.

This allows it to be modelled to cling silkily to the figure before it flutes out in soft, deep skirt flares.

The bodice drapery is interesting and typical of the advance styles.

A scarf-like piece is looped through the top of the front bodice, and forms a deep cowl at the back.

Many of the newest evening coats are longer, and show a deeply curved hem-line.

No. 1466 shows how becoming is this line. It's quite a simple little coat from the front, but beautifully cut and fitted, and with sleeves ruched above the wrist.

Then into the centre seam of the back is inserted a shaped and softly gathered fold, and the coat immediately becomes a thing of sophistication and distinction.

Surprising how simply the most interesting effects are achieved, isn't it?

Dress No. 1467

The dress has flared frills starting below the hips and cascading down each side of the back skirt, which re-echo the line of the bodice.

The coatee is a very demure affair from the front, with the neckline frankly high.

The loose magyar sleeves are three-quarter length and puffed at the wrist.

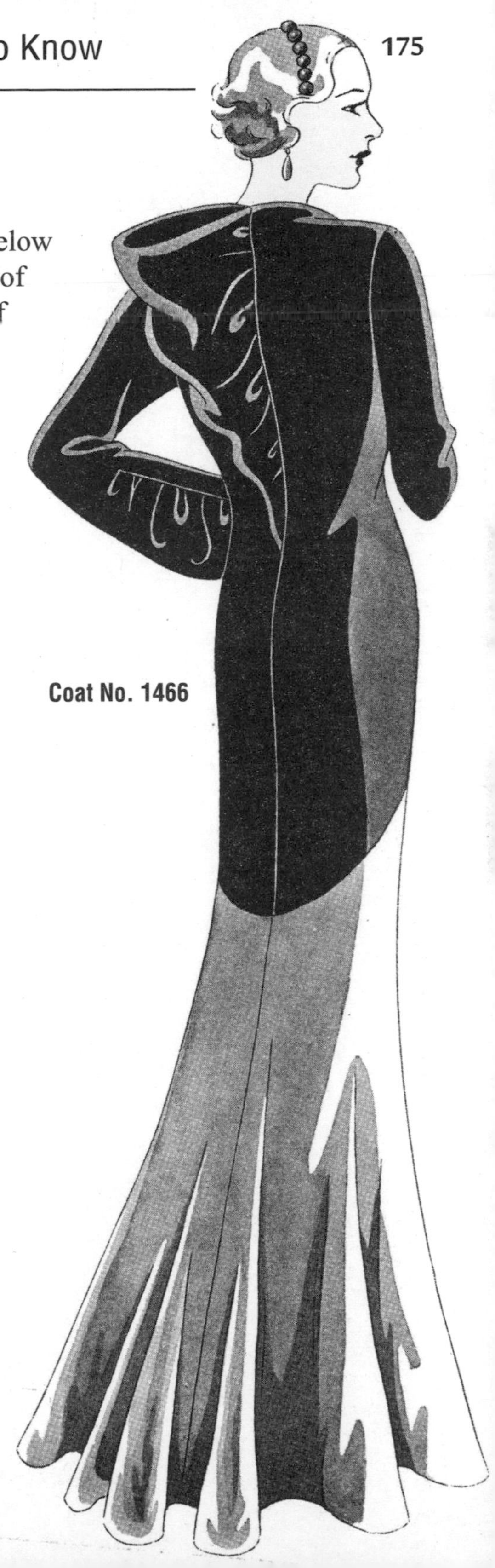

Coat No. 1466

Front/back views

A Frock For Every Party

Lillie London — 1930s

PARTY and evening frocks are delightful things to wear — and just as delightful to make. There's a fascination in working with their delicate fabrics, and with a Lillie London pattern to follow you will find everything just goes together.

For homely little parties or important ones you will find here something new and charming and typical of the new season's favourite styles.

At the left, Dress No. 1023 is a frock for quite simple parties.

You could make it in printed or plain silk, crepe, or satin, with the vest and sleeve frills in a contrasting shade.

Its most important features are the new drawn neckline of the vest and the slimming line at the top of the skirt.

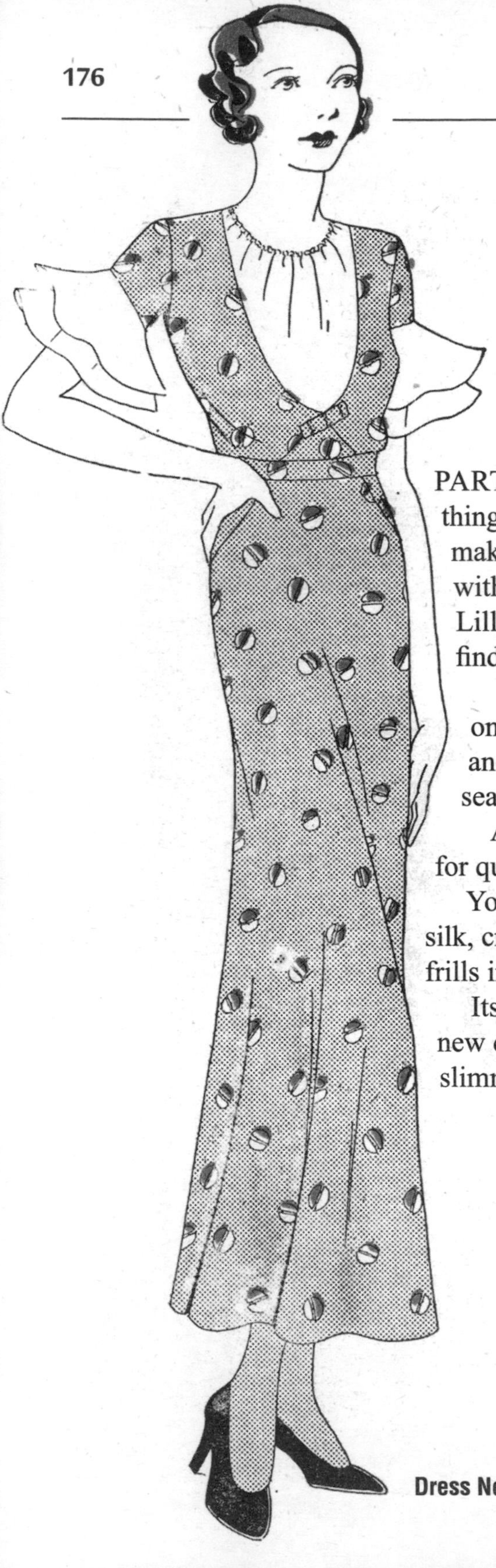

Dress No. 1023

Notice the centre back godet of No. 1024! That swinging line at the back, allied to a slimly cut skirt, is very new and elegant

The bodice has a becomingly low-cut back, and the shoulders are cut wide to give the merest suggestion of sleeves.

Wonderful in heavy satin!

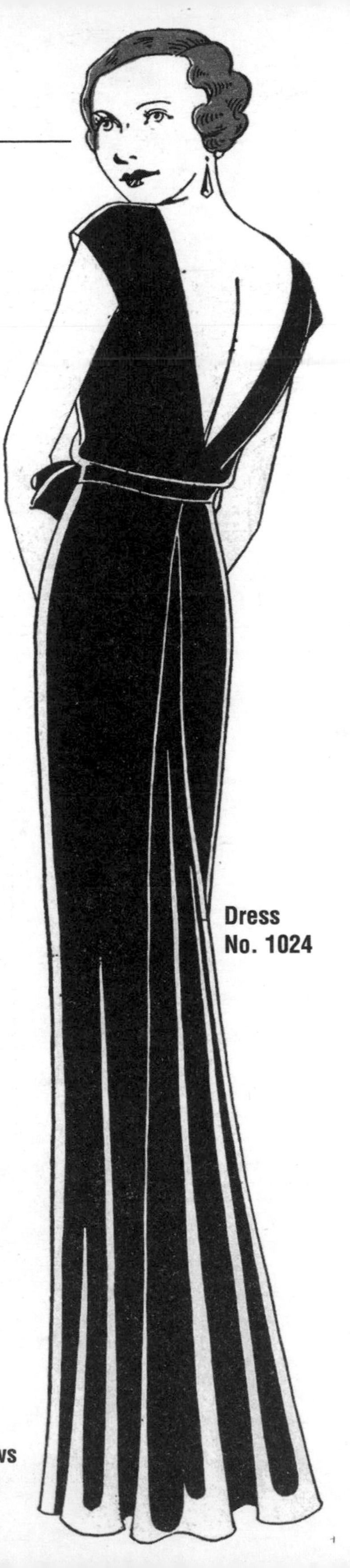

Dress No. 1024

Front and back views of 1023 and 1024

A Frock For Every Party

Lillie London — 1930s

Dress No. 1025 could be worn for semi-dress affairs, or, with a longer skirt, for dances.

Its bodice has a becoming frill from the shoulders and novel sleeves.

The skirt fullness is arranged to come at the six seams.

Georgette or soft satin would be my choice for making up this model.

Dress No. 1025, front and back

For the girl who goes a-dancing is Dress No. 1027.

Picture it in organdie, with the three-tiered circular sleeves in a contrasting shade.

The skirt is cut up in a point at the centre front and down in a low and vastly slimming point at the centre back, the bodice being cut to meet it, with only little groups of side tucks to mark the waistline.

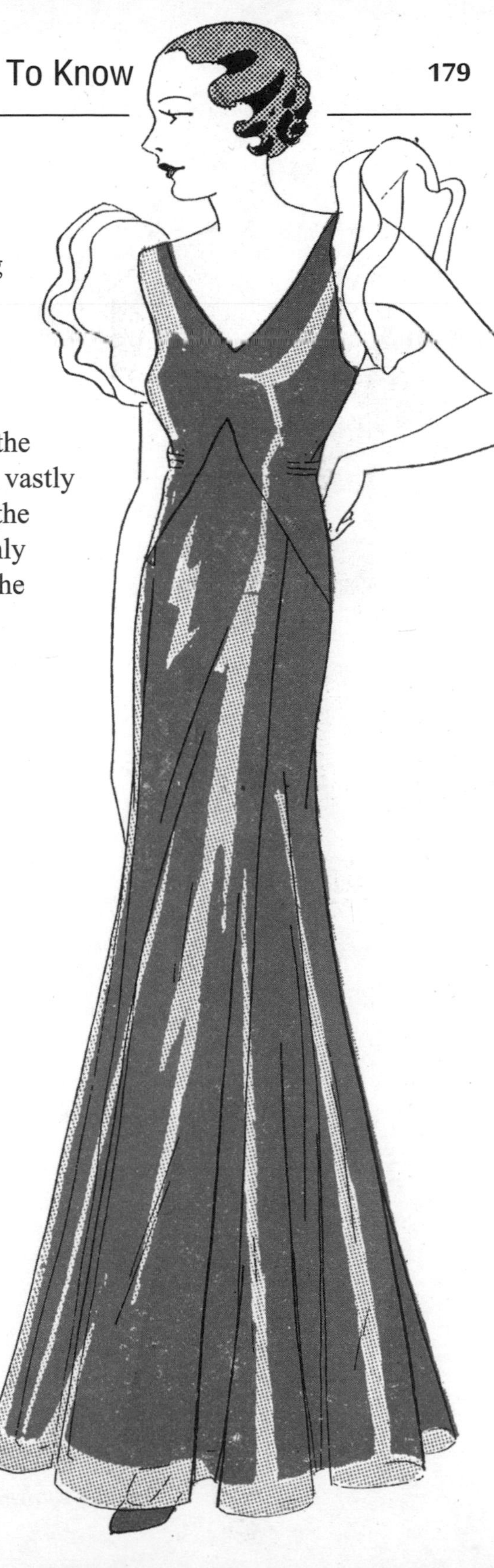

Dress No. 1027, back and front

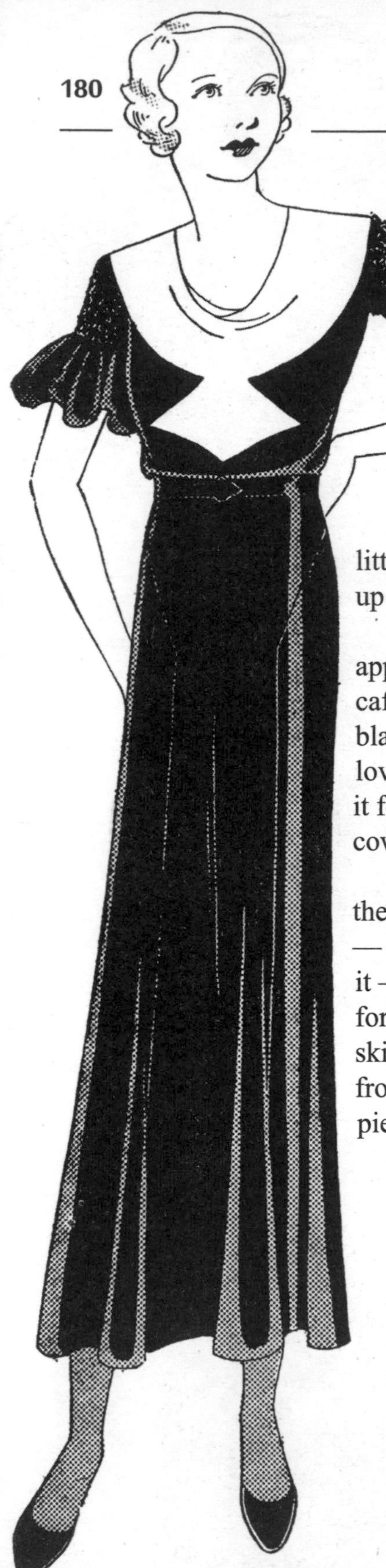

A Frock For Every Party

Lillie London — 1930s

At the left (Dress No. 1026) is a delightful little party frock which I'd like to see made up in satin.

Bottle green, with oyster for the yoke, appeals, don't you think, or brown and cafe au lait; and, almost as a matter of course, black and white suggests itself. The yoke is a lovely one, rounded until the centre front, where it forms a diamond shape; it is ever so slightly cowled at the neckline.

The sleeves are enchanting; they show the popular shirring — a good deep band of it — with the lower part forming a soft frill. The skirt has a panel at back and front, with slim-making side pieces inset at each side.

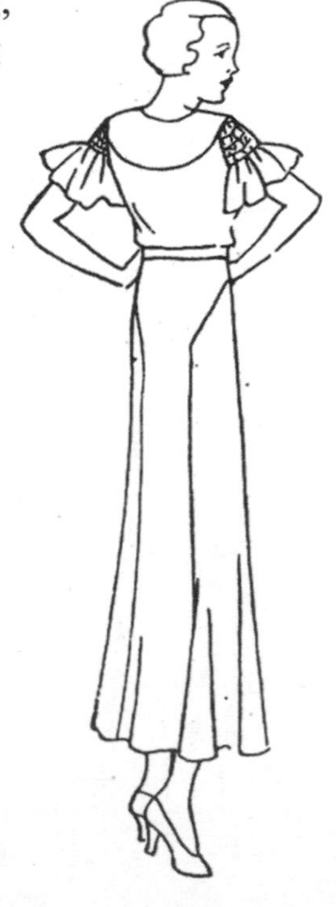

Dress No. 1026 front and back

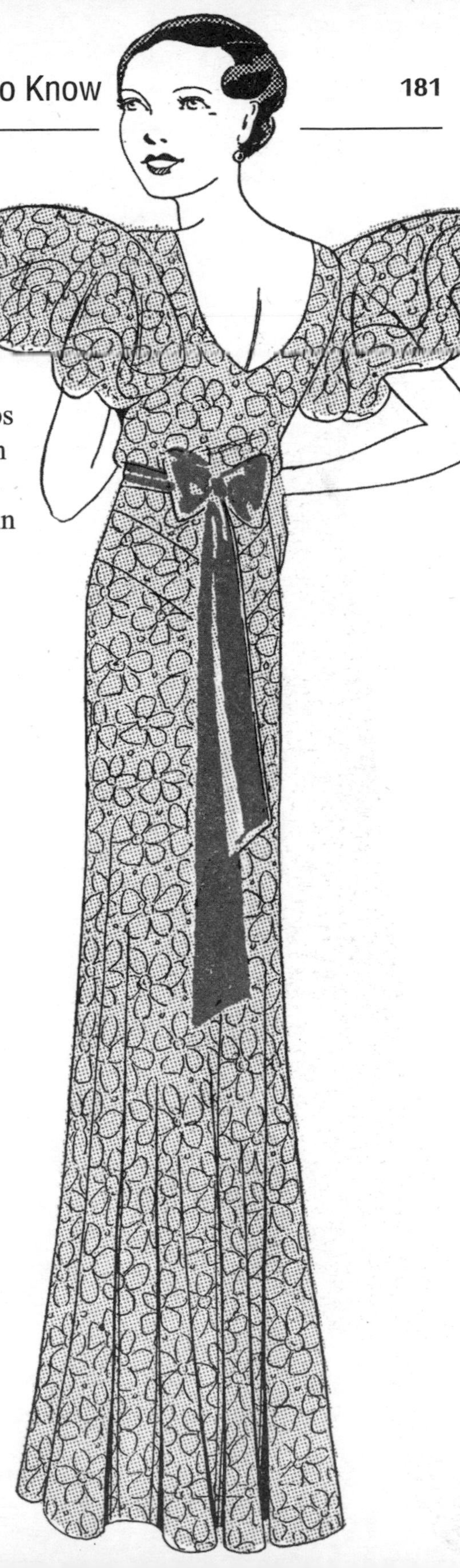

Lace is an unfailing favourite for evening wear, and is ideally suited to model Dress No. 1028.

A shaped band set low on the hips gives a wonderfully smooth and slim line, and the big puffed sleeves give an attractive air to the otherwise plain bodice.

A couple of flowers, made from scraps of lace, would make a new note of decoration, and a soft sash of velvet would complete a very charming gown.

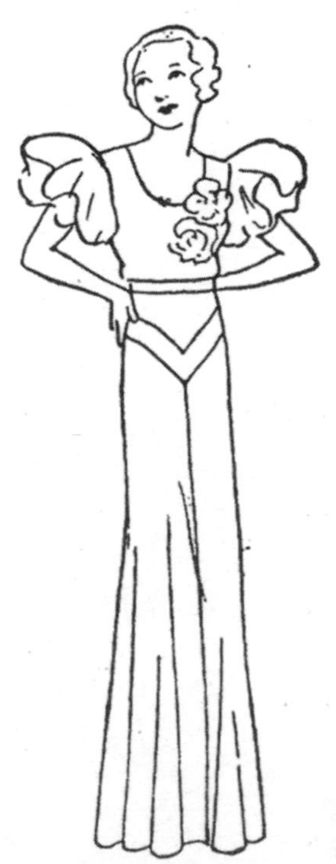

Dress No. 1028 front and back

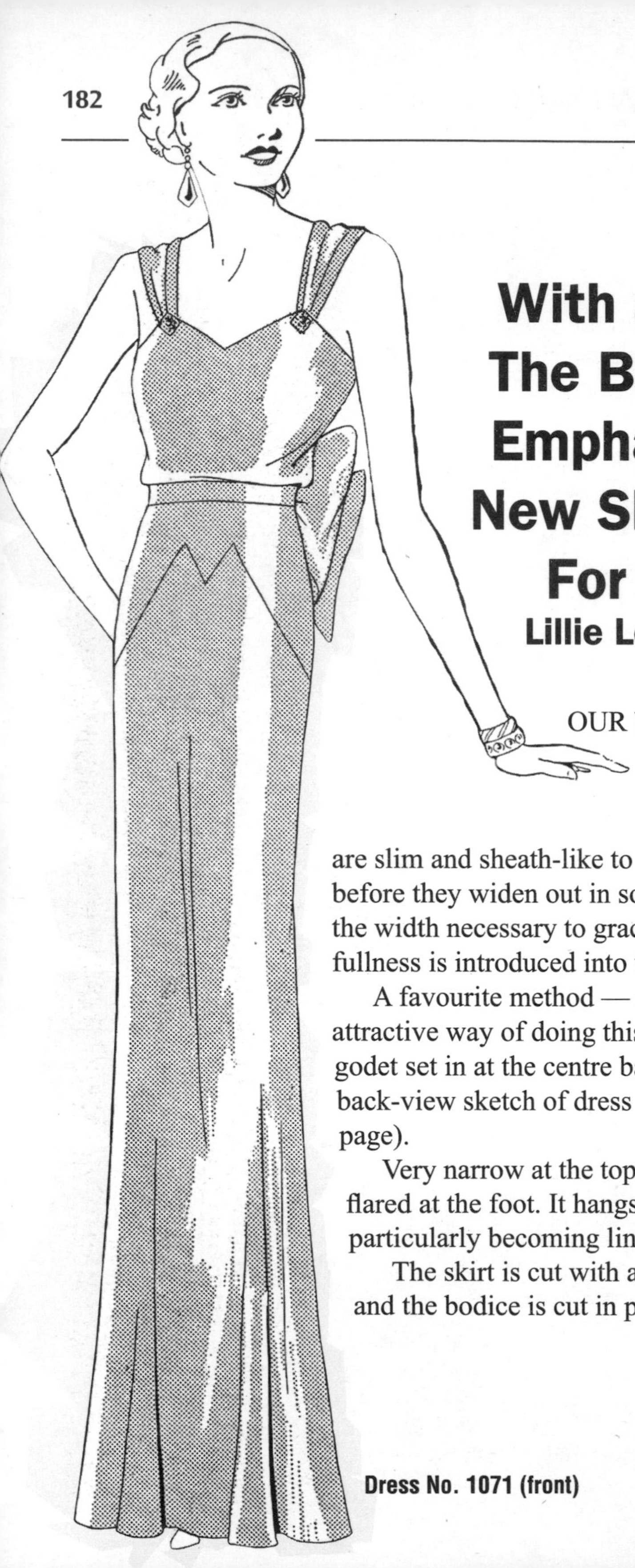

With a Bow At The Back — To Emphasise The New Sheath-Line For Evenings

Lillie London — 1930s

OUR back views promise to be very interesting this winter.

Evening-dress skirts are slim and sheath-like to practically knee length before they widen out in soft flares, so to give us the width necessary to grace and comfort additional fullness is introduced into the back of the skirt.

A favourite method — and quite the most attractive way of doing this — is by means of a godet set in at the centre back, as is shown in the back-view sketch of dress No. 1071 (opposite page).

Very narrow at the top this godet is fully flared at the foot. It hangs beautifully and gives a particularly becoming line.

The skirt is cut with a shaped yoke in front, and the bodice is cut in points at the top held up

Dress No. 1071 (front)

by softly-draped shoulder straps.

These are sewn to the side pieces of the back bodice and continue almost to the waistline where they meet a very large bow of the material.

I suggest satin or satin beaute for this dress; the rich gleaming texture of that fabric will show to particular advantage in its lovely classic lines.

A pair of little diamante clips or "twin" brooches worn at the base of the shoulder straps would give the only touch of decoration the dress requires.

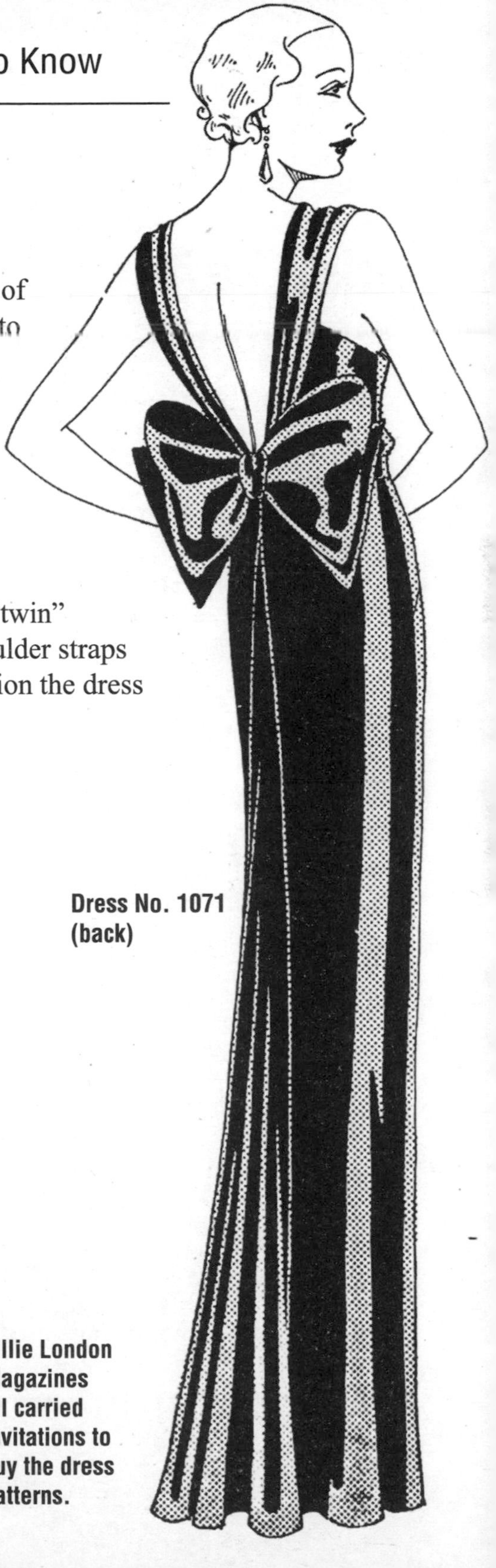

Dress No. 1071 (back)

About the Patterns —

The designs on this page are merely sketches to show the general trend of the new season's styles.

For all the designs in the following pages Lillie London Hand-Cut Paper Patterns can be got, each in a range of sizes, for sevenpence each, post free.

And you WILL write to me personally if I can be of any help to you with any kind of dress problem, won't you?

Lillie London

Lillie London Magazines all carried invitations to buy the dress patterns.

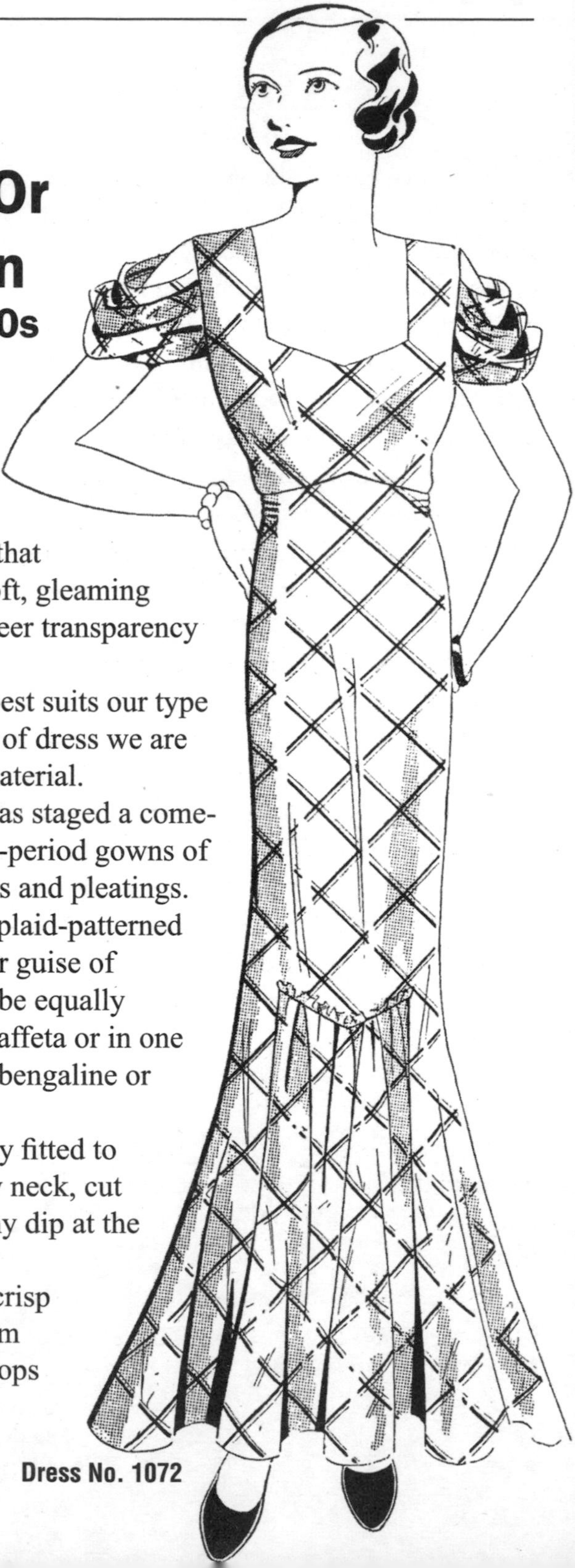

Crisp Taffeta Or Clinging Satin

Lillie London — 1930s

MATERIALS for evening dresses are always fascinating, and this year they are most accommodating, for crisp, stiff fabrics, soft, clinging ones that swathe the figure and hang in soft, gleaming folds, and airy-fairy wisps of sheer transparency are equally in favour.

We need just decide which best suits our type of looks and figure and the type of dress we are planning, and choose the best material.

Taffeta is a material which has staged a come-back, and it is ideal for the semi-period gowns of the moment, with their stiff folds and pleatings.

Dress No. 1072 is shown in plaid-patterned taffeta, perhaps the most popular guise of this material, although it would be equally successful in plain or flowered taffeta or in one of the new ribbed silks, such as bengaline or ottoman.

It has a simple bodice, snugly fitted to the figure, and a moderately low neck, cut square back and front, with a tiny dip at the centre of each.

The sleeves are interesting, crisp folds that give the new upper-arm width and leave uncovered the tops of the arms.

Dress No. 1072

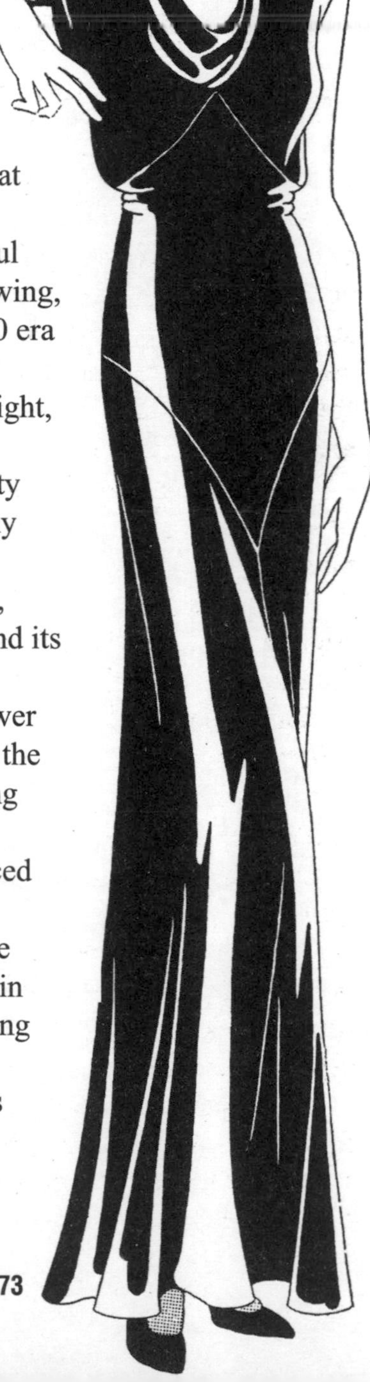

The skirt is cut in a slightly pointed line in front, and has a little group of horizontal tucks at each side to define the waist. It is slim and sheath-like to well below the hip line, where it develops a full flare, and accentuates that with inset panels at the centres of both back and front.

This is an easy dress to make, and a delightful one to dance in because the skirt hangs with a swing, and it rustles — a fascinating feature of the 1900 era that is coming back into favour!

In direct contrast is the frock shown on the right, No. 1073, which has been designed for satin or velvet. Its lines are almost Grecian in their beauty and simplicity, and will show to advantage in any soft, shimmering material which drapes well.

The bodice is cut with rather wide shoulders, which gives the effect of very minute sleeves, and its moderately high neckline is gracefully cowled.

The centre section of the dress makes the lower part of the bodice, which comes up in a point to the base of the cowl, and the deep and very slimming hip yoke.

Here again little groups of tucks are introduced to mould the waist-line.

The skirt is a four-piece, with seams at centre back, centre front and at each side, and it hangs in long gracious folds, which give a delightfully long and slender line to the figure.

I suggest Righton's satin beaute or Righton's ring velvet, both lovely and inexpensive fabrics for making up No. 1073.

Dress No. 1073

Party Fun, Games ... And Lipstick

IT all seems so innocent. Carefree, fancy-free...like everyone was a character from a black-and-white movie starring Audrey Hepburn, that involved falling in love round a log fire with some dashing young fellow, while carol singers softly intoned Silent Night outside.

Was it really like that?

Most of the games and party tricks described here are simple, homely, jolly-good-fun things that perhaps speak of a time that was itself a more simple, innocent era.

Though it must also be said that some of the things that party guests were asked to do would put them off ever going to a party again.

The articles get a harder edge, perhaps they even become more cynical, as the years go on.

According to the evidence here, you might say it must have been at some point during the 1960s that society changed so much that innocence and simplicity went out of fashion.

But the most important question is — can you pick up a chair while leaning your head against a wall?

What Shall We Do At Our Party?

My Weekly — 1957

"WHAT a wonderful party!" That's what we want our friends to say when it's all over. A party for them — and you — to remember because it was such a go-with-a-swing affair.

A wonderful party doesn't just "happen." It has to be planned if you are to avoid those awkward pauses when everyone stops and wonders what to do next.

Have a programme, that's the golden rule. Write down a list of games; a funny one to break the ice, like "Smartest Artist" (below); a quiz for the thoughtful guests to enjoy while they are all recovering their breath, and later, that good old party favourite, a rousing sing-song.

Dancing in the soft light of Christmas candles is a wonderful way to round off the party evening. When you write your party programme, remember to choose small prizes for the winning guests in the games.

Make a separate list of eats and drinks and note down all the items you have to buy, so that you can get most of your shopping done in one trip.

You see the idea? Get everything down on paper, and cross out each item when you have dealt with it.

What about decorations? That's easy. Holly, mistletoe, streamers, and all the lovely Christmas decorations are there to command, but for an extra traditional touch, dress up a Yule Log (search in the cellar for a suitable piece of wood) with fancy bows, streamers and sprigs of holly, to be carried in and burned with due ceremony early in the evening.

It's sure to be a wonderful party.

We Can Play Games

SMARTEST ARTIST — Here is a team game packed with fun and laughter. All you need is a nice large hat — or if that is too precious an empty box will do! And a pencil for each team and a fairly large piece of paper for each guest. A person in charge should have prepared slips of paper with two rhyming words on them such as: Funny Bunny, Bent Gent, Marriage Carriage, Bandy Dandy, Weird Beard, Half Calf, Tubby Hubby, Jolly Lolly, Shocking Stocking, Odd Cod, Sinister Minister, Corker Porker.

The rhymes are placed in the hat and the guests divided into teams. At the command "Go" the first person in each team rushes to the hat, pulls out a slip of paper, picks up a piece of paper and draws a picture to illustrate the rhyming words she has pulled from the hat. If you pulled out Corker Porker, for instance, all you need do is draw a really fat pig. You show this to your team, who must guess what your illustration is meant to convey.

When they have done this correctly the next player in the team then rushes up to the hat and pulls out another slip. The team to finish first wins the race. You can't draw? So much the better! That's what makes the fun.

TISSUE PAPER RACE — Divide your guests into teams — four people in each team. Have at one end of the room a tumbler for each team and in each a tablespoon.

At the other end lay out the same number of pillows or cushions on which are small pieces of tissue paper about 2 inches square, allowing three pieces for each person.

The idea is that at the word "Go," one member from each team rushes down the room, takes the tablespoon and runs to the pillows at the other end of the room. There he tries to lift a piece of tissue paper on his spoon and must then walk back and drop it into the tumbler. If the paper falls off on the way, he must begin again.

If he succeeds the spoon is passed to the next member of the team, and so on. After, say 15 minutes, everyone must stop, and the team with the most pieces of paper in the tumbler wins.

SMILE, PLEASE! — All the "props" you'll need for this are a shiny tablespoon and two guests. Before you begin the game take aside two guests and let them into the secret — they then work as a team. One guest pretends to be a photographer and while his partner's back is turned he "photographs" another guest with his camera — the tablespoon.

He then tells the audience his partner will now identify the "subject" of the picture. And this he does much to the surprise of the other guests. The "secret" is that the "photographer" assumes the same position as that of the person he snapped — if he is sitting legs crossed, the photographer does so, or if he is smoking the photographer does, too.

In this way it is easy for his partner to look round the room for the guest who is doing exactly the same as the "photographer" and at once identify him as the subject of the picture.

We Can Sing

One of the highlights in a Christmas party is a sing-song. It's good fun to split up the party into three sections, one section to sing the choruses, another section to "play" the music, different guests pretending to play the trumpet, the piano, the drums, and so on.

Once the sing-song gets going, the songs will roll out and everyone will have a marvellous time, but just the same, make a mental note of several well-known choruses so you can lead off if there's a pause.

This is a very special time of the year, and no Christmas party would be really complete without the lovely carols which express the real spirit behind Christmas.

So round off your sing-song on a quieter note. There's something heart-warming and appealing about singing round the Tree in the soft glow of candles, and these may well be the moments your guests will remember best and treasure most long after the party is over.

Woman's Way — December 27, 1941

IT'S Christmas-time and some of the boys are home, and it's not the sort of weather to go out. What are we going to do? The answer is a PARTY!

("A party!" says mother. "And who's going to provide the food?") "They'll bring their own food, mums," is the solution to that one, and if not, what's wrong with a cup of tea and anything that's lying around?

There's not much that can beat a night of fun and games in the home, is there? And privately no one is more pleased about it than Mum herself! So let's suppose the crowd's arrived and you're all set.

How to START? Here's a new "Icebreaker" we've heard of, and it sounds really good. We've not actually tried it out, so don't sue us for damages if anything goes wrong, please!

It's called **JIGSAW HIGH JINKS**. Write on fairly large pieces of cardboard all sorts of crazy high jinks, like "Do an Apache Dance," or "Sing 'My Lovely Russian Rose' in Opera Style." That's the sort of thing. I'm sure you'll be able to think up some beauties!

Cut the pieces in two, jigsaw fashion, and separate the halves, one pile for girls, another for boys. On arriving each guest draws a half card, then searches the room for the person who holds the other half. When jigsaws are all matched, each couple must perform the stunt their card orders.

And after that, of course, there's all the usual fun — a dance to the wireless or a gramophone, "taking sides" games and hosts of others you all know which are still as good as ever. How about a conjuring trick? They always go down well and provide a breather. Here's one tried and tested. If this doesn't bamboozle your friends, then nothing will!

MAGIC WRITING — Request members of the company to call out their surnames, each of which you write on a separate piece of paper. The papers are folded and dropped into a borrowed hat.

Invite someone to take a paper from that hat. It bears, we'll suppose, the name "Duncan." Put the paper in an ash-tray, and ask someone to set fire to it. Then turning back your sleeve, you lift the charred remains of the paper, and rub them on the inner side of your forearm, just above the wrist. To everyone's astonishment, the name "Duncan" appears on your arm in black letters!

Now for the secret. Before starting your performance, you write "Duncan" on your arm, using a water-colour paint brush dipped in milk. The writing becomes invisible once the milk is dried. When the ash of the burnt paper is rubbed on your arm, it adheres to the milk, causing the writing to appear. (Or you can write the name in soap.)

But how is it that "Duncan" is drawn from the hat? Well, you know Duncan will be among your audience, so while pretending to write everyone's name, you write his name on ALL the papers!

MESSAGES — Choose any letter (B, for example) and we'll assume you are sitting round the fire in a ring. The one at the end starts and has to think of something beginning with "B" — Bath would do. He then says, "I went to town to do some shopping, and the first thing I bought was a BATH." The next one thinks of something beginning with the same letter, and when he says his piece he has to mention what the one before him bought: "I went up to town to do some shopping and I bought a BATH and a BOOK." So it goes on until the list grows and you find yourself, as one person after another adds her own shopping, with a line of things to remember as long as your arm! If you can't remember one of what has already been bought you must drop out. No prompting allowed, please. There's more fun if mistakes are made.

REDS OR BLACKS — Hand someone a pack of cards, and ask him to divide it into two heaps, one consisting of the red cards, the other of the black. Then, spreading both heaps face downwards on the table, jumble the black and red cards together again. Members of the audience are invited to point to any card, and instantly you tell whether it is red or black, although you cannot possibly see.

Here's how it's done. At the start of the trick give yourself a chance to bend the red heap slightly forward, and the black heap slightly backwards. When the cards are laying face down, you can easily distinguish red from black according to which way they are curved.

Don't make it too obvious, or you'll give the game away!

Weekly Welcome — 1909

DO children nowadays have as good fun as their fathers and mothers used to have when they were kiddies? Looking at the splendid toys the young people of to-day receive from indulgent friends, you would be sure to say "Yes," but comparing a children's party of to-day with one in the "good old times" you are inclined to say "No."

There is often too much "starch" about a modern children's party; the little ones are so tricked out in fine dresses that they are not free to romp about, and they have so many fancy dishes to eat that they suffer afterwards.

In order to give a successful children's party, several points should be borne in mind. Firstly, children much prefer doing to watching and are really much happier playing simple games than having elaborate entertainment made for them by adults.

Then they are never quite at ease until they have had "something to eat," so the party should begin with tea, and not be carried on after supper, which should be given quite early. It is a great mistake to keep up children's parties until the mites are tired out; three or four hours; amusement is enough.

Instead of the ordinary big table, six or eight tiny tables daintily arranged will prove infinitely more satisfactory to the children's minds, especially as each table should be provided with a Lilliputian teapot, and the chicks should be allowed to pour out for themselves.

The cakes should be plain, chiefly of the sponge cake variety, and diminutive slices of bread and butter cut from rolls and farthing buns are also much appreciated, for children love small things to eat. Very milky tea should be provided for the babies; more grown-up tea for the others. When tea is over a good round game may be set afoot finally to clear off any shyness that lingers amongst the guests.

Musical games like the "jolly miller" or "musical chairs" are calculated to thaw out the last remnants of reserve.

When a game is going on the hostess should be finding out the capabilities of each child in the way of singing, dancing, and reciting. It is much better to get a promise to "do something after this game" in a quiet way than to ask a child in the hearing of all the others to undertake a little performance.

Some children require to be pressed to sing; others will lead off without any hesitation, and a tactful hostess knows how to start the less bashful ones first.

Dancing is an accomplishment that most children have nowadays, and so a number of quadrilles and lancers should be thrown in. If any of the small people can do solo dances try to get the proper music provided; nothing delights children more than to watch a pretty hornpipe or Highland fling executed by one of themselves.

That first variation of the first quadrille figure called "ninepins" is a splendid dance game, and even little ones who are not expert dancers can be taught to join in, and will very much enjoy the teaching.

Right and left, set and turn, promenade across and back is the fourth movement; the four girls go into the centre, and five boys dance round about them, jing-a-ring fashion.

Then the music stops suddenly, and each boy tries to secure a partner. Of course, there is an odd man out, and he pays a forfeit. Then the game goes on, but this time it is an extra girl who comes in, and the five girls dance round the four boys.

As a great finish up to a night's enjoyment nothing surpasses a Christmas tree. The presents on it need not be expensive, but it is always something to take home and show to mother, and that counts a great deal with a good-hearted child.

Party Fun And Games

Weekly Welcome — December 24, 1955

YOU want your party to go off with a real swing, and everyone to get that jolly, friendly feeling right away, don't you? Here is a bright idea for pairing off your guests without the delay and formality of special introductions.

Before the girls come into the room, let the young men, one at a time, take a piece of string with a card bearing a funny saying or invitation on its end, and drop the line over the door where the ladies will enter.

As each girl comes in she takes hold of the card. Not until she sees the man holding the string does she know who her partner may be.

On the other hand, of course, the man doesn't know what luck he has until the girl appears from behind the door!

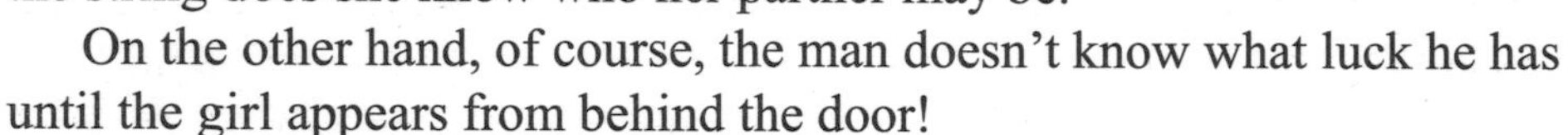

WHAT'S YOUR LINE? — Half the company leave the room. Then those inside decide what particular job they are going to do in mime and select one person to do the actions. Typical mimes are setting and lighting a fire, bathing a baby, making a cake, papering a room. Then call the first victim in. He watches the actions and then has to do the same for the next person called and so on until the last person comes into the room and has to guess what the others have been doing. It's amazing how it finishes up as nearly everyone guesses the mime wrongly. Then the sides change.

BALLOON FOOTER — Two teams are chosen, each with a captain. They line up on opposite sides of the room, with the captain behind his team, and one of them holding a large balloon. The game begins with the balloon being tossed in the middle of the room. The players on one side try to blow it into "goal" behind the opposing side, while the defenders puff it away.

PARCEL POST — This favourite game is played to music. The players sit or stand in a circle, and toss a small soft parcel, containing a prize, from one to another. When the music suddenly stops the guest in possession of the parcel is counted out, while the player last left in retains the parcel and the prize.

BLACK-OUT ARTISTS — This is good fun for grown-ups and kiddies. You'll need pencils, paper and darkness. Arrange the players round the room. Each one should have paper ready on a table or a book. When the lights go out, one person gives the instructions. They may be asked to draw a house. Then go on something like this. "Now put a chimney on the house." "Now draw some smoke coming out of the chimney." "Now a cat sitting on the roof." Sounds simple … doesn't it? But you try it yourself in absolute darkness, and see how.

STATUES — A favourite at any party. One guest is chosen as "spinner." He takes each person in turn, and spins them three times round, then lets them go. They've to "freeze" in whatever position they land. Then the spinner goes round and judges which is the best statue. When you've got a room full of folk perched on one leg, and all just dying to howl with laughter — well, try it!

DISAPPEARING COIN — Rub a piece of soft soap on the corner of a hanky. Lay the hanky out on the table (soap corner up). Ask for sixpence, lay the coin in the middle of the hanky. Fold over the corners to the centre. Pick up the hanky and shake, and the coin will seem to have disappeared. The trick is to fold over the soaped corner first, which sticks to the sixpence. The hanky can be shaken well but the coin will be stuck in the corner. Be sure to pick up the handkerchief so that the coin will be on the side nearest to you.

OUT OF THE ZOO — For this game a row of chairs is placed down the centre of the room. These are the "cages" of the Zoo animals, there being the same number of chairs as players. Each player is a Zoo animal or bird. The game begins when all the animals are sitting quietly in their cages until Percy the Parrot escapes from his cage and calls on his pals. As he reaches them he calls, "Come on, Donkey" or "Come on, Lion," and so on. Each animal then follows him on a tour round the cages, making their respective calls or howls! Suddenly, Percy yells — "Here comes the keeper!" Everyone scampers for a cage, but one player finds that somebody has taken away his cage to be cleaned. He is counted as captured and drops out of the game, which then carries on as before, a cage being taken away at each escape. The last animal to evade capture is declared the King of the Zoo and is rewarded with — a big bun!

THE IRON ARM TRICK — A trick by which you can reveal amazing strength is to invite 10 or 20 of the party present to push you against a wall. This trick really seems astonishing, and like so many mystery stunts, is actually easy. It causes a lot of fun. You, as a person who is to be pushed against the wall, face the wall with your arms outstretched and hands touching the wall. Those who push you are to work in a linked system so that the more they push the better you seem able to resist them. The solution is merely this — when you stretch your arms in the position noted, you form an arch with your arms. Your body becomes the keystone of the structure and, as such, is the strongest part of the arch. The more the 10 or 20 people push against you the more you are able to resist them.

WHERE HAS IT GONE? — Cut a slot in the end of the tray of a match box large enough to pass a halfpenny. Ask for coin, place in box for all to see and close. Wave box about, when the halfpenny will slip out into the hand. After suitable actions and patter, open the box — which will be found to be empty.

Some of the tricks you can do at a party are so simple that it's astonishing to realise that few know them.

The Sunday Post — 1950

LADIES — here's a good game to put on at the Christmas party. For most women can do it — and most men can't. All you need is an ordinary chair. Pick a blank bit of wall and stand facing it, about two feet away.

Now get someone to place a chair between you and the wall with its back to the wall. Bend forward over the top of it until your forehead rests against the wall.

Pick up the chair with both hands — just a few inches off the ground is enough — and try to walk away with it. You mustn't move forward or sideways, only backwards.

The men of the party all laughed me to scorn when I said they couldn't do it. One after another they had a go. Honestly, you'd have thought some of them had glue on their foreheads! They were stuck to the wall.

Again and again they heaved and heaved. Faces turned puce with effort. Two or three of them, by super-human efforts, got their heads two or three inches of the wall. Then forward they'd go again with a wallop.

But when it came to the ladies — that was a different story! Quite gently and easily they did it. It made the whole thing look silly. They just picked tip the chair — and walked off with it.

The men were furious. For a solid hour they tried. Eventually some got the knack. But no sooner had they got it than they lost it again! And, believe me, there were some mighty sore heads by the time they'd finished.

Here's a Game the Girls Will Win Every Time

LADIES—here's a good game to put on at the Christmas party.

For most women can do it—and most men can't.

All you need is an ordinary chair.

Pick a blank bit of wall and stand facing it, about two feet away.

Now get someone to place a chair between you and the wall with its back to the wall. Bend forward over the top of it until your forehead rests against the wall.

Pick up the chair with both hands—just a few inches off the ground is enough—and try to walk away with it. You mustn't move forward or sideways—only backwards.

The men of the party all laughed me to scorn when I said they couldn't do it.

One after another they had a go.

Honestly, you'd have thought some of them had glue on their foreheads!

But when it came to the ladies—that was a different story!

Quite gently and easily they did it.

It made the whole thing look silly. They just picked up the chair — and walked off with it.

The Sunday Post — December 1974

Now, How Did You Get That Lipstick On Your Collar?

ALAS, the time is fast approaching when some husbands (like mine!) tend to kick over the traces in the Christmas/New Year festivities.

The following hints may be of assistance to less-experienced members of my sex.

First manifestation of trouble will probably occur after his office Christmas party, around December 21.

Your lord and master's intentions will, as always, be honourable.

Not for him the Bacchanalian revelry indulged in by younger members of the staff.

The result is, he will weave his way up the garden path long after tea-time and may well trip over the front doorstep to wish you A Merry Chrishmash!

Though you won't be feeling merry, resist the temptation to clonk him with a saucepan. He probably wouldn't feel the pain, anyway.

Save your wrath for next morning when he's looking and feeling like something the cat brought in.

Tell him next time he comes home with lipstick on his collar, he can wash his flaming shirts himself. He will protest there was no lipstick on his collar. You will show him the proof.

He will protest again, proclaiming his love for you.

Little does he know you smeared the lipstick on after he fell asleep.

This ruse should be enough to keep him in check over Christmas and ensure you get a far better gift than he'd intended giving you.

The period between December 28 and January 1 will be fraught with temptations such as:— The New Year draw at his golf, bowling, social club. A session with an old pal he just happened to bump into. The annual night when the boss stands his hand.

From each of these he may return full of the joys. Don't plan meals for him during this period, for his joy may not be long-lived.

Hogmanay is the most perilous time. By about 11.30 he'll have the light of battle in his eye.

By 3 a.m. he will have:

1 — Insulted your Labour neighbours with a furious denunciation of Anthony Wedgwood Benn.

2 — Told your elder sister three times to stop talking while he's interrupting.

3 — Told another neighbour two dubious stories picked up at the golf/bowling club, oblivious of the fact that said neighbour is a kirk elder.

4 — Emptied the house by insisting on entertaining the company with an incoherent arrangement of *It's A Sin To Tell A Lie.*

Again save your wrath for next morning when he is grey-faced and moaning feebly.

Point out that, in view of the amount he has poured over his throat recently, he is obviously not short of a bob or two.

Slap in a quick claim for extra housekeeping money. That'll get him back on the rails for the next 11 months. — **Mrs R. J.**

The Songs We Used To Sing

PERHAPS it's the music we remember best of all. It helps, of course, that some of the words stick so strongly in the memory that they are difficult to forget even today.

These are the songs your mother and father sang. These were the songs you heard when the call went up that everyone was to do "a turn".

A lot of them, of course, we saw on TV. There wasn't Christmas wall-to-wall television coverage, in the old days, of course. But there were some shows that had great songs, there was Val Doonican, The Alexander Brothers — and there was The Weekly News.

We watched and listened to the performances on TV, and The Weekly News printed the lyrics to the songs so we could sing along. It was karaoke, without the video backing tracks.

And what songs they were. Val Doonican was a treasure, a true gentleman who came across wonderfully well on TV — a genial, friendly fun-loving man. He was a huge star in the 1960s and '70s. His versions of the comedic ***Paddy McGinty's Goat*** and ***Delaney's Donkey*** (lyrics printed here) should be more celebrated than they are as classics of British entertainment history.

If only there were more like Val now.

The Alexander Brothers, too, were wonderful to watch. Great entertainers, and famous for outselling The Beatles in Scotland, they did shows that moved people to tears, took them back to their childhoods or broke their hearts.

There are few things that give a lump in the throat more than when you think of Christmases past and hear ***Nobody's Child*** on the radio.

Val Doonican
Walk Tall

All through the years that I grew up Mom taught these things to me;
But I was young and foolish then and much too blind to see,
I ignored the things she said, as if I'd never heard,
But now I see and understand the wisdom of her words.

CHORUS:
Walk tall, walk straight and look the world straight in the eye,
That's why my mother told me when I was about knee-high.
She said, "Son, be a proud man and hold your head up high,
Walk tall, walk straight and look the world right in the eye."

I started going places where a youngster shouldn't go,
I got to know the kind of girl it's better not to know,
I fell in with a bad crowd and laughed and drank with them
But thru' the laughter, Mama's words would echo now and then.

CHORUS.

I got in trouble with the law and I'm in prison now,
But through these prison bars I see things so much diffr'nt now.
I've got one year left to serve and when my time is done,
I'll walk tall and straight and make Mom proud to call me son.

CHORUS.

Val Doonican
Delaney's Donkey

Delaney had a donkey that ev'ryone admired;
Tempo'rily lazy, permanently tired;
A leg at every corner balancing its head.
And a tail to let you know which end it wanted to be fed.

Riley slyly said "We've under-rated it.
Why not train it?" then he took a rag.
Rubbed it, scrubbed it, oiled and embrocated it,
Got it to the post and when the starter dropped the flag,

CHORUS:
There was Riley pushing it, shoving it, and shushing it,
Hogan, Logan, ev'ryone in town,
Lined up attacking it, shoving it and smacking it,
They might as well have tried to push the Town Hall down.
The donkey was eyeing them, openly defying them,
Winking, blinking, twisting out of place,
Riley reversing it, ev'rybody cursing it,
The day Delaney's donkey ran the half-mile race.

The muscles of the mighty, never known to flinch,
Didn't move the donkey quarter of an inch.
Delaney lay exhausted, hanging round its throat
With a grip just like a Scotchman on a twenty-shilling note.

Starter Carter, lined up all the rest of them,
When it saw them it was willing then.
Raced up, braced up, ready for the best of them;
They started off to cheer it but it changed its mind again.

CHORUS:
There was Riley pushing it, shoving it and shushing it;
Hogan, Logan, Mary Ann Macgraw,
She started poking it, grabbing it and choking it;
It kicked her in the bustle and it laughed "Hee-Haw!"
The whigs and conservatives, radical superlatives, lib'rals, tories, hurried to the place,
Stood there in unity, helping the community,
To push Delaney's Donkey in the half-mile race.

The crowd began to cheer it, Rafferty the judge,
Came up to assist them, still it wouldn't budge.
The jockey who was riding, little John Macgee,
Was so thoroughly disgusted he went home to get his tea.

Hagan, Fagan, students of psychology,
Swore they'd shift it with some dynamite;
Bought it, brought it;
Then without apology, the donkey gave a sneeze,
And blew the darn stuff out of sight.

CHORUS:
There was Riley pushing it, shoving it, and shushing it,
Hogan, Logan, all the bally crew,
P'lice and auxiliary,
The Garrison Artillery,
The Second Inniskillings and the Life Guards, too.
They seized it and harried it, picked it up and carried it,
Cheered it, steered it to the winning place.
Bookies all drew aside, and committed suicide,
Because Delaney's Donkey won the half-mile race.

Val Doonican
Paddy McGinty's Goat

Now Patrick McGinty, an Irish man of note,
Fell in for a fortune and he bought himself a goat,
Says he "Sure of goat's milk I'm goin' to have me fill"
But when he brought the nanny home he found it was a bill!

All the young ladies who live in Killaloo.
They're all wearing bustles like their mothers used to do!
They each wear a bolster, beneath their petticoat,
And leave the rest to providence and Paddy McGinty's goat.

Missis Burke to her daughter said "Listen Mary Jane,
Who was the man you were cuddling in the lane?
He'd long wiry whiskers a-hanging from his chin"
"'Twas only Pat McGinty's goat," she answer'd with a grin.

She went away from the village in disgrace.
She came back with powder and paint on her face.
She'd rings on her fingers, who wore a sable coat,
You bet your life she didn't get those from Paddy McGinty's goat.

Now Norah McCarthy the knot was goin' to tie,
She washed out her trousseau and hung it out to dry,
Along came the goat and he saw the bits of white;
And chewed up all her falderals, upon her wedding night.

"Oh, turn out the light quick," she shouted out to Pat.
"For tho' I'm your bride, sure I'm not worth looking at.
I had two ev'rything, I told you when I wrote,
But now I've one of nothing all thro' Paddy McGinty's goat."

Mickey Riley he went to the races t'other day,
He won twenty dollars and shout "Hip-hoo-ray!"
He held up the note shouting "Look at what I've got!"
The goat came up and grabbed it and swallowed up the lot.

"He's eaten me banknote," says Mickey with the hump.
They went for the doctor and they got a stomach pump.
They pumped and they pumped for the twenty dollar note,
But all they got was ninepence out of Paddy McGinty's goat.

Now ould Paddy's goat had a wondrous appetite,
And one day for breakfast he had some dynamite,
A big box of matches he swallowed all serene,
Then out he went and swallowed up a quart of paraffin.

He sat by the fireside, he didn't give a hang.
He swallowed a spark and exploded with a bang
So if you go to heav'n you can bet a dollar note,
That angel with the whiskers is Paddy McGinty's goat!

Val Doonican
If The Whole World Stopped Lovin'

Have you ever stopped to wonder
What kind of place this would be
If the whole world stopped lovin'
The way you stopped lovin' me?

If ev'ry heart was broken
The way that you broke my own,
And the world stopped lovin'
How long would livin' go on?

Hear the church bells in the steeple
As they ring their song through the air,
If the whole world stopped lovin'
There'd be no steeple bells there.

The tears would fill the rivers
'Til the rivers flooded the sea
If the whole world stopped lovin'
The way you stopped lovin' me.

Val Doonican
I'm Just A Country Boy

I ain't gonna marry in the Fall,
I ain't gonna marry in the Spring;
For I'm in love with a pretty little girl
Who wears a diamond ring, and:

CHORUS: I'm just a country boy,
Money have I none,
But I've got silver in the stars
And gold in the morning sun,
And gold in the morning sun.

I'm never gonna kiss the ruby lips,
Of the prettiest girl in town; •
I'm never gonna ask her if she'd marry me
For I know she'd turn me down, 'cause:

CHORUS.

I never could afford a store-bought ring
With a sparkling diamond stone;
All I could afford was a loving heart,
The only one I own.

CHORUS.

The Alexander Brothers
Donald, Where's Your Troosers?

I've just come down from the Isle of Skye,
I'm no' very big and I'm awful shy,
And the lassies shout when I go by,
"Donald, where's your troosers?"

CHORUS:
Let the wind blow high,
Let the wind blow low,
Through the streets in my kilt I'll go,
And all the ladies say, "Hello,
Donald, where's your trousers?"

A lassie took me to a ball,
And it was slippery in the hall,
And I was feart that I would fall,
Fur I hadnae on ma troosers.

CHORUS:
Let the wind blow high,
Let the wind blow low,
Through the streets in my kilt I'll go,
And all the ladies say, "Hello,
Donald, where's your trousers?"

I went down to London town,
And I had some fun in the underground,
The ladies turned their heads around, saying
"Donald, where are your trousers?"

CHORUS:
Let the wind blow high,
Let the wind blow low,
Through the streets in my kilt I'll go,
And all the ladies say, "Hello,
Donald, where's your trousers?"

To wear the kilt is my delight,
It isna wrong, I know it's right,
The Islanders would get a fright
If they saw me in the troosers.

CHORUS:
Let the wind blow high,
Let the wind blow low,
Through the streets in my kilt I'll go,
And all the ladies say, "Hello,
Donald, where's your trousers?"

They'd like to wed me everywan,
Just let them catch me if they can,
You cannae tak the breeks aff a Hielan' man,
And I don't wear the troosers.

CHORUS:
Let the wind blow high,
Let the wind blow low,
Through the streets in my kilt I'll go,
And all the ladies say, "Hello,
Donald, where's your trousers?"

The Alexander Brothers
A Guid New Year

A guid New Year to ane an' a'
And mony may ye see,
An' during a' the years to come,
O happy may ye be;
An' may ye ne'er hae cause to mourn,
To sigh or shed a tear,
To ane an' a' baith great an' sma'
A hearty guid New Year.

CHORUS:
A guid New Year to ane an' a'
An' mony may ye see;
An' during a' the years to come,
O happy may ye be.

Now let us hope our years may be
As guid as they ha'e been;
And trust we ne'er again may see
The sorrows we ha'e seen.
And let us wish that ane an' a',
Our friends baith far an' near,
May aye enjoy in times to come,
A hearty guid New Year.

CHORUS.

The Alexander Brothers
The Old Rugged Cross

On a hill far away stood an old rugged cross,
the emblem of suffering and shame;
and I love that old cross where the dearest and best
for a world of lost sinners was slain.

REFRAIN:
So I'll cherish the old rugged cross,
till my trophies at last I lay down;
I will cling to the old rugged cross,
and exchange it some day for a crown.

O that old rugged cross, so despised by the world,
has a wondrous attraction for me;
for the dear Lamb of God left his glory above
to bear it to dark Calvary.

REFRAIN

In that old rugged cross, stained with blood so divine,
a wondrous beauty I see,
for 'twas on that old cross Jesus suffered and died,
to pardon and sanctify me.

REFRAIN

To that old rugged cross I will ever be true,
its shame and reproach gladly bear;
then he'll call me some day to my home far away,
where his glory forever I'll share.

REFRAIN

The Alexander Brothers
Bonnie Wee Jeannie McColl

CHORUS:
A fine wee lass, a bonnie wee lass, is bonnie wee Jeannie McColl,
I gave her ma mither's engagement ring and a bonnie wee tartan.
shawl.
I met her at a waddin' in the Co-operative Hall,
I wis the best man and she wis the belle o' the ball.

The very night I met her she wis awfy, awfy shy,
The rain cam' pourin' doon, but she was happy, so wis I;
We ran like mad fur shelter, an' we landed up a stair,
The rain cam' pourin' oot o' ma breeks, but och I didna care.

CHORUS

Noo I've wad ma Jeannie an' bairnies we hiv three,
Twa dochters and a wee, wee fellah that sits upon ma knee.
They're richt wee holy terrors an' they're never still for lang,
But they sit and listen every nicht while I sing this sang.

CHORUS

The Alexander Brothers
Nobody's Child

AS I was slowly passing by an orphan's home one day,
I thought I'd stop a little while just to watch the children play.
Alone, a boy was standing, and when I asked him why,
He turned with eyes that could not see and this was his reply.

CHORUS: I'm nobody's child, nobody's child.
I'm like a flower, just growing wild.
No mommy's kisses and no daddy's smiles,
Nobody wants me, I'm nobody's child.

People come for children to take them for their own,
But they seem to pass me by and why I never know.
I know they want to take me, but when they see I'm blind,
They always pick some other child and I am left behind.

CHORUS:

No mommy's arms to hold me and soothe me when I cry,
Sometimes I feel so lonely, I wish that I could die.
I'll walk the street of heaven where all the blind can see,
Then I'll be like other kids, There'll be a place for me.

CHORUS:

A Wartime Christmas

THERE is unavoidable hard fact that must be remembered when you read reports of what Christmas is like for the troops who are away from home fighting on land, sea and air. It is that only good news is allowed.

There were government restrictions on what could be said, there was the nation's morale to keep up...and there was good, old-fashioned common decency that kept editors from telling terrible tales of sons, husbands and fathers suffering and homesick a long way from plum duff, Santa's visits and festive spirits by their own kitchen hearth.

ARMY OF TO-DAY'S ALL RIGHT!

British troops on duty in home commands on Christmas Day will receive an egg with their bacon for breakfast.

Dinner includes roast pork or poultry, potatoes, sprouts and Christmas pudding, while tea-time will bring cake and mince pies.

Entertainment is to be supplied by Ensa parties and military concert parties, together with an Army mobile cinema service.

The accounts of Christmas at war, on a Dreadnought, airfield or Army camp, are upbeat. They sound wonderful — games of football, dances in the evenings and even an extra egg.

The reality was probably, in many cases, a little bleaker.

On the other hand, no punches are pulled in the clearly war-weary complaint of the food situation on the home front (page 222) from 1943. The war had been going on for a long time, and there was no end in sight.

It was tough going.

However, the last article, Goodwill Towards Men, from Christmas 1945, after the Second World War was over, is a message of fresh hope and reconciliation for the world. It is one of the best examples in this book of an expression of the true spirit of Christmas.

Christmas On A Dreadnought On The North Sea

The Weekly News — December 12, 1914

Merry Christmas

"ROUSE out, there! Rouse out! Turn out, there! Turn out; show a leg or a purser's stocking!"

This is the summons which, at half-past six on Christmas morning, makes "Jack Tar" roll out of his hammock and stow it away in double-quick time — quicker than usual, for at seven he is to sit down to the breakfast of the year — ham, eggs, sardines, fish, fruit, and other delicacies, which he never sees any other morning.

Of course, in many cases, some difficulties have to be overcome, and many strange devices resorted to, to provide the "handy man" with a decent Christmas.

For on board ship you cannot send out for any little thing you are short of, for the special occasion.

But, as a rule, wherever he may be, "Jack" makes the best of things and enjoys himself thoroughly on Christmas Day.

Decorations Aboard.

Naturally, preparations begin on Christmas Eve, if not before.

The fire in the cook's galley is allowed to remain alight all night, and boiling and stewing and roasting goes merrily on till the small hours.

Busy hands are at work with coloured paper and glittering tinsel, holly and mistletoe, and anything else the sailors can get hold of, covering the grim walls of the Dreadnought and making everything look festive.

Christmas Day breakfast over, and the necessary clean-up properly done, the sailors, looking immaculate in white duck (from the Dutch doek, meaning linen or canvas), are mustered for morning inspection and Divine service.

A few hymns and prayers and a very short sermon complete the service, and the men are at liberty to go ahead and get ready for the function of the day when the captain and officers visit their messes.

Meanwhile, by an old-established custom, a kind of topsy-turveydom reigns on deck.

For the posts of the principal petty officers are taken by the smallest boys, and the little chaps masquerade for a time in unaccustomed dignity, and give their superiors a taste of that discipline which they themselves have to undergo for 364 days in the year.

The Captain's Inspection

Eight bells are struck, the band strikes up "The Roast Beef of Old England," and the captain and his officers pay their state visit to the messes.

As the captain reaches each mess, all the men spring to attention alongside their tables, while two sturdy fellows, with samples of their good fare, stand at the head of the board, groaning under such delicacies as hams, fat geese, or fowls.

When these are not obtainable, ordinary rations, supplemented by liberal purchases from the ship's canteen, take their place, and Christmas puddings.

For Jack, no matter what happens, will not be deprived of his beloved "plum-duff."

Cheers

Captain and officers sample these puddings amid deafening cheers, wish the men a "Merry Christmas," and retire, leaving the men free to enjoy themselves in their own way.

And when appetites are satisfied, toasts have been drunk, and jokes told and exchanged, Jack gets out his pipe, for Christmas Day is the only day in the year when it is permitted all hands, even the boys, to smoke on the lower deck.

Smoking Concert

Then, towards evening, an ancient salt will walk aft and, touching his forelock in true nautical style, requests the honour of the company of the captain and his officers to a smoking concert, that will be held on the lower deck.

This request is never refused, and at the time appointed the captain and officers assemble to enjoy an exhibition of "local" talent — hornpipes, sea songs, and recitations — supplemented by the band.

And sometimes an officer obliges with a song, which, needless to say, is received with intense enthusiasm and encored again and again.

And so the hours slip away, till "Out pipes" is sounded, and "Jack Tar," tired and contented, at last tumbles into his hammock.

Still on Guard.

But let it not be thought that even for such a great occasion is the huge floating fortress allowed to take care of itself.

Even a great national festival must not interfere with the safety of a million pounds' worth of complicated mechanism, carrying nearly a thousand souls on board.

The look-out men are at their station; the officer of the watch paces up and down the bridge; stokers are busy below feeding the furnaces; the engine-room staff dart about, keeping a close eye on whirring machinery.

Thus the great ship keeps up the traditions of the Navy, and even on Christmas Day, as on all other days, is "Ready! Aye, ready!"

Christmas In The Army

The Weekly News — December 27, 1941

THE Army has now put the final touches to its preparations for Christmas.

The festive season represents the peak of the entertainment period; many units will produce pantomimes or special Yuletide productions, and Army dance bands will provide nightly entertainment from Christmas to the New Year.

Officers and men with special knowledge of production have rehearsed the troops. Where the services of a soldier have not been available the War Office have been able, in many cases, to arrange for a civilian producer-manager to act in this capacity.

Since the outbreak of war every encouragement has been given to units in the Army to provide entertainment for themselves.

Some units have a number of musicians in the ranks, others a number of talented performers, with the result that in the Army of today there are more than 1,000 organised entertainments which are equally divided between Regimental Concert Parties and Regimental Dance Bands.

Grants have been made by the War Office for the purchase of musical instruments, costumes and properties.

Troops fed in mess on Christmas Day will have pork instead of beef, and arrangements are also being made to allow one egg per man.

A special allocation of fruit was made to N.A.A.F.I. for Christmas puddings and mince pies.

No Additional Trains at CHRISTMAS

The Minister of War Transport directs that no more passenger trains are to be run between 21st and 29th December, inclusive, than on any ordinary day in December.

The public is warned that if more people seek to travel than can be accommodated, they will find themselves stranded.

NO RESTAURANT CARS OR BUFFET CARS will be run in England and Wales between December 21st and 29th, inclusive.

BRITISH  **RAILWAYS**

RAILWAY EXECUTIVE COMMITTEE

Christmas With The Air Fighters

The Sunday Post, 1941.

DESPITE war-time restrictions, it will still be a merry Christmas at R.A.F. fighter stations.

The festive spirit will be displayed in a variety of ways, and the men who guard the air will celebrate the season in as traditional a manner as the war permits.

At one station the ball will be set rolling on the Saturday before Christmas with a party for children of married personnel. This will include tea, a cinema show, and games.

On Christmas Day the airmen will have dinner in the main dining hall, and, serenaded by the station orchestra, will work their way through a meal which will owe not a little of its excellence to their own "Dig for Victory" efforts.

After dinner at another operational station, where the time-honoured custom of the officers waiting on the men will be observed, the wives and children of airmen living locally will be entertained by the officers to a Christmas party.

Games and tea will be provided, and Santa Claus will give to each of the children a present from a gaily-decorated tree. For Christmas night, community carol singing, together with a film show, has been arranged.

On Boxing Day, after lunch, the officers will meet the airmen in a game of football, and as the station has a formidable record of victories a keen game is anticipated. Another attraction will be a boxing display, and in the evening a dance and concert will compete for patronage.

At yet another station the Christmas dinner will be followed by a dance, to which airmen will be able to bring their wives. In the evening an E.N.S.A. concert party will provide an entertainment, and the show will be followed by a dance in the sergeants' mess.

Not overlooked in these festivities are the W.A.A.F., whose own Christmas dinner will be followed — but not too closely — by a dance.

Despite the festivities, Christmas will lead to no relaxation of vigilance at fighter stations, and if Jerry should decide to gate-crash he will speedily be shown that he is an unwanted guest.

The Sunday Post — Christmas 1944

" You've had it!"

Our Food Could Be Better

The Sunday Post, December 19, 1943.

FIFTH winter of war has started badly with a flu epidemic.

The country's in need of a tonic — something to tide us over the testing time ahead.

Nothing would help more than wider variety of food. Especially sunshine fruits like oranges and lemons, rich in vitamin C, and fats providing vitamin D and reinforced resistance.

These foods are available in distant parts of the world. We're not getting them because the ships allocated to food cargoes haven't the space.

We are told it is all a question of priorities. Munitions of war must come first.

Agreed, but a decline in the health of the people would be equal to defeat in a dozen battles.

Experts say that, in spite of rationing, the nation is healthier today than ever, and that a large percentage of the people is getting better and more varied diet than before.

The important thing is not what the health standard was two or three months ago, but what it's going to be when winter's over.

The flu epidemic suggests that, in spite of all assurances, there has been a lowering of tone.

We have to face facts like these

(1) Britain has been at war far longer than any other Allied Country now actively in the fight.

(2) We have behind us four and a quarter years of war strain. Effect has been cumulative.

(3) Our food position can't be compared with America, Canada, Australia, New Zealand, and South Africa. Most of these have only just begun to feel the pinch. They all have fruits and fat in far greater measure than we have.

(4) Even Germany hasn't done so badly in this war. Her fats position is bad, but up to a year ago she had the orchards, vineyards, and orange and

lemon groves of North Africa, Sicily, and Italy to draw upon. She still has direct land link with orange-growing Spain.

These facts have played their part in the resistance of the German people.

Our experts have worked out a formula.

They say this meets the nation's health needs. But formula feeding is not necessarily enough. Needs change with time and increased strain. Formulae don't.

What was adequate for 1943 may not be enough for 1944.

Another point. Official statistics always show a lag. And because of this any falling off in health might only be detected when too late.

The Services, quite rightly, have had good food and plenty of it. It has paid good dividends.

In total war the health of the civilian is as important as that of the fighter.

If the allocation of a few more food ships would mean the difference between robust national health and a lowered tone, these ships should be found.

It isn't enough to keep our people ticking over. They need energy and vigour as never before.

Of course, we need every ship that can be spared for big operations ahead. But we now have a lot more ships than we could have counted on even nine months ago.

Cargoes we counted on losing have got through. Our stocks of food must be higher than at one time seemed probable.

Isn't it possible, then, to offer a well-earned war bonus in the shape of foods which build and maintain health?

Wouldn't the result more than justify the risk — if it is a risk?

Goodwill Towards Men

Evening Telegraph — 1945

DURING the past six Christmases slaughter has gone on upon a scale and with more fearful weapons than the modern world has ever seen.

While great armies were locked in battle, death dropped from the skies on peaceful civilians, not sparing women and children.

The worst of the struggle is over now, though eddies of the great storm which swept the world are still being seen and heard. But peace has come or is coming.

For goodwill among men we shall have to wait longer.

Not goodwill but hate has ruled the world for six terrible years and hate takes long to die down. When shall we be able again to think well of Germans?

Another great effort is about to be made to secure the world's future against such fratricidal folly as has devastated it during the past six years.

But at the beginning at least, it will have to be an armed peace. If something better is to come out of it, international goodwill will have to take the place of international hatred.

The fresh effort after a League of Peace may succeed or fail but towards it the Christmas message will always be an inspiration. The hope of one day realising it is one humanity will not let go.

Grim memories of the ordeal through which we have passed will mingle with our thanksgivings today for the end of the Great War. Its austerities are still with us as the Christmas tables bear evidence and this can hardly be "A Merry Christmas."

About that we dare not grumble for hundreds of thousands in Europe will not fare so well.

And the worst of our ordeal is over. If some family reunions are yet delayed, many more will be possible than on any Christmas Day for six years.

At some of these there will, alas, be vacant chairs, never to be filled again. The men who died to make this a peaceful Christmas will claim their share of remembrance and will go on claiming it on this day every year till kindly oblivion descends on our loss.

For many that will not come until they too have passed into the unknown.

But in spite of these sad thoughts and the uncertainty that hangs over the future of so many returned serving men, this should be a happy Christmas.

Fear for friends who are risking their lives in battle no longer sits an unwelcome guest at the Christmas table as he has done for six years. We have endured much and the spirit that carried us through can be trusted not to desert us now.

We are being given a great opportunity to make a fresh start with renewed knowledge of how much man can do to shape his world to his will.

All that has been yielded in the war years has not been lost. So we keep this Christmas strong in the faith that it will be the first of many still happier Christmases to come.

No fitter date than Christmas Eve can be imagined for the announcement from Moscow that the "Big Three" Foreign Ministers have so far reached agreement about the manner of drawing up the peace treaties with Italy, Hungary, Bulgaria, Rumania, and Finland that it is possible to conceive the summoning before May 1 of a peace conference of the twenty Allied nations specially concerned to consider the terms agreed upon.

There will be controversy about which of the Big Three has got most of its own way, and some of the decisions will not be welcomed in France.

But the big fact remains that the difficulties which broke up the London conference of the Big Five have been overcome and that co-operation between Britain, the U.S.A., and the U.S.S.R. is to be resumed and it may be hoped to continue.

That should provide happier auspices for the first Assembly of the United Nations meeting in London early in the New Year than looked at one time to be possible.

Altogether, the announcement is a welcome Christmas gift from Moscow.

The True Spirit Of Christmas

FOR many decades, The Sunday Post has carried the Francis Gay column. It is famous and much imitated, but the original has never been equalled. It was a series of anecdotal little stories, one for each day of the week.

To describe in just a few words exactly what makes Francis Gay so special is somewhat difficult. He isn't a clergyman, or a social worker, or a benefactor, or a welfare officer or a wise old head or a philosopher — but somehow he is also all of these things.

Francis, and his Lady of the House, were ideally suited to Christmas. This is the time of year when the column really came into its own.

He used to accept donations to his "Operation Coalbag", which was intended to buy coal to heat those who would nowadays be described as experiencing "fuel poverty". This coal fund was also Francis's pot of donations for good deeds, which bought gifts for orphans, deprived children, poor pensioners and lonely folk. There were no rules governing which directions Francis would spread his good will in.

Kind-hearted souls would give a little to the fund. But with a readership touching one-and-a-half million at The Sunday Post's peak, there were quite a few of these donations, ranging from a few shillings to a share in the wills of deceased readers. Francis did a lot of good work.

There was never a boastful "look what I have done" element, though, far from it. Francis Gay's column was, and still is, at root a humble, down-to-earth listener, sympathiser and spreader of good tidings.

The column, in a wider sense, carries an extremely powerful message. It is a representation of all that is good and kind and — most especially — selfless in the human race. It is Christmas.

1959

SEVEN DAYS HARD
By Francis Gay

WHEN I arrived home the other night, the Lady of the House was sitting at my desk with columns of figures on a sheet of paper in front of her. She had that "don't-disturb-me-while-I'm-counting" look on her face. I took the hint and retired to the kitchen to put the kettle on.

But hardly had I done so when the door burst open and her ladyship whooped in. "Francis," she cried. "We've reached one thousand six hundred!" And, by George, so we had.

A parcel will arrive this week at the homes of no fewer than 1,600 worthy folk who have no idea it's coming. It'll contain shortie, Christmas pudding, tinned fruit and soup, sweets, tea, sugar, cheese and biscuits. For me and the Lady of the House — and perhaps the 1,600 people, too — the parcels will be the climax to a wonderful Christmas week.

Once again we have been almost overwhelmed by gifts from you all — £250 from a Perthshire reader, a cheque for £100 from Edinburgh, £50 from Barra, 10s from a Scots soldier in Cyprus — aye, right down to the 2s 6d in stamps from an old-age pensioner.

And the parcels! My goodness, the Lady of the House and I have never known such a flood. The one that touched us most of all was the packet of sweeties we received for Christmas Rose — the wee orphan girl I told you about last week, who was born on Christmas Day in Nazareth.

Together, friends, we will take into hundreds of homes some of the joy and excitement that Christmas should bring. Thank you — and a Merry Christmas to you all!

1963

DON'T worry they won't get away with it! For more winters than I care to remember, Francis Gay has been running "Operation Coalbag" — a coal-for-old-folk scheme that has gone from strength to strength. Frankly, I'm more than a little proud of it and of the folk who make it possible.

So you can imagine what I felt when a letter arrived on my desk to tell me somebody's trying to steal our thunder! Yes, under the slogan, "A Warmer Christmas," the boys of the 17th Ayr (Castlehill) Boys' Brigade and the girls of the Brownie packs teamed up and footed the bill for more than a ton of best coal.

Last week, with two borrowed vans to help them, the B.B. lads went round the homes of 20 old folk and humped a hundredweight of coal to each of them. Then, with a cheery shout of "Merry Christmas", they were off on their rounds again.

But, as I say, nobody steals a march on Francis Gay and gets away with it — and the lads and lassies of Ayr are no exception. So, do you know what I've done? I've sent a letter to Mr Munro, minister of Castlehill Church, drawing his attention to the matter — and enclosing £10 to be passed to the Boys' Brigade to buy another ton of coal for the old folk.

You see, between you and me, I'm just as proud of their "Operation Coalbag" as I am of our own!

1961

IT happened on a Christmas night not long ago in a little Perthshire village. An old woman sat by the bed of her husband, whose life was peacefully drawing to an end. Neither spoke, for all that had to be said had been said long before. Midnight chimed and, soon after, the old man closed his eyes for the last time.

His wife knew it was all over. She stretched out her hand and smoothed her man's hair. Then, with a long, last look, she rose slowly to her feet, and went down the stairs.

The kitchen range still glowed with warmth and, lifting her beloved tabby cat in her arms, the old woman sat down in her chair to await the morning. What she thought of in the hours that passed, I do not know, nor would I tell you if I did. For surely the memories of over 60 years that must have come to her as she sat there are too precious to share.

At length the dawn broke, and the first light of day told her the night she had dreaded most was now passed.

So, sadly, the old body put on her coat to tell the neighbours that her man had gone . . . and as she closed the front door behind her, she closed it on the life she'd lived and loved for so long, and went forwards alone to face the years that are left.

1977

OH, I suppose you can explain it away if you like.

But this is the story of Mrs Shepherd's Christmas miracle — and it was a miracle for her. She lives at 8 Elphinstone Crescent, Airth, and she says herself that she's getting on in years and life hasn't been easy since her husband died a year past.

When she went to bed the other night, she tells me she prayed that she might, somehow, have enough to give her grandchildren and her great-grandchildren a small present each for Christmas. But in her heart, she didn't know how she was going to manage.

Now, that evening, her daughter had asked her if she had an old box big enough for a certain present. Mrs Shepherd recalled one in her husband's side of the wardrobe, so she went and pulled the box out. When she got up next morning, the daylight was bright enough for something on the floor by the wardrobe to catch her elderly eyes.

To her amazement, it was an old wallet. She must have pulled it out with the box. When she opened it, her prayers were answered. For inside were sixty pounds, tucked away by her husband. No doubt carefully saved by him for the Christmas they never shared last year.

It was, says Mrs Shepherd, as if he had come back and put it there for her — just when her hopes were at their lowest.

1960

IF ever Francis Gay felt compassion, it was last Monday.

By bus, train and car, two hundred mothers, fathers and relations arrived at Royal Victoria School. Newcastle, for the last day of term. They had come to take their blind children, who are pupils at the school, to spend Christmas with their loved ones at home. By evening all fifty children had gone . . . all, that is, except Sandra, a little girl of eight. She had heard all the happy hubbub as the other children met their parents; then she heard the door close as the last of them left on their home-going and . . . I wonder what her thoughts were as she turned away in her darkness, the only child left in the big, silent school?

I am sorry to say Sandra had nowhere to go.

She has no mother, and her daddy, who is also blind, is ill in hospital. I wonder if she learned in that moment — perhaps for the first time — that loneliness goes deepest when you are young? Maybe she did, but it must be, oh, so hard to understand when you are only eight.

Of course, Sandra was still surrounded by love and care. The good folk who run the school were still there and they couldn't have done more for her. Right away she was moved from her empty dormitory to share a room with her house mother, and I know a search was begun for someone to take her home for Christmas.

How glad I am to tell you the quest was a success — for may God forgive us if at Christmas there is even one lonely child.

1965

DECEMBER is a busy time for wives and mothers ... so rushed, so many things to see to, so much to remember besides the household chores and the special shopping.

So tired, perhaps, you might even begin to feel a wee bit sorry for yourself. But, allow me to say very gently: How would you like it if you had nothing to see to?

I am thinking of what an old grandmother said to the Lady of the House only the other day — "My dear, I have a room of my own in this lovely home where everybody is kindness itself. I have no need to fuss or rush or do things. The staff see to everything.

"I cannot go out and shop even if I wanted to — I'm not able to walk, as you know. But, oh, I'd give all I have to be hurrying and scurrying, doing this and that, getting tired out if only I had somebody to do it for."

It's bad enough being too busy — but at this season it's worse not being busy enough.

1954

A GENTLE, quiet, comforting Christmas to you if you have loved and lost . . . I am thinking of all who, like Mrs Mary Hunter, 94 Western Road, Aberdeen, face this Christmas with a fresh sense of loss.

In 1940, Mrs Hunter's husband was reported missing, presumed killed in France. For 14 years she has had no other word, but all that time she has prayed that one day the uncertainty would end and she would learn where her loved one rests.

Now has come the news that her husband's grave has been found, and one day she hopes that she and her boy will be able to go there and lay a flower of remembrance.

To all such as Mrs Hunter this will be a Christmas of longing and sad memories. But even for them I am sure it can bring a reminder that God knows and cares and that He will give them the oil of joy for mourning.

The following week, The Sunday Post carried this story:

LAST Sunday Francis Gay told how the grave of an Aberdeen soldier has been found in France, 14 years after his death in action.

The soldier's widow is Mrs Hunter, of Woodside, Aberdeen. For those 14 years she has prayed that one day the uncertainty would end, and she would learn where her husband was buried.

Now Mrs Hunter has received a letter from an air pilot in England. It reads:— "Dear Mrs Hunter, It was with distress I read the account of your sorrow at this time. After so much patient faith it must indeed be a sad blow, doubly so at this time of year and particularly so for your boy.

"Boys in particular need a father in their growing years. My father was killed in World War 1 and I, too, knew the wistful longing for a father's understanding and help.

"Perhaps you will let me help. I am an airline pilot, now, flying on long-distance routes. Each year I am entitled to four weeks' annual leave with free air travel. "As I am single and unattached (my mother died 14 months ago) would you accept the two seats for you and your son normally reserved for me in my holiday period?

If you will let me know where your husband lies, I will gladly arrange your travel from the airport at Orly or Le Bourget. I was born in Scotland, though brought up in Australia. To me you are a soul in need and a fellow-Scot. I try to be a Christian, and those are my only reasons.

"The travel voucher will be available for you any time after June 1.

"You will need a passport for yourself and son, and sufficient money for your hotel accommodation. I will look after your booking, coach travel, &c., so your journey will be uncomplicated.

"It should not be necessary for you to have to meet me in connection with this offer, so please don't feel embarrassed at accepting. May I wish you both a Merry Christmas and a happier New Year with a mind at rest."

1941

I WISH you a Merry Christmas!

You may reply sourly — "That's all very well, Mr Gay, but if you'd lost as I have, if you had my trouble, if the war had meant to you what it has meant to me, you'd find it impossible to talk so lightly."

Friend, there's something in what you say; but I venture to think the war has meant much heartbreak to me, and a great deal of sorrow, anxiety, and disappointment. For all that, I say to you, A Merry Christmas!

Listen — There's the worst of wartime Christmas — AND THERE'S THE BEST!

It can be a Merry Christmas if you be gallant enough to make it so. It can be a Merry Christmas if you keep your faith, if you look for the best; if you try to make happiness for those at home, for your neighbour, for anyone who looks like having a thin time.

It can be a Merry Christmas if you set your sorrows and your worries behind, turn your face to the Light of Christmas Morning, begin to sing a Christmas carol about the day (which certainly will come) "When peace shall over all the world its ancient splendours bring," and if you will let a Little Child lead you into cheerful service.

A Merry Christmas to you — even if your heart is breaking! A Merry Christmas — a Christmas with peace in it, in spite of the war.

A Christmas of kindliness and courage and neighbourliness, a

Christmas which brings us into God's presence that He may light a happy candle in our hearts.

A Merry Christmas to every reader of this page! God bless you all!

1970

I DON'T know whether to be sad or angry.

A friend who works with the R.S.P.C.C. has been keeping an eye on an Edinburgh family. The parents are not deliberately cruel to their only child, a little girl of eight. But both are alcoholics.

Poor Moira is sadly neglected, and there is no affection from her father or mother. So, when my friend called the other day and found Moira alone in the house, he asked her what she'd like most of all for Christmas. She looked at him, her face solemn. "I'd like to go into a children's home for Christmas," she replied.

My friend was astonished. "But why?" he asked. "Because," she said, "Santa Claus always goes there, and he never comes here. Because there's a Christmas tree there, and there's never one here. Because there might even be a party."

As I say, I don't quite know what to feel. Angry, that parents can care so little for a child that she actually wants to go into a home for Christmas, and receive from strangers the love that she has never had from her own father and mother. Sad, that neither she nor they have ever known the magic of a Christmas morning.

Be that as it may, Moira's wish has been granted. Her stocking will be full when she wakes. And, between you and me, Santa plans to make it a very happy Christmas indeed!

1971

MUCH has been said and written about the tragedy of Ireland.

More, I fear, will be heard in days to come. But I'd like to share with you something that passed almost unnoticed in Edinburgh last week. To do so, I must take you back to a dark day in September when a young Army officer was called to deal with a bomb outside the hall in Castlerobin, Belfast.

Thinking, perhaps, of his own little girls of two-and-a-half and four months, the first thing he did was shepherd a group of children to safety. Then he went forward, knowing he risked his life, to try to make the bomb safe. A few minutes later he was dead, the victim of a cruel trap.

Well, the children of Castlerobin knew nothing they could do would ever make up for his death. Yet they wanted to do something. Believe it or not, they collected no less than £250 for the soldier's children.

And they still remember. A few days ago, minister from Castlerobin made the journey from Belfast to the soldier's home in Edinburgh — a home that should have been so happy this Christmas.

With him, he brought two gold bracelets for the little girls, gifts from the children of Castlerobin. He said simply, "They'll never forget the man who saved their lives."

Of course, the children are too young to understand. Yet surely in those gold bracelets lies a Christmas message for Ireland . . . that where there's courage and kindly hearts, there must also be hope.

1943

LAST Christmas Day I called at a little house in a poor, dull street, where four small children were making Christmas for themselves.

It was a gallant and pathetic attempt. Father was abroad — he's been killed since. Mother was full of good intentions, but rather indolent. Big sister (and she's only ten, at that) was in bed with a temperature, and Bobbie, Michael, and Mildred were left to make the best of a sad business.

For the stockings were empty!

They'd been hung up with such excitement, so much hope, such bright visions . . . and in the morning they hung limp before the fireplace.

Even mother had been a bit conscience-stricken that morning, and had eventually found some buns and dominoes.

But it was all unfortunate till wee Michael proposed to be Father

Christmas himself. It meant putting on his overcoat, and bringing in some empty boxes . . .

Then I arrived. I had a little load of surprises with me and I was the real Father Christmas. They hugged me, and they clapped their hands, and they laughed and cheered . . . though I came away very near to tears.

I tell you this, folk, so that if you think there's any child anywhere this Christmas whose stocking will be empty of delight you may go now, NOW, to fill it.

1979

IN December, 24 years ago, Glasgow was in the grip of fear.

A savage killer had committed a string of gruesome crimes. Eventually Peter Manuel was arrested, tried and convicted. But until then, he was as feared as the Yorkshire Ripper is today. People wouldn't venture out after dark, especially in the Mount Vernon area.

Rev James Lees, now of North Berwick, was in a Glasgow charge at that time.

On an evening before Christmas, he went out with a party of carol singers, mostly young people from his congregation. Accompanied by two men with lanterns they toured the streets, singing carols.

Every now and then Mr Lees counted heads to make sure no one had lagged behind. At one street corner he thought he'd miscounted. He counted again. He now had fifty-one carol singers instead fifty! Then he spotted the stranger, a teenage girl in the middle, singing away.

He asked where she'd come from. She explained she was on her way to visit her granny. She'd missed her bus and had begun to walk. But the dark, silent streets frightened her and she kept thinking about the murderer.

Then she heard the carol singers. She hurried towards the singing and joined the group. She'd been among them for several streets, hoping they'd eventually get to where her granny lived.

Needless to say, Mr Lees made sure the group went right to Granny's door. But it isn't it an eerie echo of the violence that so sadly still casts a shadow over the brightest Christmas?

1958

HAVE you noticed there are times when we are mysteriously led to do something even against our own judgment? A remarkable example has just come to me in the case of Archie Stewart.

Archie is a grocer in Dunipace, and a little over a month ago, he bought a Christmas present for his mother. It was a beautifully-carved trinket box of Italian workmanship, with that delicate beauty that made it just right as a gift for someone he loved.

Archie naturally intended to hide the box till Christmas came. But an unaccountable thing happened. On the evening of Saturday, November 15, he took out the box, and there and then he gave it to his mother — more than a month before Christmas.

Why did he do it? Archie doesn't know. He just felt he wanted to.

And when he saw the happiness on his mother's face, he was sure he had done right.

Next day, Sunday, Mrs Stewart went to church as usual, and took her accustomed place in the choir. Then, with horrifying suddenness, on the way home from church, she collapsed. Within a few hours she was dead.

When the first shock and grief had passed, Archie thought again of the trinket box. What had made him give his mother the gift so early just the night before she died? Archie will never know.

But although it will be a sad Christmas for him, he does feel that in some mysterious way he was led to give his mother a last precious moment of happiness.

1980

JOAN ROBERTS was exhausted. She'd spent all morning in a throng of Aberdeen shoppers trying to find acceptable Christmas presents at a reasonable price. She'd cleaned the house in the afternoon, baked gingerbread, shortbread and a Dundee cake that hadn't turned out right. It was five o'clock and she hadn't even made a start to tea.

She'd meant to write out the Christmas cards that evening, but she didn't think she could face it, Oh, well, she'd give the address book to husband Jim. He could do it for once in his life!

Jim came home early and she apologised for his tea not being ready and explained about the busy day and the Christmas cards. Could he address them while she made the meal?

"No bother," said Jim and went upstairs. She heard him hunting around in his wardrobe and when he returned, whistling he was carrying a stack of envelopes. "Last year's cards," he explained sheepishly.

"I didn't dare tell you that I'd forgotten to post them!"

Before Joan's astonishment changed to words of rebuke, Jim — crafty fellow — agreed she'd had a busy day, telling her to forget tea, he'd take her out for a meal.

What's more, they could post the cards on the way. Joan was lost for words, but not for laughter.

Suffice it to say they'd a lovely meal and folk on the Roberts' mailing list can rest assured they'll get a Christmas card this year!

1968

IT'S a parable, Francis," said the Lady of the House when she read the letter. "It's your Christmas parable!"

The letter came from Mrs Jean Andem, one of our friends from across the Atlantic, who lives at 23 Oak Road, Milton, Massachusetts. And though the parable, strictly speaking, isn't about Christmas, I believe it has a special meaning just now.

At four o'clock one morning Mrs Andem was wakened by her cat, Jim, rushing in through the open window. She rose to investigate, and found Jim in the bathroom, chasing a mouse round the inside of the bath! Bad enough — but as she stood wondering how she could cope, in came Pete, the cat next door, and joined in the fray.

Normally, Jim and Pete are good friends, but sharing a mouse was a different story.

The two began to fight, fur flew in all directions, and the poor wee mouse ran in and out and around them.

Then Mrs Andem had a brainwave. She held a metal waste basket in the bath. The mouse ran into it, and Mrs Andem carried it to the front door and saw it scamper off gratefully across the lawn.

When she returned to the bathroom, she found the two cats sitting in their own fur in the bathtub, looking foolishly at one another, and wondering what had happened to the mouse!

The moral is surely this — those who would be selfish deny themselves most of all.

1975

DAVID GORDON will sit down in his home in Clarkston on Thursday with his family.

His grandchildren will be there, too. And just before they begin their meal, one of them will place her hands together and say the children's grace: —

Thank you for the world so sweet,
Thank you for the food we eat.
Thank you for the birds that sing,
Thank you God for everything.

You'd see David's lips moving, too, as he silently repeats the words. Just as he's done at every meal for 32 years — at home, in restaurants and hotels, even at big important dinners, and over a sandwich and a cup of coffee.

For his thoughts will be 6,000 miles away in Burma. He was a prisoner of war there, in a harsh jungle camp.

Men died all around him. Many were on the verge of starvation. December 25, 1943, was like any other day, except perhaps worse, for Christmas seemed a mockery.

Then, as David and Sandy, his comrade from Inverness, ate their meagre rations of rice, a plump jungle sparrow swooped down and hopped fearlessly up to Sandy.

David held his breath.

Given half a chance, any man there would have caught and killed it, and roasted it over the stove in his hut. Instead, Sandy took a few crumbs of rice, from his own tiny portion, and shared it with the bird.

As they watched it, he smiled. "After all, Dave," he said, turning to his compatriot, "it's Christmas."

And it was to be Sandy's last, for not long after he died. But David never forgot the incident. That day he began saying his silent thank you for blessings always to be found, even amid squalor and starvation, for his survival, and the sacrifices of those who gave so much.

And he has said that simple grace ever since, at every meal, a tribute to a brave and gentle Highlander he will never forget.

1954

CHRISTMAS can't be Christmas without secrets! That's more than half the fun. That's nearly all the excitement.

The Lady of the House won't be 18 next birthday — but she still does things behind my back at Christmas time.

And though I am by no means as young as I was 20 years ago, or longer, I'm still a laddie enough to surprise my wife on Christmas Day and all because I smuggled my gift for her into the house when she wasn't looking.

Silly? Well, I dare say it is in one way.

But it's going to be a sad day when we cannot pretend and forget business and worries and wear a paper hat and sing carols and tie up parcels and prove to our wife or our husband or our children or Aunt Kate that we are still young in spirit and experts in keeping secrets and plotting kindly conspiracies.

For it is in precisely this way that we make Christmas truly Christmas.